TEACHING DOG OBEDIENCE CLASSES

The Manual for Instructors

TEACHING DOG OBEDIENCE CLASSES
The Manual for Instructors

By JOACHIM VOLHARD
and GAIL TAMASES FISHER

Drawings by Melissa Bartlett

FIRST EDITION

HOWELL
BOOK HOUSE
New York

Macmillan General Reference
A Simon & Schuster Macmillan Company
1633 Broadway
New York, NY 10019-6785

Library of Congress Cataloging-in-Publication Data

Volhard, Joachim.
    Teaching dog obedience classes.

    Bibliography: p. 379
    Includes index.
    1. Dogs—Training—Study and teaching—Handbooks, manuals, etc.   2. Dogs—Training—Handbooks, manuals, etc.   I. Fisher, Gail Tamases.   II. Title.
SF431.V63   1985   636.7'083'07   85-27172
ISBN 0-87605-765-2

Printed in the United States of America

Contents

PART IV PROBLEM SOLVING

JOACHIM VOLHARD

GAIL TAMASES FISHER

About the Authors

F OR ALMOST TWO DECADES, **Joachim ("Jack") Volhard** and **Gail Tamases Fisher** have taught dog obedience classes, Jack as an avocation and Gail as a vocation. For the past ten years they have given seminars in America, Canada and England teaching others how to instruct. In addition to these weekend workshops, they conduct one or more five-day instructor school training camps each year which have been attended by individuals from beginners to experts, amateurs to professionals, who have come from almost every state of the Union, Canada, England, Puerto Rico, the Republic of Singapore and the West Indies. They are recognized as the nation's leading teachers of instructors and trainers.

In 1983 Jack and Gail collaborated in writing **TRAINING YOUR DOG—The Step-by-Step Manual** (Howell Book House, 1983) which was widely hailed as the best training book ever, and received the Dog Writers' Association of America award for Best Book on Care and Training in 1983.

Gail also developed and teaches a college course on dog obedience instructing at the University of New Hampshire.

Foreword

THIS IS A BOOK that trains trainers to train their clients to train their dogs. If that sounds too complicated and if you have to read the sentence again, you probably shouldn't be running obedience classes. Training dogs and people is a terribly complex task, one that calls for a full measure of patience, tact, humor, technical skill and optimism. Here is a book that handles the complexity of dealing with dogs and their owners in a cohesive and intelligent manner. It is a manual for instructors that will be treasured reading and a trusted guide.

When I teach seminars, regardless of the area of the country I am speaking in, I usually ask how many people in the audience consider themselves full- or part-time instructors. Usually three-fourths of the room raise hands. This is always interesting to me. Most of these souls teach, perhaps, one Tuesday night class at the local "Y" or taught one several years back. Yet they consider themselves "professional" instructors. I then ask how many in the audience are like myself and make their living, their *whole* livelihood strictly and solely by working with dogs. Perhaps one or two hands go up. These people are remarkable individuals! It is a great sacrifice to dedicate one's whole work life to helping dogs and their owners. The experience of the truly full-time trainer usually outdistances his part-time comrade, yet there is no reason for even a part-time professional to run a poorly-organized class. All trainers must meet high standards in my opinion. Our dogs and their owners deserve no less. There can be no such thing as an "informal" dog obedience class or an instructor who plans his or her class from week to week. Jack Volhard and Gail Fisher have now made excuses for bad classes highly suspect. Instructors are called to extremely high standards in this book, challenged to be innovative, urged to be totally professional whether they work on a full- or part-time basis.

I join with the authors in urging instructors to become more proficient in evaluating not just their canine students but the human handlers they teach—to put themselves in the place of the distraught owner, to recognize owner characteristics and become skilled in helping the owner restructure his or her approach to the dog. There is a new wave of canine professionals in America today who place equal emphasis on dog *and* owner. Dog training is no longer just for dogs. Through this sterling manual we see clearly that it is a human skill that is *taught*. And that teaching might as well be done correctly.

We must realize that dog training in general, both in the literature that has been produced (and still *is* being produced, with few exceptions) and in the folklore that is still being handed down, is where child-rearing was about 100 years ago—before Anne Freud and the advent of child psychology, before Dr. Benjamin Spock, before any real enlightenment took place in the field. This is our challenge as instructors and helpers of dog owners, and it is a challenge taken up so admirably in this fine manual. In my opinion, we will never change the way dogs are treated in our society unless we change the way we instruct their owners. This book, then, is a precious gift to all instructors, and by extension to all owners and to our dogs themselves.

Jack Volhard and Gail Fisher are professionals who have aided countless dogs and their owners through seminars, clinics, classes and especially through their award-winning book **TRAINING YOUR DOG— The Step-by-Step Manual.** Now they reach out to you, the full- or part-time instructor or would-be instructor, offering you a tightly organized, sensible and workable approach to working with canine and human students. You will love the economy of words in the fine writing here. You will go into your classes with renewed vigor and verve, supplemented by new-found knowledge and special tips that will make your "work" as an instructor a joy and pleasure. Read this book with gratitude, for yourself, for your human students and especially for the dogs you teach. This is a major contribution to canine literature, and I'm honored to have been asked to write a foreword for as fine a book as **TEACHING DOG OBEDIENCE CLASSES—The Manual for Instructors.**

JOB MICHAEL EVANS

author **The Evans Guide for Counseling Dog Owners, How to Be Your Dog's Best Friend** (with the Monks of New Skete) and monthly columnist, *Dog Fancy.*

Acknowledgments

First and foremost, we are deeply indebted to the inspiration, dedication, innovation and enthusiasm of the late Olive Point. It was Olive's strong belief in the importance of understanding not only sound principles of dog training, but also the mechanics of teaching people that laid the foundation for this book.

Through the years, our students have been a constant source of encouragement and incentive to us. From beginner through obedience competitor, they have challenged and inspired us to innovate and grow.

Our special thanks to those students and their dogs who volunteered their time for the photograph sessions: Sue Auger, Joanne Baker, Nancy Barnes, Ria Barrows, Myrian Bergeron, Wendy Bergeron, Lynda Carter, Sue Daly, Connie Draper, Rosemary Duggan, Margaret Foster, Gary Gordon, Amanda Jones, Frederick Jung III, Jenny Liedkie, Ken Martin, Gary Netsch, Cindi Olson, Patrice O'Neil, Cindy Salsbury, Lyn Scribner, Stuart Sill, Roxanne Spillman, Pat Symons, Afton Sweigert, Debbye Tardiff, Doris Thibeault, and Gail Tompkins.

The photographs in this book were taken by our students and friends, to whom we are grateful—Joanne Baker, Cindi Olson, Desiree Vaughn and Constanze Volhard.

And to Jocelyn Hartley, who has helped in innumerable ways, our gratitude.

Melissa Bartlett has done illustrations for a number of our articles, and helped to make our first book a success. Her contribution to this book is again immeasurable. Her insight and humor are a refreshing addition to a book entitled a "manual."

Finally, we are grateful to our spouses. Wendy's and Howard's support and encouragement have made this book possible.

Introduction

For NEARLY TWO DECADES we have been teaching obedience classes and giving instructing seminars throughout this country, and in many other parts of the world. Wherever we teach, we are constantly reminded that knowing how to train a dog bears little, if any, relation to being a good instructor. An experienced trainer can make everything look easy, but this is of no help to someone just starting out.

Our approach to instructing is not based on personal aptitude, preference or speculation. Instead, it rests on scientific research on how people learn a new skill combined with a thorough understanding of canine behavior and learning.

Our goal, in writing this book, is to provide the instructor with a manual for the successful operation of dog obedience classes. In many cases, the obedience class is the last stop before euthanasia. Success in teaching is the key to a mutually enjoyable relationship between owner and dog, and a rewarding career or hobby for the instructor.

Uppermost in our minds is the belief that dog training should be fun for both the trainer and the dog. The obedience instructor has the ability to make it so.

Joachim J. Volhard
Gail Tamases Fisher

PART I

The Student's Dog

"If our approach to training is based on moral ideas regarding punishment, reward, obedience, duty, etc., we are bound to handle the dog in the wrong way."

Konrad Most
Training Dogs

1

Understanding Canine Behavior

INTRODUCTION

The dog's ability to function in a human society is in part due to his outstanding ability to understand the silent communication of body language and facial expression. The dog is able to recognize minute postural changes, facial expressions and physical innuendoes.

The dog knows when we are angry—not, as some people believe, because he is aware of his own transgression, but because he reads our body language and facial expression. Conversely, when we are happy, he recognizes those body signals as well.

In addition to his ability to recognize our emotions, he has the ability to communicate his feelings through his body postures and facial expressions.

The dog's view of the world is shaped by the combination of his innate behaviors, or instincts, and the experiences he has throughout his life.

In this chapter we will discuss the critical periods in the dog's life, during which his behavior is shaped by his experiences, and the method of communication of the dog—body language, facial expression and vocalizations.

17

CRITICAL PERIODS

A critical period is a special time in the dog's life when a seemingly insignificant experience may and often does have a great effect on later behavior. While there may be physical changes marking the beginning or end of a critical period, these are periods of *social* development.

The specific ages are not absolute, but generally apply to most puppies and dogs. The early critical periods are the same for all dogs, regardless of size or breed. The ages of the later critical periods will vary depending on the size and breed of dog.

The Early Critical Periods

Neonatal Period (Birth to 12 Days)

The Neonatal Period, from birth to 12 days of age, is devoted to two functions: obtaining nutrition by nursing, and staying warm.

A puppy is not physically self-sufficient when he is born. He needs the warmth of his environment to control his body temperature. He needs physical stimulation to urinate and defecate. He has neither sight nor hearing, and is deficient in his senses of smell, taste and touch. He reacts to hot and cold, and to some extent to pain. He also reacts to the smell of mother.

He moves by crawling forward in a circular pattern, moving his head from side to side in an attempt to locate mother. He may vocalize while he's searching, which stimulates mother to nuzzle him and let him know where she is.

The environment affects him only inasmuch as it touches him. While the puppy grows rapidly in size and strength during this period, his behavior patterns remain virtually the same throughout. EEG's taken during the Neonatal Period show no difference between the puppy's brain waves when he is asleep and when he is awake.

Transition Period (13 to 20 Days)

The Transition Period is from 13 to 20 days and is marked by a number of physical changes in the puppy.

At the beginning of this period, the puppy's eyes will open, at an average of 13 days. While his pupils will react to light, the retina is still undeveloped, and he is unable to see objects or movement until around 21 days of age.

The puppy will begin to crawl backward as well as forward, and a few days later he will begin to walk in a wobbly fashion, falling as often as he takes steps forward. Once he starts walking, the puppy no longer crawls.

18

The first teeth erupt at around 20 days, and he begins to bite and chew. Tail wagging also begins during this period, indicating that tail wagging is not reliant upon seeing and hearing, since he cannot yet see or hear.

He begins to react to sounds at an average of 19.5 days, when he startles at a noise, but is still unable to locate the source of the sound.

This critical period is one of rapid physical changes. Over a period of just a week, the puppy has changed from a Neonate who cannot hear, walk, move his bowels without stimulation, keep warm by himself or eat other than by sucking, into a puppy who can do all of these things.

Awareness Period (21 to 28 Days)

The Awareness Period is from 21 to 28 days. This is the first week during which the puppy is able to use his senses of sight and hearing. Because the change in his sensory perceptions happens so abruptly, over a 24-hour period in most puppies, he needs a stable environment. Now he has the greatest need for his mother and for a familiar environment. Weaning or moving the litter to a new location at this time in all likelihood will psychologically scar the puppies.

Learning begins during the Awareness Period. It is the time in the puppy's life when he learns what it is to be a dog.

Canine Socialization Period (21 to 49 Days)

The period from 21 to 49 days, or three to seven weeks, is the Canine Socialization Period, when the puppy learns to use the species-specific behaviors that make him a dog.

To reach his genetic potential, the puppy must stay in the nest with his mother and littermates throughout this time. During this period he will practice body postures, facial expressions and vocalizations, and learn their effects on his siblings, mother, and any other dogs he comes in contact with. He learns how it sounds to bark and be barked at; how it feels to bite and be bitten.

He learns the various behaviors that make him a dog: chase games—imitating the chase necessary to catch and bring down game—teach him coordination and timing; greeting behavior teaches him the body postures of greeting; fight games teach him the use of his body, body postures and expressions to elicit various responses. For example, during play, when a fight might begin, the puppy learns that a submissive body posture has the effect of turning off the aggression of his littermate.

During this critical period the puppy learns one of the most important lessons of his life—to accept discipline. He learns it from his mother, who through discipline teaches the puppies not to bite so hard, or, during the weaning process, to leave her alone. This is a learning experience for the puppy. Unfortunately, it is cut short by many breeders under the mistaken assumption that because the dam disciplines the puppies, she no longer wants to be with them. Quite the contrary. A normal mother will set up the puppies so she **can** discipline them.

We have a lot to learn from observing the manner in which the dam disciplines a puppy. When the puppy has committed a transgression, perhaps something as simple as coming too close to the mother when she doesn't want to be bothered, she will give him a warning—a meaningful look, often accompanied by an almost imperceptible wrinkle of the nose or twitch of the lip. If the puppy has not yet learned the meaning of the look, or is determined to pester Mom, he will push his luck. At that point she will give him a noisy scolding, accompanied by a nip on the nose. The scolding consists of a growly snarl, and the nip is rarely hard enough to hurt, much less draw blood. But the lesson is well learned. The chastised puppy quickly rolls over onto his back, screaming "I've been killed!" Mom immediately stops the discipline and assumes a benevolent and haughty expression, looking much as if she wished she hadn't had to do that, but after all he is such a bothersome little fellow.

The discipline is swift, to the point, and is over as quickly as it started.

The puppy learns several lessons: He learns to respect the facial expression which forewarned the discipline; he learns that he can be and will be disciplined in his life; he learns to assume a submissive posture, and that when he does, it has the effect of stopping the scolding. Most important for our purposes, the puppy learns to accept discipline.

These lessons have far reaching implications. Once the puppy has learned to accept discipline, it can be carried over to a new master.

It is also during this period, at around three weeks of age, that puppies will begin relieving themselves away from the sleeping area.

This, the Canine Socialization Period, is when the formation of strong attachments begins. The puppy bonds not only with his own species, but others as well. Socialization with people and with other species, such as cats or farm animals, is ideally begun during this period.

The period from 21 to 49 days is a time when the puppy is learning the behaviors which make him a dog. If deprived of this opportunity, he will never again be able to fully learn these lessons.

Puppies that are removed from the nest too early tend to be nervous and to bark and bite, and often cannot accept discipline. They are frequently aggressive with other dogs, and sometimes will not breed. A puppy taken away to a new home or to a pet shop before seven weeks of age will not realize its genetic potential as a dog and companion.

20

Mother's discipline.

EARLY CRITICAL PERIODS

1. Neonatal, 0-12 days

Responds to warmth, touch and smell. The pup cannot regulate body functions such as temperature and elimination

Neonatal Period.

2. Transition, 13-20 days

Eyes & ears are open, but sight + hearing are limited. Tail wagging begins. The pup can now control body functions

Transition Period.

3. Awareness 21-28 days

Sight and hearing function clearly. The pup begins to learn he is a dog and has a great need for a stable environment.

Awareness Period.

4. Canine Socialization 21-49 days

By interacting with his mother and littermates, the pup learns the various behaviors which make him a dog.

Canine Socialization Period.

5. Human Socialization, 7-12 wks.

The pup has the brain waves of an adult dog. This is the best time for going to a new home

Human Socialization Period.

6. Fear Impact, 8-11 wks.

Try to avoid frightening the puppy during this time, since traumatic experiences can have a lasting effect during this critical period.

Fear Impact Period.

23

Human Socialization Period (7 to 12 Weeks)

The best time to bring a puppy into its new home is during the Human Socialization Period, from 50 to 84 days, or seven to twelve weeks. It is also the best time to introduce him to those things that will play a role in his future life. For example, if he has not already been exposed to farm animals and it is necessary for him to interact peacefully with them, it is at this age that he should meet them in a positive, non-threatening manner. If the breeder has not already introduced him to the sounds of the vacuum cleaner, car engines and city traffic, he needs to be exposed to these now. Children, men with beards, women in floppy hats, and senior citizens, while all people to us, appear different to the dog. His education and socialization should include exposure to many types of people of all ages.

At seven weeks of age a puppy's EEG shows the brain waves are the same as those of an adult dog. His capacity for concentration is not yet adult and his attention span is short. But he can learn. Not only can a young puppy learn, he *will* learn whether we teach him or not. This is the age when the most rapid learning occurs. Everything he experiences makes a greater impression on him now than it ever will again.

Learning at this age is permanent.

Because of the relative ease of teaching at this age, because the puppy has not yet learned any bad habits that will later have to be cured, and because the puppy is just a fraction of his adult size and weight, this is the ideal time to begin obedience training in a positive, non-punitive manner, taking into account his physical limitations and short attention span. The instructing program described in Appendix I is designed for dogs of any age and has been successfully used for countless puppy classes.

Fear Impact Period (8 to 11 Weeks)

During the Fear Impact Period, from eight to eleven weeks, any traumatic, painful, or frightening experience will have a more lasting impact on the puppy than if it had occurred at any other time. It is the puppy's perception of the experience that is important, not that of the owner.

For example, a trip to the animal hospital during this period, if unpleasant, could forever make a dog apprehensive about going to the veterinarian. By taking along a toy and some treats and making the experience pleasant and fun, the potentially negative impact is alleviated.

Under no circumstances should elective surgery such as ear cropping or hernia repair be undertaken during this period.

If the puppy is taken to obedience class during this period, it is important that the classes be non-stressful for the dog.

Seniority Classification Period (13 to 16 Weeks)

This critical period, from thirteen to sixteen weeks, is also known as the "Age of Cutting"—cutting teeth and cutting the apron strings.

It is at this age that the puppy begins testing to see who is going to be the pack leader. From thirteen weeks on, if the puppy attempts to bite, even seemingly in play, it is an attempt to dominate. Biting behavior is absolutely discouraged from thirteen weeks on. (See "Biting" in Chapter 12, Behavior Problems.)

Dogs play by the rules, if they are spelled out clearly. One of the rules is that there is only one top dog, one pack leader. The pack leader is listened to and obeyed. Knowing who is the pack leader is important to the dog. If there is no person in the household who is willing to assume this responsibility, then the dog will take over.

During the Seniority Classification Period, the dog attempts to clarify and resolve the question of leadership. The more dominant the dog, the more important it is that there be a strong and consistent leader. The more submissive the dog, the more willing he is to listen to any master, even an ineffectual and inconsistent one.

Obedience classes teach the owner to be his dog's pack leader. Pack leadership is something that the handler learns through training—through specific exercises designed to teach the dog who is in charge. If training has not been undertaken prior to this period, it must be started at this age to avoid serious problems later.

Later Critical Periods

The ages of the following critical periods may vary depending on the size of the dog. Small dogs tend to experience these periods earlier than do large dogs.

Flight Instinct Period (4 to 8 Months)

The Flight Instinct Period occurs sometime between four and eight months of age. This is the time when a puppy will test his wings. He will venture off on his own and may turn a deaf ear when called.

The Flight Instinct Period lasts from a few days to several weeks. How the dog is handled during this stage will mean the difference between a dog who doesn't come when called and one who responds readily. Because most dog owners are not aware of this naturally occurring developmental stage, they react incorrectly, thereby creating a problem for themselves.

When the dog goes through the Flight Instinct Period, the training organization gets its first call from the frantic owner. Prior to this, the

The flight instinct period is rather taxing.

Flight Instinct Period.

puppy was small enough to be carried or held if he didn't respond to a command; he was still cuddly and puppyish, and he always came when he was called. Now he is getting too big to carry, he has begun to change into a gawky teenager and, darn it, now he doesn't even come when called.

Not only is he not coming when called, he may be learning a very harmful lesson—if he does come, he gets scolded and perhaps even hit. The scenario goes something like this: Konrad is let out for a romp early in the morning, as he has been for weeks. A few minutes later, Dad, in his dressing gown and slippers, goes to the door to let him in. Konrad, who has just noticed the smell of a bunny who ran across the lawn earlier that morning, decides to check out the source of this interesting scent before going in to get breakfast. So, instead of responding to Dad's call, he takes off on the trail of the rabbit. Dad, in dressing gown and slippers, takes off in hot pursuit of Konrad.

Konrad thinks this is wonderful. Dad wants to chase the bunny too! Dad's yelling and screaming must be his hunting call. After a short while, Konrad decides he's more hungry than curious about the rabbit, so he turns to Dad, as if to say, "Let's go home. This isn't worth missing breakfast for." Whereupon Dad, furious and exhausted, grabs Konrad by the collar, hits him a few times, tells him what a bad puppy he is, and drags him home where he is isolated in the bathroom as a lesson not to run away again.

Lesson learned? Yes, but the wrong one! The lesson Konrad learned is: When I run away, it is best to stay away as long as possible, because Dad doesn't like it when I go back to him.

The emergence of the Flight Instinct is another reason for starting puppies in obedience class before this age. If the owner is training the puppy when the Flight Instinct Period begins, he is able to continue training him to come in a positive fashion, on leash for several weeks, and then try him off leash again. If, when let off the leash, the puppy doesn't respond to the command to come, he is put back on leash for several more weeks. Since he is always praised when he comes, he learns that coming when called is pleasant.

There is a physiological change that corresponds with the Flight Instinct Period—teething. The puppy has lost his milk teeth between four and six months, and his beautiful, white adult teeth are plainly visible. Most owners heave a huge sigh of relief at that time, thinking that they've made it through teething without any of the horror stories they've heard, such as dogs destroying kitchen cabinets, tearing down walls, pulling out doorjambs, eating couches and the like. "Whew!" they think. "Konrad isn't such a bad dog after all."

Then one day, when Konrad is about eight months old, they come home only to find that Konrad has chewed a large chunk out of a kitchen cabinet. Why has he done this? He made it through teething without doing anything horrible. Why now?

The reason is that Konrad hasn't yet made it through teething. While the adult teeth come through the gums prior to six months of age, they don't set in the jaw until between six and 10 months. It is *then* that Konrad will chew. Not only will he chew, but he *must* chew. There is a physiological need for him to exercise his mouth at this time, and he will do so on whatever is handy. Lock him in an empty room, and he'll destroy the door or the walls.

Dad's opinion of Konrad is deteriorating even more. He doesn't come when he's called, his gawkiness makes him look as though he can't get out of his own way, and now he's starting to cost big bucks in repair bills. So Dad gives Mom an ultimatum: Either train that dog or out he goes. This is when Mom calls the training organization, and Konrad goes to school.

Unfortunately for Konrad, this usually corresponds with the next Critical Period.

Second Fear Impact Period (6 to 14 Months)

This Fear Impact Period, also called the Fear of New Situations Period, is not as well defined as the first. The Second Fear Impact Period corresponds with growth spurts. Hence it may occur more than once as the dog matures.

What marks the Second Fear Impact Period is a change in the behavior of the now adolescent dog. He may suddenly be reluctant to approach something new, or be frightened of something or someone familiar.

When a dog is exhibiting fear or reluctance, he should not be forced into a confrontation, bullied into being brave, or reinforced in his fear through soothing tones and petting. Force can frighten the dog further, and soothing tones only serve to encourage his fear. What the calming, praising voice says to the dog is, "Mom pets me and coos at me when I'm frightened. It's good to be afraid."

His fear should be handled with patience and kindness. The dog is permitted to work it out for himself without being forced to deal with something he perceives as dangerous. Training during this period puts the dog in a position of success, so his self-confidence will be built up.

Gail knew one of her dogs was in the Second Fear Impact Period one day when she heard furious barking coming from the bathroom. She went in to see what was amiss, only to find her eight-month-old puppy barking furiously at the toilet as if she had never seen it before. Laughing, Gail sat down on the fear-producing object, and the pup's expression immediately changed, as if to say "Oh, that's what that is! I didn't recognize it without you on it."

Because the Second Fear Impact Period corresponds with the age at which most dogs are brought to obedience class, it could have far-reaching implications. If the dog perceives the class as a frightening place, he may generalize this fear to all situations where there are groups of dogs, such as dog shows and obedience trials, or he may generalize this fear to the specific event, for example, training, or the particular location.

If, on the other hand, the dog's perception of class is that it's a nice place and that training is fun, the positive ramifications are obvious. It underscores the importance of starting puppies in class before the onset of the Second Fear Impact Period.

Since most students wait until the dog is older than six months before enrolling him in class, the need for selecting training techniques and running the class in such a way as to reduce the dog's anxiety becomes clear.

Maturity (1 to 4 Years)

Many breeds, particularly the giant breeds, continue growing and physically changing beyond four years of age, so maturity refers to sexual maturity rather than full growth. For the average dog, maturity occurs sometime between one and a half and three years of age, with small dogs maturing earlier and giant dogs maturing later.

This critical period is often marked by an increase in aggression and by a renewed testing for leadership. The increased aggression is not necessarily negative. Often it means that a previously overfriendly dog becomes a good watch dog and barks when people come to the door. It may also mean, however, that Konrad and Argus, who used to be good friends, now start fighting every time they see each other.

When, at maturity, the dog tries to test leadership, he should be handled firmly. Regular training throughout this testing period, praising him for the proper response, and giving him no inroads to the top dog position will remind him that the issue has been settled.

SUMMARY

Although many dogs will not undergo any noticeable changes during these periods, the importance and impact of the Critical Periods on the dog's behavior are beyond question. While the obedience instructor can do nothing to change the earlier critical periods, understanding the impact on the dog enables him to help the owner understand and deal with his dog's behavior.

CANINE COMMUNICATION

During the critical periods, the puppy is learning to communicate and to understand communication through body language, facial expression and vocalizations. He practices various body postures and learns what responses he gets from his mother and littermates.

Dogs understand one another's communications, regardless of breed, size, hair cover or cosmetic surgical procedures such as ear cropping and tail docking. The Japanese Chin can communicate with the Welsh Terrier as easily as can a French Bulldog and an English Mastiff. The language of dogs is universal.

At the same time, dogs presume that we understand their system of communication. When a dog is communicating with us, and we misunderstand his message, problems occur. For instance, a dog who assumes a submissive posture in response to his master's anger is punished because the master interprets the look as "guilty." If this happens repeatedly, the dog may become overly submissive, even urinating when frightened.

We knew such a dog. He was frequently chastised for lack of housetraining. When he assumed a submissive posture it was interpreted by the owner as "knowing he had done wrong," and resulted in his being further punished to teach him a lesson. This dog became so confused that he began urinating anywhere at any time—on the couch, on the bed, on the floor—and he wouldn't move away when he was urinating. He would lie in his own urine with a submissive expression, which was further interpreted as guilt.

Once this dog's owner learned the significance of the submissive posture—that the dog did not know why he was being chastised—and stopped chastising him, within a matter of days the dog stopped the inappropriate urination.

Understanding canine communication helps the obedience instructor in many ways: to recognize both the overt and subtle expressions of mood or feelings, to tailor exercises to the specific reactions of the dogs, and to understand what constitutes normal behavior. It is only through the understanding of what is normal that abnormal or aberrant behavior is recognized.

The following body postures and behavior patterns explain the moods and expressions of the dog.

Neutral Posture & Expression

In neutral body posture the body is relaxed with the tail at rest, hanging down from the body. The head is held high with the ears up, but not pointing forward. The mouth may be open or closed, and the corners of the mouth are neither pulled back nor brought forward.

This is most often how we see dogs in a comfortable situation such as at home, or even in class once they become accustomed to the environment.

Alert Posture & Expression

When the dog is alert, he will hold his head up, pointing the ears forward and focusing his attention on whatever has alerted him. His mouth is usually closed or just slightly open.

He will stand tall on his toes, with his tail almost straight out from his back. Sometimes there will be slight piloerection of the hair along his spine.

This posture indicates interest. What happens next depends on what has aroused the dog's interest and how he reacts to it. He may find that there is nothing of concern, and he will go on about his business; he may see that it is Dad returning from work and go into Greeting Behavior; he may discover that it is the dog next door who is in season and behave appropriately to that, or discover some other event of interest. Alert posture is a prelude to another behavior.

Offensive Threat

When a dog is exhibiting Offensive Threat posture and facial expression, he is dangerous, aggressive and ready for attack. This dog will attack at the slightest provocation.

In this posture, every part of the dog is brought upward and forward. He stands tall on his toes, increasing his stature. The hackles, the hair along the spine from the base of the tail to the ears, are up, increasing his size. His tail is brought up and forward over his back, and may be wagging stiffly. Ears are up and forward.

The aggressive dog's facial expression is nasty. His nose is wrinkled, exposing his teeth with the corners of the mouth brought forward. He is usually vocalizing—a low, throaty growl which sounds as serious as he means it to be.

Defensive Threat

The dog exhibiting Defensive Threat posture is also dangerous; however, he will attack only as a last resort. A dog exhibiting Defensive Threat is being self-protective. This dog will bite if cornered, but would choose to run first. He is frightened and can be provoked to bite.

The body posture of the defensive dog is lowered and pulled back. The ears are back, the tail is back and down, generally tucked under the dog's belly, and while the hackles are up, the stature of the dog is lowered and

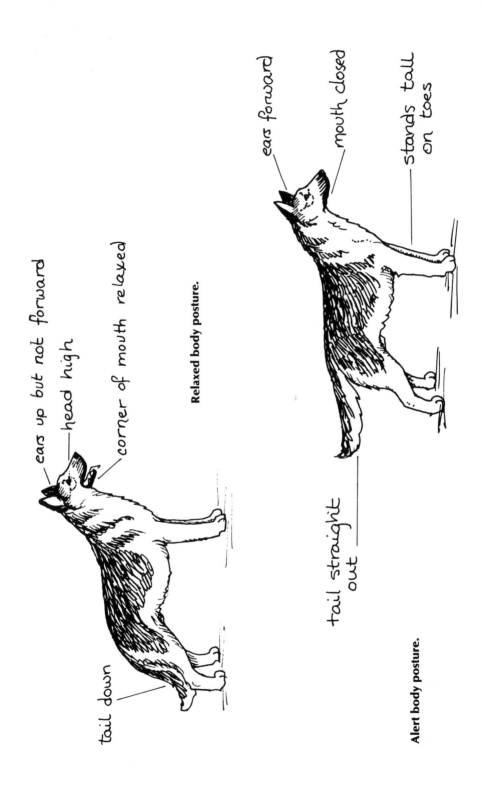

ears up but not forward

head high

corner of mouth relaxed

tail down

Relaxed body posture.

ears forward

mouth closed

stands tall on toes

tail straight out

Alert body posture.

tail up
and stiff

hackles up

ears forward

nose wrinkled

corner of mouth forward

stands tall + forward
on toes

Offensive threat posture.

hackles up

ears back

pupils dialated

wrinkled nose

corner of mouth back

body lowered

tail
tucked

Defensive threat posture.

leaning backward. There are similarities in the facial expression of dogs exhibiting offensive and defensive threat. Both have exposed their teeth by wrinkling the muzzle, but in defensive threat the corners of the mouth are pulled back. This dog may be growling or whining, and his pupils will be dilated.

Submissive Posture

There are two expressions of submission: active and passive.

Active Submission

In active submission the body posture of the dog is low, croup lowered with the tail tucked under, possibly against the belly. The front end of the dog is lowered as well.

The facial expression is non-threatening. Everything is pulled back—the ears, the corners of the mouth, the corners of the eyes, and the forehead is smooth. The dog will avert his eyes and avoid making eye contact.

Movements include groveling and moving around in front of another dog or person. While in this posture, the dog will lick at the mouth of the superior dog.

Passive Submission

In Passive Submission, the dog is still. He rolls over on his back, tail tucked tightly against the belly. He will hold his head over to one side, straining to avoid eye contact. He may urinate while in this posture, but he doesn't move. He may lick his lips or nose.

Greeting Behavior

There are several aspects of greeting behavior. There is the greeting that takes place between pack members, human and canine, and between strangers on neutral territory.

Pack Member Greeting

When a person belonging to the dog's household comes home, he is greeted by his dog like a returning member of the pack. The dog wags his tail on a horizontal line, and may whimper or bark. The dog will jump up in an attempt to lick the person's lips.

Some dogs will grin in greeting. Their lips will be pulled back, exposing the front teeth in what some people mistake as a snarl. This is probably the closest imitation the dog can come to smiling.

34

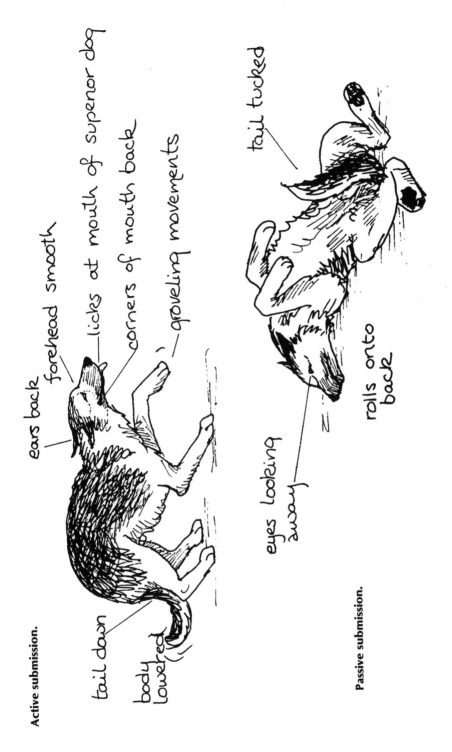

Active submission.

ears back
forehead smooth
licks at mouth of superior dog
corners of mouth back
groveling movements
tail down
body lowered

Passive submission.

tail tucked
eyes looking away
rolls onto back

When dogs in the same pack greet one another, the tail carriage indicates the status in the pack hierarchy. The higher the tail carriage, the higher that dog is in relation to the others. The lowest member of the pack will, during greeting behavior, wag his tail quite low, often with his body posture lowered as well. It is common to observe active submissive behavior in the greeting ritual.

Neutral Territory Greeting

When two strange dogs of the same sex meet on neutral territory, they go through a ritualized series of movements, almost like a choreographed dance. If both dogs exhibit normal behavior, have received the proper canine socialization and have learned to use and read body language, the greeting behavior is non-combative. They will approach each other curiously, check out the sex and scent of the stranger and go through a series of movements to establish who is dominant and who is submissive. One may place his head across the withers of the other, and then vice versa. They may move in a circular direction, continuing to sniff and establish their own hierarchy. Then, when the ritual is completed, they may go off individually to lift a leg (in the case of males), or they may begin to play together.

If allowed to go through the greeting ritual on their own, there is rarely a fight. Fighting between strange dogs on neutral territory is almost always caused by human intervention. A dog owner will panic at the sight of another dog and will frighten his own dog into fighting, or will try to pull his dog away by the leash. The leash is probably responsible for most dog fights on neutral territory.

When a dog's owner holds on tightly to the leash during greeting, or tries to pull him away from another dog by tightening up on the leash, several things happen.

First, the tight leash causes an aggressive response. Secondly, by pulling backward on the leash, the owner is inadvertently changing his dog's body posture. His dog may be aware that he has to show deference to a more dominant dog by lowering his body posture just at the moment that his owner pulls on the leash, thereby pulling his dog's head up, increasing his stature, and sending the message to the strange dog that he is trying to be dominant.

Being able to sniff each other to learn sexual status and dominance is often important to two dogs on neutral territory, such as in an obedience class. When, for instance, there are two dominant males in a class who indicate that they need to learn about each other, they can be put in a position of being able to greet without danger to either dog.

In our classes, two experienced handlers, usually the instructor and an

tail up

ears up

front
end
lowered

Play bow.

assistant, take the two dogs away from the owners, walk them up to each other on *loose* leashes, and allow them to sniff for *three seconds*. After three seconds, both dogs are simultaneously *called* away, not pulled away, by their respective handlers, and are walked back to their owners.

By taking the dogs from the owners, we eliminate the possibility of owner anxiety causing an adverse reaction. Since most owners cannot maintain a loose leash in that situation, we don't take a chance on their not being able to do it correctly.

Three seconds is sufficient for these two dogs to establish what they need to know about each other, and they will then be able to participate in the class without straining to get to one another.

Play Soliciting Behavior

In Play Soliciting Behavior the dog's body posture is lowered in front in what is called the "Play Bow." He will wag his tail on a horizontal line

37

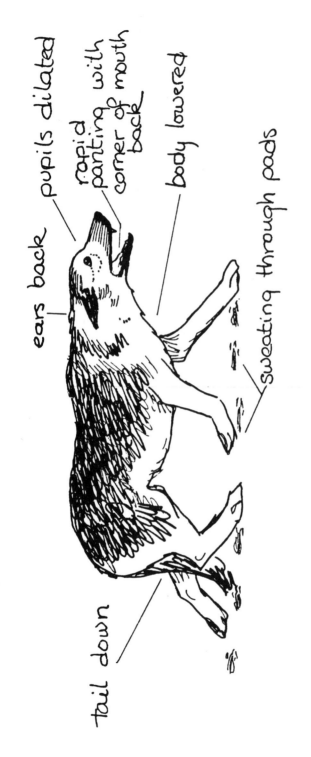

ears back

pupils dilated

rapid panting with corner of mouth back

body lowered

sweating through pads

tail down

Stress.

with his back, or slightly higher. His facial expression is quite happy, ears up, and mouth open in what looks like a smile. He may bark and run around in small circles with his tail down, croup lowered.

It is possible to imitate this posture and often encourage a dog to play.

Stress

While stress is not really in the category of body signals, it is important for us to recognize its signs. When a dog is under stress, his body posture is lowered, his tail is down, ears are back, corners of the mouth pulled back. He will likely be panting or licking his lips. He will sweat through his pads, and wet paw prints will be seen on the mat if he is in class, or floor. His pupils will be dilated.

When the dog is under stress, learning stops. Therefore if you recognize these signs during training, instruct the handler to stop and give the dog a rest.

CONCLUSION

For obedience instructors, being able to read the dog's body language is critical. We are able to understand his moods and what he is trying to communicate to us. Understanding the dog allows us to deal with him correctly and intelligently.

2

How the Dog Learns

INTRODUCTION

Dogs are such popular pets because they have so many seemingly human qualities. They are honest—dogs don't lie; they are trustworthy—at least once they have been trained; and they are loyal—that all-redeeming quality. Dogs are social creatures who enjoy our company as much as we enjoy theirs. In times of need they comfort us, and in general mirror our moods.

HOW THE DOG DOES *NOT* LEARN

Precisely because dogs seem so like us the novice trainer tends to anthropomorphize. He attributes human qualities to his dog and if the dog does not live up to these, the owner becomes angry and frustrated.

Owners tend to have varying theories about how their dogs learn and why they should respond as expected. The three main ones are:

The "primrose path" theory;

the "promise of future reward" theory; and

the "threat of future punishment" theory.

The "primrose path" theory goes something like this—"how could you do this to me? I house you, I feed you, I take care of all your veterinary bills, and I give you frequent baths! Don't you have any gratitude?" The painful lesson is that the dog does not have any gratitude. He also has no sense of duty, no conscience and only does what he perceives to be to his own advantage.

The "promise of future reward" theory goes like this—"if you behave yourself today and don't jump on anybody when they come through the door, I will buy you a Big Mac. I know you like Big Macs because every time we drive by the Golden Arches you drool." Unfortunately, this theory, too, does not work. The dog does not understand and his behavior will not be influenced in any way by such promises.

Finally, we have the "threat of future punishment" theory which is just as ineffective as the previous two. Saying to the dog "if you don't behave yourself, I will really let you have it," will not influence his behavior in the least. As much as the owner would like to think otherwise, his dog is an animal. Dogs are not dumb, by any means. They are exceedingly smart, but animals nevertheless.

Instructors are also fighting what we call the "Lassie" syndrome—"my dog understands everything I say." And, the owner thinks he has proof. He will tell you, "When my dog has done something naughty, he has guilt written all over him. He **knows** he did something wrong. Why is he acting guilty if he does not know he misbehaved?"

One instructor we know demonstrated the fallacy of the "guilty look" to her class with her own dog. She would bounce a ball for her dog, who loved balls. The dog would longingly look at the bouncing ball, following it with his eyes, and showing to everyone that he really would like to have the ball. She then placed the ball on the ground, pointed to it accusingly and remonstrated "did you do that?" whereupon the dog would shrink back in horror, exhibiting all the signs of guilt in his repertoire. It made an important point to the students. It is the owner's **attitude,** especially his body posture, which elicits the look of guilt and not what the dog may or may not have done.

What the owner has to learn is that attempting to shame the dog into good behavior will not work, nor will punishing the dog after the fact. Consider the following: The owner is preparing supper. A succulent steak is on the kitchen counter and he has to go to the pantry for some other ingredients. The dog, who up to now has been sleeping in the corner, recognizes that opportunity knocks only once. He snatches the steak and devours it. When the owner returns, he immediately sees what has happened. The dog is summoned. "Shame on you! How could you?" The dog looks dutifully ashamed of himself and the owner is convinced the dog knows what he did wrong. But does he? The answer is no. The dog

THREE "THEORIES"
OF HOW DOGS LEARN

The "primrose path" theory of learning.

The "promise of future reward" theory of learning.

The "threat of future punishment" theory of learning.

understands only that the owner is upset with him, but he does not understand it because of the steak he ate. The dog's doleful appearance is a reaction to the owner's attitude and not his feelings of remorse for what he did. The dog thoroughly enjoyed the steak and would do the same thing again, given another chance.

HOW KONRAD LEARNS

In our training book **"TRAINING YOUR DOG"** (Howell Book House, 1983), we referred to the dog as *Konrad* and for the sake of consistency we will continue to call him that.

What our students have to understand is that dogs learn through experience, pleasant and unpleasant ones. They learn principally through the faculty of memory. This is not to say that dogs are unable to "think" or work out problems for themselves. But in the context of what we try to teach them, we rely mainly on memory. The dog will try to avoid unpleasant experiences, those he perceives as disadvantageous to himself, and he will unwillingly pursue pleasant experiences, those he perceives as advantageous.

In Jack's house the dog biscuits are kept in a kitchen cupboard. No matter where his dog may be in the house, such as lying in front of the fireplace watching the football game, when that cupboard is opened, he appears out of nowhere. He perceives it to his advantage to do so, because he may get a biscuit.

Jack also has a Siamese cat, experienced in dealing with all kinds of dogs. When necessary, she will stand her ground and any dog that gets too fresh is severely disciplined. Claws are sharp and they hurt. The over-zealous dog quickly learns that it is to his advantage NOT to pester the cat.

These are examples of experiences the dog views as advantageous and disadvantageous to himself.

Training a dog is no more than showing him what is to his advantage and what is not.

The objective of obedience training is to develop the ability to communicate with the dog in a manner that does not violate his dignity and results in a harmonious and mutually enjoyable relationship. It is accomplished by creating an association between primary and secondary stimuli.

PRIMARY STIMULI

Primary stimuli are those directly responsible for a given response by the dog, either voluntary or involuntary. For example, a dog can be coaxed to come to his owner, if the owner kneels down, thereby reducing his body

The dog quickly learns what is to his advantage and disadvantage.

Dogs learn through pleasant and unpleasant experiences.

posture and making himself appear more inviting to the dog. On the other hand, if the dog is on a line and the owner wants him to come, all he has to do is reel his dog in. The dog has no choice and the response is involuntary.

Inducive Training

Eliciting a voluntary response from the dog is called *inducive* training and is accomplished through encouragement, body posture, praise and food, all of which are perceived as pleasant by the dog, with food usually being the most gratifying. On the basis of experience, the dog will learn that it is to his advantage to do what his owner wants him to do. For example, if the owner wants to train his dog to come when called, he can reward the dog with a treat every time the dog responds to the come command.

Can inducive training override instinctive behavior, such as a male dog's pursuit of a female in season, or the hunting dog's following the trail of game? Our experience has been that it cannot.

Compulsive Training

Compulsion is defined as the state of being forced to perform some action which appears to be without rational reason. Compulsion ranges from mild to strong.

Mild compulsion, such as physically placing the dog into a sit, need not be unpleasant. Even though the dog does not understand why he is being made to sit, he is nonetheless being compelled to do so.

Strong compulsion, such as firmly checking the dog to remain in heel position, is highly unpleasant. The dog does not understand the reason for the compulsion, but quickly learns what he must do in order to avoid it.

Compulsion can be used to train a dog to do something he would not do on his own, and to teach him to refrain from something he would do on his own, but which is considered objectionable.

Training for Action

When compulsion is used to teach the dog something he would not do on his own, such as to sit on command, or any other obedience exercise, it is immediately followed by an agreeable experience. As Konrad Most put it in *Training Dogs*, a book written in 1910, "[t]he sharp contrast between the disagreeable experience . . . and the agreeable . . . makes it easy for the animal to appreciate where his advantage lies, and he learns very quickly."

The agreeable experience can be in the form of praise, a treat, fondling the dog, or another exercise the dog likes. To maintain the dog's enthusiasm for training and foster a positive attitude, the agreeable

46

The inducive method.

The compulsive method.

experience, whatever it is, must match the degree of compulsion. **The stronger the compulsion, the greater the agreeable experience has to be that follows it.**

Dogs differ in what **they** consider agreeable. For example, it is generally assumed that dogs like to be petted or fondled, which is not necessarily the case. Some dogs merely tolerate it and others do not like it at all, in which case it would not be a pleasant experience. Some trainers confuse violent pounding on the dog with petting or fondling. The dog's response will tell the trainer whether he considers it pleasant or not.

Similarly, some dogs do not consider praise or food particularly agreeable and instead prefer something like retrieving a ball or a stick. Even so, most dogs can be conditioned to accept praise and food as something agreeable. The point to remember is that just because *we* think the dog should perceive what we are doing as agreeable, does not necessarily mean the *dog* will perceive it as such.

When the dog is introduced to a new exercise, only the mildest compulsion to get the desired response is used so as not to produce any unnecessary anxiety. The general rule is: regardless of the stage of training the dog is in, only **the least amount of compulsion necessary to get the desired response** is used. Compulsion in excess of that will cause apprehension, intimidate the animal and needlessly prolong the time it takes the dog to learn the exercise.

Training for Abstention

Compulsion is also used to teach the dog to refrain from behavior we consider objectionable. But now the rules change.

First, the degree of compulsion must be such that it immediately suppresses the objectionable behavior. Ideally, it only has to be used **once** to arrest to offending conduct. If three tries are not enough, either the type of compulsion used is not correct, or it was not used properly.

Second is the timing of the compulsion. The ideal time of impressing upon Konrad that we don't want him to chase the cat is when he is thinking about it, **before** he has a chance to get started. Once he is in full chase, any disciplinary action will not diminish his pleasure in the chase, but will only undermine our relationship with the dog.

We can spare the dog much grief if we can get the owner to understand the correct time to impart discipline. It is without a doubt the most important lesson for the establishment of a mutually enjoyable relationship. It is also the single most important area of misunderstanding of how a dog learns and what influences his behavior.

Remember to reward the dog with something he finds enjoyable.

Dogs differ in what they consider agreeable.

The correct time to stop undesirable behavior is:

(1) When Konrad is thinking about it. To know what a dog is thinking is not difficult. Dogs are wonderfully predictable creatures. Having paid attention to what they have done in similar circumstances in the past tells us when they are likely to do the same thing again. The fixed stare, the tensing of the muscles, a slight change in body posture, the intent facial expression, are all telltale signs of his thoughts.

(2) When Konrad begins the objectionable behavior.

The incorrect time to try to deal with the objectionable behavior is:

(1) During fruition.

(2) After the fact.

Third, the disagreeable experience of compulsion is **not** followed by an agreeable experience, because it would only confuse the dog and nullify the effect of the compulsion.

Let's review Konrad's interest in the cat. The cat appears on the scene and we see Konrad's beady little eyes begin to focus. Based on prior experience, we know that whenever he has that expression, evil lurks in his heart. At that precise moment we convince him that it is to his distinct disadvantage to even think about chasing the cat. Konrad averts his eyes and looks at us. Since he may still be thinking "darn, I wish I could chase the cat," we say nothing, because praise at that moment might encourage him to try again, the very thing we don't want.

How do we know that Konrad has learned his lesson? He will tell us! On the next occasion the cat makes an appearance, we observe Konrad's reaction. If Konrad immediately looks up at us as though to say "I don't see any cat—there is no cat anywhere in sight," we know he has learned to leave the cat alone. We now can tell him what a good fellow he is for ignoring the cat. If, on the other hand, he continues to stare at the cat, it does not take a genius to figure out what he has in mind.

The lack of understanding of when to use compulsion for abstention, that is, **when** and **how** to discipline the dog, is no doubt what causes the beginner trainer the most problems for himself and his dog. It starts with housetraining or with training the dog to come when called.

Puppy has an accident in the house and the owner angrily points to the mess and either verbally or physically chastises the puppy. "Did you do this? Shame on you! Don't you know this is a brand new rug? How could you do this to me?" Smack, smack, smack! Such after-the-fact discipline will not teach the puppy not to make a mess in the house. Dogs who are housetrained by this approach become clean in spite of and not because of

The correct time to intercede is when the dog is <u>thinking</u> about misbehavior rather than after he has completed it.

The correct time to stop undesirable behavior.

the training. The correct time to intercede is when the puppy **begins** the action or when he is **thinking** about the action—before he completes it or before he has a chance to get started.

The second most common example of improper discipline is when Konrad does not come when called. Picture the following: Konrad likes to chase cars and once he is on his way, there is nothing the owner can do to get him to come back until Konrad gives up the chase. He returns only to find a master who is livid and who takes him by the scruff and thrashes him, all the while uttering threats of serious bodily harm, should he ever do that again.

The problem with this approach is that it is not only ineffective in teaching Konrad not to chase cars, but it undermines any hope we have of teaching him to respond to the "come" command. What was unpleasant for Konrad was not the chase, but the homecoming. He will continue to chase and, since he gets punished for coming home, he begins to stay away longer and longer in an effort to delay the inevitable.

One of the first instructions we give our students is **NEVER punish your dog when he comes to you no matter what he has done.** And, never do anything that the **dog** may perceive as unpleasant, such as giving him a pill, after he has responded to the "come" command. If he has to have a pill, call him, reward him with a treat and praise when he comes, and *then* give him the pill.

In the case of some obedience exercises, it is not clear cut whether we are training for action or abstention.

Here is a little teaser. When we teach the dog to heel, are we training for action or abstention? Are we teaching him to remain in heel position or not to leave heel position? The answer is both, at least in the beginning. The distinction is not, however, of such import as to require adherence to the rules concerning training for abstention and the exercise is treated as though we are training for action, that is, following the use of compulsion with an agreeable experience.

What about the Stay? Are we teaching the dog to remain in place or not to leave? The answer is we are teaching him not to leave and the rules of training for abstention apply. If reinforcement of the stay command becomes necessary, it is not followed by a pleasant experience in the form of praise. The dog is not praised until the conclusion of the exercise.

Discipline

1. Verbal reprimand.

For many dogs, especially puppies, a barklike and emphatic verbal reprimand, such as "Stop it!" or "Ah, ah!" is sufficient. To be effective, it is

One of the first instructions we give our students is NEVER punish your dog when he comes to you no matter what he has done.

When the dog responds to the come command, he is always praised.

given once and at the onset of, or when the dog is thinking about, the offending behavior. We do not use the word "no" for two reasons. One, by the time we get the dog in class, he has been "no'ed" to death. In many cases, it is the only word the dog has heard—"no, this, no, that." The dog has learned to tune it out. Second, it is used too often in human conversations and hence might cause confusion for the dog.

2. Shake by the scruff of the neck.

Young puppies, and some older dogs, respond well to a shake by the scruff. Accompanied by a verbal reprimand, it imitates how the mother dog disciplines her pups.

3. Eye contact.

For prepubescent dogs and young adults, an effective approach to discipline is to grasp the hair and loose skin at the side of the neck, near the face, with both hands, one on each side, lifting the dog's front end off the ground, establishing eye contact and issuing a verbal reprimand. Eye contact is maintained until the dog looks away, after which he is released.

4. Smack on the muzzle.

The severest form of discipline we use is a smart smack on the *top* of the muzzle, administered with either the hand or preferably the loop end of the leash. It is reserved for instances of aggression towards people or other animals and conduct that has been resistant to other forms of discipline.

Timing of discipline is more important than the nature of discipline. Even aggression can often be checked with a verbal reprimand, if given when the dog is thinking about the undesired behavior. **The further removed in point of time, the less effective the discipline will be.**

Whichever disciplinary measure the situation calls for, if three tries do not produce the desired response, either the technique is not being used correctly, or it is the wrong technique under the particular circumstances.

We view discipline as being inverse to motivation. The definition of motivation is perceived rewards minus perceived costs. In order for the dog to stop chasing cars or cats, the perceived costs must outweigh the perceived rewards. As long as they do not, the dog will continue the objectionable behavior. Put another way, it must become more costly to chase than not to chase. When that point is reached depends on the dog and on the handler's willingness to deal with the problem. Successful training is often no more than who is more persistent, the dog or the trainer.

A Final Word About Compulsion

Some behaviorists and authors of training books refer to the disagreeable experience of compulsion as "punishment," which is not only unfortunate, but also incorrect. Punishment implies that the recipient **knew** right from wrong when he committed the act for which he is being punished. The dog, however, even once trained, can never know right from wrong.

The use of words like "punishment" and "misbehavior" and "correction" in connection with training dogs connotes culpability where none exists! These words are anthropomorphic and inappropriate.

The dog is trained to abstain from behavior he would do on his own, but which is considered objectionable, through the use of disagreeable experiences, that is, compulsion, period! **THE DOG IS NOT PUNISHED.**

The dog is also trained to do things he would not do on his own through the use of disagreeable experiences. Again, **THE DOG IS NOT PUNISHED.**

The dog never misbehaves. He either engages in behavior that is considered objectionable or he fails to respond to a command. In either case, it is *our* job to train him properly.

SECONDARY STIMULI

Secondary stimuli are commands or signals. During training, the dog is conditioned to associate secondary stimuli with primary stimuli. The dog is considered trained once he responds reliably to the secondary stimulus— the command or signal.

Once we have gotten to that point, we never have to worry about the dog again, right? If only it were so.

The association between the primary and the secondary stimuli will weaken with each successive non-reinforced repetition, ultimately making the dog unreliable. A non-reinforced repetition is a command or signal unaccompanied by the primary stimulus. How quickly the association weakens depends on the extent to which the particular exercise is in harmony with the dog's instincts. For example, once a Sheltie has learned how to heel, the need to reinforce the exercise by means of the primary stimulus will be significantly less frequent than with a Siberian Husky.

The need for periodic reintroduction of the primary stimulus is referred to by some as "retraining" the dog. It is not so much retraining the dog as reestablishing the association between the primary and secondary stimuli.

This principle can baffle and frustrate the inexperienced trainer and unless he understands it, he will be tempted to overcome it by increasing the amount of compulsion. After all, the dog did it yesterday, the day before and the day before that. Today, he is just being stubborn. Bam!

Unfortunately, this method of training does not work.

secondary inducement

PRIMARY inducement

The dog becomes conditioned to associate secondary inducements with primary inducements.

Making the association.

The dog is neither stubborn, nor recalcitrant. The association between the primary and secondary stimuli has weakened and all that is necessary to reestablish it is to briefly go through the training progressions used to teach the exercise to the dog. It is a review, necessary whenever we deal with memory, not dissimilar from your having memorized a poem and then not reciting it for a few months. You, too, would have to refresh your recollection before you could recite it perfectly again.

CONCLUSION

The dog learns mainly through the faculty of memory. By creating an association between primary and secondary stimuli, we teach him to respond to commands. This association can be created through inducive or compulsive stimuli. When compulsion is employed to train for action, only the least amount necessary to get the desired response is used. When the dog is trained for abstention, the compulsion used depends on the dog and the situation so long as there is no doubt in the dog's mind that his behavior, or intended behavior, is unacceptable.

3

Influences on Learning

INTRODUCTION

How readily a dog will learn a particular exercise, or refrain from conduct considered objectionable, depends on a variety of factors. These fall into two broad categories: intrinsic influences on learning, that is, those that emanate from the dog himself, and extrinsic influences on learning, which emanate from the dog's environment.

INTRINSIC INFLUENCES ON LEARNING

Breed Characteristics

Pure-bred dogs were developed through selective breeding for particular traits, such as herding, guarding, hunting, or just being a good lap dog. As the popularity of the dog grew, breeding objectives began to change. Appearance came to be considered more important than function. It also became more important for the dog to fit in as a family pet than to be a natural hunter or herder. The dog has to be a pal for the kids and "a little protective." The very traits for which the dog was originally bred, become "objectionable behavior" in the increasingly urbanized setting where he is now expected to live. In many breeds the result has been to select for less instinctive and more juvenile traits, making the modern-day dog easier to manage than his predecessor.

The giant breeds are a good example. By selecting for a fairly tranquil and docile animal, the dog becomes a good pet. A high-powered, spirited Newfoundland, for instance, will require more commitment, not to mention expertise, than the average owner is willing to invest.

The traits, however, are still present in varying degrees of intensity and depending on what we want to teach the dog, will be a help or a hindrance. If the desired response coincides with the dog's instincts, he will learn it easily; if it is not, learning it will be more difficult.

The ease or difficulty of training a dog depends on the extent to which the exercise being taught is in harmony with his instincts.

Many times we have heard dogs being labeled "stubborn" for one reason or another. But this so-called stubbornness is often no more than a strong instinct which runs counter to what the owner wants the dog to do. A Beagle, for example, with a strong hunting instinct is easily distracted by the scent of a rabbit and will try to follow it. If this happens while the dog is supposed to heel, he will obviously be more interested in giving chase than in walking at his owner's side. A Beagle whose hunting instinct is less developed will be more easily taught to ignore rabbit tracks while heeling than the dog with the strong hunting instinct.

The presence of a strong chase instinct, so often found in the herding breeds, explains the fondness for chasing cars, bicycles and joggers. To teach such a dog to come when called when faced with a moving object can require herculean measures on the part of the owner and much support by the instructor.

Understanding the influence breed characteristics have on teaching various exercises to the dog will help the instructor put his students in a position where they can succeed.

Temperament

Temperament means different things to different people. What is considered desirable by some is viewed as objectionable by others. My dog is aloof; your dog is shy. My dog is assertive; your dog is aggressive. My dog alerts; your dog is noisy.

Temperament is defined as the dog's suitability for the specific task or function **for which he has been bred.** As such, there are no "good" or "bad" temperaments; there are suitable and unsuitable temperaments.

In the context of training, temperament is affected by willingness, first, to do the job for which the dog was bred and, second, to do something

59

Intrinsic influences on learning.

The presence of a strong chase instinct found in the herding breeds explains the fondness for chasing cars.

Instinctive behavior.

for his owner. This, too, is largely breed specific and can be in conflict. A dog may have a great willingness to do the job for which he was bred, such as pull a sled, but a lack of willingness to do something for the owner, such as come when called.

Some breeds are more typically independent than others and dogs of these breeds see little need, if any, to do what the owner wants. They will take longer to train than a dog who is less independent.

Sensitivity

The dog's sensitivity to touch, sight and sound, as well as his mental sensitivity, also influence learning and how he responds under any given circumstance.

Touch Sensitivity

The main primary compulsive stimulus used to train dogs is the check on the leash. The dog's response to the check depends on his touch sensitivity or pain threshold. A dog that is touch insensitive will not feel the check the same way as a dog that is touch sensitive. **Unless the check is a disagreeable experience, it is not a primary compulsive stimulus and will not accomplish its objective.**

Touch sensitivity tends to be breed related. Picture the Labrador Retriever sitting in the boat. His master fires and a duck falls into the icy water, 30 feet from the boat. His master gives the command "fetch!" Our dog just sits there as if to say "that water is co-o-o-ld. You shot it, you get it!" Or imagine the hunting dog rushing through the underbrush after the wounded pheasant. A thorn gets stuck in his foot and he gives up the chase with "ouch, that smarts!"

If this happened in real life, these dogs would not be selected for hunting or breeding hunting dogs. They would either get a new home or not be around very long. To do their job, they have to be touch insensitive, almost oblivious to physical discomfort.

Touch sensitivity is affected by the dog's interest in a particular activity at a given moment. A Beagle, although normally medium touch sensitive, will not feel the brambles or the cuts inflicted by the low branches, while in pursuit of a hare. Similarly, when two dogs get into a fight, their pain threshold increases.

When the instructor is faced with a student who is not getting the desired response to the chosen stimulus, that is, the check is not working, he has two options. He can increase the strength of the stimulus by recommending the pinch collar, or he can recommend a change in stimulus, such as to food.

Touch sensitivity would be a disadvantage to retrievers required to fetch ducks under all manner of adverse conditions

Touch sensitivity.

The point to remember is that it is not how **we** perceive the effect of a stimulus on a dog, but how the **dog** perceives it. There is no difference in the perception of the check between the touch sensitive Sheltie being trained on the dead ring of the collar and the touch insensitive Labrador being trained on the pinch collar.

Sight Sensitivity

The dog's sensitivity to visual stimuli will affect his response in the presence of moving distractions. To the Yorkshire Terrier, it is imperative to investigate every moving leaf or blade of grass, which makes heeling off leash somewhat of a nerve-racking exercise.

For handlers with sight sensitive dogs there is a premium on correct handling so as not to confuse the dog with extraneous movements and they have to be instructed accordingly. The emphasis here is on calm and smooth handling, keeping body movements to an absolute minimum. Leash handling and hand position are critical to the efficient training of the dog.

Sound Sensitivity

Most dogs are medium sensitive to sound and have perfectly normal responses to auditory stimuli. Some dogs, however, are sound sensitive and loud noises literally hurt their ears. In hunting dogs, it is called "gun shy." The dog is not really shy of the gun, it is the sound that bothers him.

Extreme sound sensitivity imposes some limitations on the dog in that he finds it difficult to concentrate and respond around loud noises. Some dogs, for example, will leave the room when the radio or television is turned on. Training for basic control, however, should not be adversely affected.

Deafness is a problem in some breeds and becomes quickly apparent. It is not to be confused with the temporary deafness afflicting the male dog when he is called to come while pursuing a female in season.

Mental Sensitivity

Dogs find it difficult to deal with human emotions such as disappointment, frustration and anger. If the owner becomes disappointed or angry over what he perceives to be some shortcoming on the part of the dog, the dog will not understand why his owner is upset. He will become anxious and learning will be impeded.

Although the coping mechanism of dogs varies, just as it does with people, negative emotions confuse the dog. **Confusion needlessly prolongs training.**

We tell our students when something goes wrong to examine how they trained the dog. Any shortcomings in the training are the owner's fault, not that of the dog.

Particularly troublesome are those instances where the dog responds to a command, but does so imprecisely. To berate him for any imperfections now, after he has tried to do what he was told, is most discouraging to the dog. The preferable course is to repeat the exercise, this time showing him what is expected.

Food for Thought

When the owner is not getting the response he thinks he should get, he becomes disappointed. Disappointment leads to frustration, which leads to anger, which can lead to violence. All of these undermine the relationship between owner and dog. The dog does not understand why his owner is feeling angry and he has difficulty coping with his master's negative emotions.

It is for this reason that instructions to the owner must be such that he is able to get the expected response and that the stimulus which has been chosen will get that response. For example, if the owner, because of the touch insensitivity of the dog, is not getting a response to the check, he will become frustrated. If the strength of the stimulus is not increased, or if it is not changed, training will not be successful!

Health

If the dog is ill, it will be difficult for him to concentrate on his lessons. Some of the more common problems that will interfere with the dog's ability to learn are described in PART IV.

What is not easily assessed is the effect medication has on how the dog will respond. The best guidance we can give is that if there is a change in the dog's behavior, or if the dog's responses are not quite what they used to be, ask the owner for a possible explanation. Try to find out if the dog has been put on medication. We have seen some strange effects in dogs under treatment for different conditions.

EXTRINSIC INFLUENCES ON LEARNING

Environment

Dogs are acutely affected by their perception of the environment. An environment the dog senses as unfriendly, or even hostile, makes him uncomfortable and anxious. Strife or friction in the family, tension or grief, all have an adverse impact on the dog's ability to learn.

Extrinsic influences on learning.

The training class, in particular, must exude a friendly and positive atmosphere. Since the first impression leaves the most lasting impact on the dog, we want it to be a positive one so that he looks forward to coming to class. Excessive noise, produced either by shouting or by barking, causes hyperactivity among the dogs which can lead to aggression. The presence of a bully in class, who tries to lord it over all the other dogs, produces a similar result. Training methods that instill fear also have a detrimental effect on the group.

By creating a calm and friendly environment, the instructor enhances the dog's ability and willingness to learn, which in turn benefits the students.

Routine

Dogs are creatures of habit. Changes in their routine produce stress which retards learning. A daily routine, consisting of regular feeding and relieving times, as well as exercise and mental stimulation in the form of training or a nice walk, will yield the best results.

Nutrition

Many dogs have adverse reactions to various substances contained in the food they ingest. Some are allergic to certain foods, chemicals or additives, and become hyperactive or lethargic. Others experience chronic digestive upsets for one reason or another. Learning is obviously made more difficult under these cirumstances and the advice of a veterinarian will have to be sought.

The Handler

Attitude

By far the most important extrinsic influence on learning is the handler's attitude toward his dog.

Obedience classes are often viewed as a last ditch effort to rehabilitate the canine delinquent. The owner would like to like his dog, but is at his wit's end on how to cope with Konrad's antics. School is his last hope—if Konrad does not shape up, it's a one-way trip to the pound. Their relationship has deteriorated to the point that no matter what the owner does, Konrad does not respond.

Then there are the students who don't want to be there at all. The husband got the dog for the kids and Mom is left with the job of taking care of him and now, training him. Or, worse yet, one of the kids is assigned to train the dog with "you take him to school, or he goes," which is unfair to both child and dog. Or, there is Dad, in class because he is the only one who can handle the dog, but who is thinking of a dozen other things he would rather be doing.

The challenge for the instructor is to mend these relationships and motivate those who don't want to be there. He meets that challenge by making the student successful, early and frequently.

Success, no matter how little, immediately changes the student's outlook. He may say to himself: "I don't believe it. The little fellow actually did what I told him to do." Or, "this isn't as bad as I thought it would be." The student's outlook begins to change. Instead of disliking Konrad, he begins to enjoy him. Instead of dreading class, he looks forward to it.

The attitude we want to foster among our students is a positive and benevolent one so that both student and dog enjoy the training and each other.

Consistency

Perhaps the toughest row to hoe for the instructor is to get across to the student that dogs do not understand "sometimes," "perhaps," "hardly ever," or "maybe." Dogs understand yes and no, pleasant and unpleasant, always or never.

This objective is accomplished by insisting on one command and one command only. If the dog does not respond to the first command, the student is instructed to reinforce, either by showing the dog what he is supposed to do, or by checking the dog, depending on the stage of training. We explain to the students that the key to training is getting the desired response to the first command. We also stress that while the dog is learning, to give a command only when they are in a position to enforce it. For example, don't give a command while you are in the bathtub, unless you are prepared to get out of the tub!

Similarly, the students are instructed to be consistent in their dealings with their dogs at all times. It is not fair to permit the dog on the couch sometimes and then discipline him when he tries to sit on a guest's lap.

Inconsistencies confuse the dog and prevent him from learning.

Unintentional Training

The most difficult negative influence on learning the instructor encounters is unintentional training. The student **thinks** he is training his dog to do one thing when he is really training his dog to do something else. At best, the student will wonder why he is not getting the expected

The attitude we want to foster is a positive one so that both the dog + student enjoy training.

Handler attitude.

It isn't fair to permit the dog on the couch sometimes + then punish him when he tries to sit on a guest.

Consistency.

response, and at worst, he gets mad at his dog when he thinks the dog has made a mistake.

As an instructor, watch for the following:

1.   Roughhousing with the dog.

Roughhousing teaches the dog to assert himself against the owner, a form of unintentional training which is not desirable. Instruct the owner to stop this form of play and teach the dog to retrieve instead.

2.   Timing of petting.

Students will often pet the dog at the incorrect moment, thereby giving the dog the impression that the behavior he is exhibiting at the time is acceptable. For example, after the return on a Down Stay, the dog gets up and the owner pets the dog. The owner thinks he is praising the dog for having stayed. What he is really doing is teaching the dog to get up when he returns.

Another example, and a much more serious one, is petting the dog when it shows signs of fear or aggression. What the owner wants to do is to reassure or calm the dog. What he is actually doing is telling the dog that it is all right to be afraid or aggressive. The owner is unintentionally reinforcing the undesired response.

Unintentional training is one of the reasons we make such a big point of when the owner can and cannot pet his dog. By making the owner aware of what he is doing, and the influence petting has on the dog, many of the potential problems of unintentional training can be avoided.

3.   Calling the dog.

Even though the students have already been told never to punish the dog when he comes, they must also be instructed not to do anything the dog perceives as unpleasant after he has come, such as calling the dog to give him a pill, or calling him to cut his toenails, or to give him a bath. When the dog responds to being called, he is always rewarded first, either in the form of praise and petting, or a treat.

4.   Training.

The most frequently asked question we get during our seminars is "how do I correct my dog's crooked sit?" Questions dealing with other training problems follow. When we ask the questioner to show us how he trained his dog for the particular exercise, invariably he will have miscued the dog. The handler has **trained** the dog to make the mistake, unintentionally, of course, usually through some oversight or the incorrect application of a training technique.

Take the example of the crooked sit at heel. By drawing the leash across his body, the handler has cued his dog to sit crooked. Since he is unaware that he is drawing the leash across his body, he blames the dog who is sitting crooked, responding correctly to the cue. Once the error is pointed out to the handler and he mends his ways, the dog begins to sit straight.

CONCLUSION

The combination of the different influences on learning will determine how readily the dog will respond. The instructor's awareness of their impact will help him guide his students through their trials and tribulations.

PART II

The Instructor and the Student

"Without any doubt at all, the writers knew their subject but they did not know how to teach it. Only in a very small percentage of human beings does knowledge go hand in hand with the ability to impart it. Knowledge is commendable; teaching an art acquired by all too few."

From *Companion Dog Training* by Hans Tossutti
(Howell Book House, 1964).

4

The Obedience Instructor

INTRODUCTION

Jack and Heidi, along with 20 other anxious handler/dog teams, presented themselves for their first lesson. Heidi was Jack's first Landseer Newfoundland and at the suggestion of a colleague, he had enrolled in the Beginner Class of the local obedience club. Twelve weeks later they graduated and, having enjoyed the training, decided to continue. Five months later, after obtaining a C.D. title, the club asked Jack to become an instructor.

This meteoric rise from beginner to instructor is not unusual. Not long ago we had a student who was an instructor for a weight reduction program. When we asked her how she had become an instructor, she said, "I lost the most weight in the last course."

What is the message here? Obtaining a C.D., or losing 50 pounds, has nothing to do with being able to teach. To be a teacher requires other aptitudes and skills. In this chapter the attributes that are necessary to make a good instructor, as well as those that are desirable, are outlined.

Monday Night.. Star pupil....

A meteoric rise from beginner . . .

Tuesday Night.. Star teacher ?

to instructor is not unusual.

ATTRIBUTES

Liking People

A good instructor **MUST** genuinely like people. While this seems almost too obvious to mention, we frequently hear comments like "I love the dogs—it's the people I can't stand." An instructor with this attitude would be better off sticking to training or considering a different career.

Ability to Teach

Training and teaching require separate and distinct skills. A dog trainer deals with dogs and uses techniques designed to train dogs. An instructor deals with people and uses techniques designed to teach people.

The adage "[H]e who can does. He who cannot, teaches" does a disservice to teachers. A good teacher excels at teaching and a good trainer at training. Placing emphasis on training aptitude as a prerequisite to *instructing* is therefore misplaced.

The essence of teaching is communication—the ability to impart knowledge to the student. To tell the student what he must do in such a way that the instructions can be successfully executed requires clear and specific articulations. It is not enough to tell the student "correct your dog." He needs to be told *precisely* what he must do to get the desired result.

Knowledge of the Subject

A thorough knowledge of dog training means knowing different techniques for any given exercise. There will be times when either the student is unable to use a technique or it will not work with his dog. Familiarity with more than one approach allows the instructor to try something else.

Having a solid working knowledge of the AKC obedience exercises from Novice through Utility permits the instructor to design a program so his students can readily participate in obedience competition, if they want to.

Understanding the different breed characteristics is necessary, since they affect how a dog will learn a particular exercise. For example, teaching the Stand to a Cocker Spaniel can be exasperating if you do not know that the breed was selectively bred to point by *sitting;* they have been bred with heavy bottoms! Armed with this insight, the instructor now knows, in all likelihood, a Cocker will take longer to learn this exercise than other dogs.

Familiarity with the developmental stages of the dog is a **must.** Program content is formulated to train dogs of **any age,** including puppies beginning at 8 weeks of age. Some people still think that a dog's training

A good dog trainer knows how to deal with dogs but is not necessarily a good instructor of people.

Instructing and training are different skills.

It helps to know more than one approach to training.

should not start until he is at least six months to a year old. By then he is probably a thorough nuisance and, if it is a large dog, he will be difficult to manage. The enlightened view, based on scientific findings, is to start the training while the dog is young.

Belief in Obedience Training

Most people enroll in an obedience class because they have a specific problem. Rover not only chases the mailman down the street, but he also won't come when called. The target of Sadie's voracious appetite includes Dad's favorite shoes, the garbage and anything else that isn't nailed down. And, Konrad's barking keeps Mrs. Smith from taking her afternoon nap.

Whether he realizes it or not, the student's principal problem is an inability to communicate with his dog. Obedience training teaches him, through various exercises, the art of communicating with his charge. If the training alone is not sufficient to solve the problem, a foundation has been laid for its solution.

It is therefore essential that the instructor believes in the value of obedience training as a means of achieving communication between owner and dog. The "you have to do this because I say so" approach does not work.

Many obedience exercises at first glance appear to have little practical application. It is the instructor's job to make these exercises relevant to the student. For example, it is a lot easier to brush a dog that has been taught to stand than one that is flailing about on the kitchen floor.

What about the need for precision, such as insisting on straight sits? Is it necessary for the pet owner? Absolutely! **The degree of precision is directly proportional to the ability to communicate, and hence the amount of control.**

Control brings freedom to the trained pet—he can be allowed to run off leash, because he will come when called; and he can go anywhere pets are allowed, because he is well behaved. **That is the essence of a good pet.**

Ability to Observe

Most obedience instructors come from the ranks of dog trainers. In this capacity they are schooled in observing the dog. Instructors, however, must teach themselves to watch the handlers, which has to be practiced until it becomes second nature.

To be successful, the student has to follow instructions. The instructor, therefore, must observe the *student* to see that he is doing what he has been told. For example, Sequence 2 of the Automatic Sit requires the student to grasp the leash snap with his right hand and check straight up as he tucks the dog into a sit with his left hand. If instead of checking straight up, the

Instructors should make obedience exercises relevant...

Rather than letting the dog flail about on the kitchen floor, encourage the student to...

use the Stand For Examination exercise.

Making obedience exercises relevant is the instructor's job.

student draws the leash across his body, the dog will not sit straight. Unless the instructor has watched the student, he will be unable to help him. **If the student's actions are correct, the dog's response will be correct.**

Impartiality

Occasionally a student will have all the qualities of a good dog trainer and the instructor will be tempted to spend more time with this individual than with the rest of the class. A similar temptation arises with the student who has the same breed of dog as the instructor.

Extra time can be given to these students, but after class. The other students will resent class time spent favoring one individual when they are entitled to an equal share of the instructor's time.

Personal Qualities

Enthusiasm, empathy, patience and a sense of humor all help to make an individual a better instructor.

Enthusiasm is contagious; empathy shows understanding; patience prevents anxiety; and a sense of humor maintains sanity.

RESPONSIBILITIES

Putting the Student in a Position of Success

The most important responsibility of the instructor is to put his students in a position that permits them to succeed.

Obedience classes are comprised of individuals with varying aptitudes and motivations. For the majority to be successful requires a program which increases the probabilities of success. If the student is sincere in his desire to train his dog, is willing to put in the necessary time and effort, he should be able to succeed.

The instructor's responsibility ends once he has put the student in a position of success. For example, if the student does not follow instructions, does not practice during the week or does not come regularly to class, he will have difficulty keeping up with the lessons. Under those circumstances, there is nothing the instructor can or should do. It is the responsibility of the student, not that of the instructor, to train the dog.

Class Preparation

Class preparation ensures that the exercises that need to be taught will be taught. Outlining ahead of time which exercises will be covered and in

An instructor should avoid giving extra class time to students with the same breed of dog as theirs.

Impartiality is important.

what order makes the difference between conducting a smooth class or standing there not knowing what to do next.

By planning the order of the exercises, the instructor helps the students in controlling their dogs. For example, in the first few weeks, the dogs tend to be excitable when they first arrive at class. By beginning the session with calming exercises such as the Sit, the Stand and the Down, the dogs quickly settle down. As the course progresses, the instructor can then begin the class with heeling.

Punctuality & Appearance

When class starts on time the students need to be on time themselves. Waiting for late arrivals encourages tardiness, and penalizes students who are punctual. Students coming late not only miss part of the instructions, but disrupt the class. If a student arrives when the class is already in progress, the dogs invariably become distracted, some of them start to bark, and everybody gets excited. This creates frustration on the part of the handlers, and resentment against the student who is late. The instructor sets a good example for the class by starting punctually.

The impression the instructor makes on the students will depend on how he dresses. Wearing the dirty blue jeans and sweatshirt worn for kennel chores shows a lack of respect for the students and the program. Club or school uniforms are the easiest way to deal with the question of what to wear and create a good impression.

DEVELOPING INSTRUCTORS

Every training organization continually faces the task of developing new instructors. Some have structured programs for this purpose, others are more casual. If the organization follows a particular approach to training, it will look to its own students for instructors. If it does not, it might look outside its own ranks. For example, we recently received an application in the mail from a local training organization looking for new instructors, which is one way of going about it.

A number of years ago, a training organization in search of a new instructor sent a committee to visit our classes to see whether it would be interested in hiring us. This is another approach to finding instructors.

By far the most common method is for an organization to look to its own students. In this section we will address ourselves to creating new instructors from the ranks of the organization's members.

The governing body for developing instructors is usually the Training Committee headed by the Training Director. Regular meetings are held to school assistants in the methodology employed by the organization. One would think that, as members of the organization, they would be familiar with its methodology. While this is true to a certain extent, the individual has learned it as a student, and will probably have forgotten all but the last training progression for every exercise. For example, when the assistant is asked how he taught his dog the Automatic Sit, he will say, "by checking the dog with the left hand." That particular sequence is the last of three, and he will have to be reintroduced to the two which preceded it.

Assisting

By assisting an instructor, the apprentice gains the experience of giving individual aid where necessary, observing the students and dealing with them on a one-on-one basis. There are, however, some ground rules to follow.

It is the instructor who gives instructions to the class. **The role of the assistant is to see that the students carry out those instructions without contradicting the instructor or giving conflicting advice.**

When helping an individual, the assistant will be tempted to improvise on the instructions. Improvisations hurt rather than help because they will confuse the student.

Occasionally, even though the student is following instructions, the technique being instructed is not working for a particular dog. When he sees this, the assistant notifies the instructor, who provides an alternative approach. As the assistant becomes more knowledgeable, this responsibility can then be given to him.

The amount of individual help an assistant gives is just enough to make the point. Too much elaboration causes the student to miss the next instructions, and is disruptive to the rest of the class. If more help is needed, the assistant suggests meeting the student after class.

Learning to Observe

The assistant observes the student to make sure that the instructor's directions are carried out. At first, he will watch only the dogs and will not see what the students are doing. Then he will try to watch everything, and consequently will miss even the most blatant errors directly in front of him. He can't see the trees for the forest.

Observing is a skill that has to be learned. Like any other skill it is learned in small steps. The beginner assistant also has to know what he is to observe. He has to watch:

1. Position of the dog
2. Collar position
3. Handler position/posture
4. Leash handling/position
5. Left hand/arm position
6. Right hand/arm position
7. Command/motion sequence
8. Pace
9. Petting
10. Action/training sequence.

The assistant also has to listen to:

1. Command voice
2. Verbal reinforcement
3. Praise
4. Verbal reprimand
5. Nagging
6. Release.

For example, Sequence 1 of the Sit Stay includes dog position (dog sits at heel), collar position (rings between ears), handler position (next to dog), leash position (folded into left hand), left hand/arm position (directly above dog's head with tension on leash), right hand/arm position (signal), command/motion sequence (signal and command, then step in front), petting (no physical praise), action/training sequence (if necessary, reinforce, step back, pause, release tension with left hand, pause, praise and release). In this particular example, the only point not applicable is pace.

The assistant listens to tone of voice (command), verbal reinforcement (if necessary), praise, no nagging (e.g., staystaystaystaystay), and the release.

The new assistant gains proficiency by first focusing on one or two points, and then increasing his sphere of observation. In addition, at first, he is assigned to observe only one student.

Getting Your Feet Wet

The transition from assistant to instructor includes conducting a class without having to assume the entire responsibility. This can be accomplished by having the assistant call some commands. The exercise most suitable is a heeling review because it does not require any new instructions and the assistant gets a feel for being in control of the class. We once had an assistant call commands for the first time who suddenly blanked out on the word "halt." She knew there was a word to stop the class, but couldn't think of it. The students kept heeling until they were out of breath when the instructor realized what had happened and came to her aid. The next step is to assign the assistant one exercise to teach. The assignment is given at least one week before it is due so that the assistant can outline the exercise and practice the articulation of instructions.

As the assistant gains knowledge about dog training and becomes familiar with the mechanics of running a class, he is assigned a class to teach under the supervision of an instructor.

CONCLUSION

A person who is an obedience instructor or who is considering becoming one will be successful if he enjoys teaching, enjoys people and enjoys sharing the knowledge and skill of training dogs. Being an instructor can be one of the most nerve racking and tiring professions, but also one of the most rewarding. The rewards are the successes of the students—establishing harmonious and mutually enjoyable relationships between the students and their dogs.

5

The Mechanics of Instructing

INTRODUCTION

Depending on the subject matter, learning takes place in different ways. When an activity, such as playing golf or training a dog, is involved, the instructing process has to take into account how people learn *physical* skills. In this regard, aptitude is often overrated. The person's desire to do well is more important than his God-given talent.

HOW PEOPLE LEARN

People learn a physical skill through practice. The quickest and most efficient way is in an orderly progression of small sequences. As each progression is learned, the next one is added, until a complete sequence of new skills can be performed.

Picture yourself learning to drive. With an automatic transmission, getting the car moving is easy—press on the accelerator with the right foot and steer. A standard transmission car requires an additional step—letting out the clutch with the left foot while depressing the accelerator with the right. And what is the result of that extra step? For the first few tries you stall the car.

Yet another step is added when you practice starting up on a hill. So that you don't roll backward, you engage the handbrake. To get the car moving now, you have to coordinate releasing the handbrake with letting out the clutch with the left foot and pressing on the accelerator with the right foot.

To begin at this step would be time consuming and frustrating.

The same principal applies to dog obedience instructing. When introducing the Automatic Sit, for example, we want the handler to think about three things: (1) the Halt; (2) the Sit; and (3) the Place. By first teaching the Sit, then the Place, and lastly, the Halt it becomes a fairly easy maneuver which even a beginner can learn to perform in just a few minutes.

ATTENTION

To teach another person, you must have his or her attention. In the majority of teaching situations, this is not a problem. In an obedience class, however, it can be, unless special efforts are made to deal with it.

The first session at which the handlers come with their dogs presents a real challenge. It is one of the most important lessons and at the same time, unless carefully choreographed, one where the student is least likely to pay attention. Since everything that follows builds on what is taught during that class, it is imperative that the student is put in a position of being able to learn.

It's not that the students don't want to pay attention. They can't. They are too nervous, too anxious. They are worried about their dogs and the other dogs. While in this state they are physically incapable of paying attention. Worse yet, the electricity in the air is sensed by the dogs who now become overexcited. A snow ball effect is created with student and dog feeding on each others' anxiety.

The first order of business, therefore, is the reduction of anxiety so that the students, both human and canine, can pay attention. Here is how it is done:

(1) The size of a class is limited to 15. If there are more than 15 students in the class, it is virtually impossible, even with good assistants, for the instructor to keep track of everyone in the class.

(2) As soon as handler and dog arrive, the dog is fitted with a training collar. The handler is given a training leash and instructed how to hold it, immediately giving him an element of control he has not had up to now. (We issue a collar and leash as part of the course to ensure that right from the start everybody has the equipment we want them to use.)

(3) The class starts by having handlers and dogs sit on the floor in a

semicircle in the center of the training area while the instructor goes through a brief orientation. He introduces himself, the assistants, if any, and talks for not less than five and not more than 10 minutes. What the instructor says is less important than that he speaks *quietly* and *slowly*. The purpose of the talk is not so much to inform, as to reduce anxiety. Information typically part of an orientation is given out in written form.

(4) The first exercises that are taught are the Sit, the Down and the Stand. The handlers have not moved from the spot where they started except that now they are on their knees. By eliminating any unnecessary moving about by the handlers, the dogs are kept quiet and under control.

Next comes sitting at heel position which is taught as a stationary exercise. It is not until the end of the session that heeling is introduced, and then only as briefly as possible. By then the dogs are not nearly as bouncy as at the beginning of class and everybody is quite relaxed.

(5) A friendly atmosphere!

By following these steps, the instructor reduces the students' anxiety so they can pay attention to the lesson.

RETENTION RATE

Research has shown that the average person accurately remembers only about 10% of what he hears. If the instructor lectures to his class for one hour, his students will remember about six minutes of the entire talk. Unfortunately, there is no way to predict which six minutes. Is it three minutes at the beginning and three minutes at the end? Six minutes interspersed throughout the talk? Six minutes of what they want to hear? Or just the funny stories?

The lecture certainly seems to be a haphazard way to impart information.

We can only speculate what the presence of the dog does to that retention rate, but it surely is not going to improve it. The moral is: unless you have plenty of time and don't mind repeating yourself again and again and again, keep lectures to an absolute minimum.

Adding demonstrations will increase retention to about 35%, and actually doing it, to about 50%.

In practical terms then, significant learning of a new skill does not take place until the student has had the opportunity of doing it himself. We like to give our students the chance to try each new maneuver three times before sending them home. Still, we have no guarantee that they will remember all

Graph of amount of information retained by students

10%

Listening to a lecture

35%

Watching a demonstration

50%

Doing it himself

I hear, I forget; I see, I remember; I do, I understand.

90

the instructions necessary to practice correctly what we have just taught them, especially since at every class more than one exercise is covered. Even after having done it three times, the retention rate does not go much over 50%.

To help the student remember what has been covered in class, we use written reminders, or **homework sheets.** These need not be elaborate. A brief reiteration of the instructions given during class—no more than one typewritten page—is all that is necessary. Homework sheets are a powerful tool to help the students recall what was taught in class, as well as serving as a reminder to practice.

You can remember the retention rate of your students with the help of the Chinese proverb "I hear and I forget; I see and I remember; I do and I understand."

AN INSTRUCTING FORMAT

A number of years ago, Glenn Johnson (*Tracking Dog,* Arner Publications, 1977) introduced us to an instructing format which we have followed ever since. It is called EDICT.

Explain
Demonstrate
Instruct
Correct
Train.

Explain

The instructor introduces an exercise with a brief overview, including the name of the exercise, its purpose and an explanation of how it is performed. For example, the instructor might say:

> The next exercise is the Down Hand Signal. It is a neat trick to teach your dog and tonight you will learn Sequence 1. With your dogs sitting at heel, I will tell you to leave your dogs. Fold the leash into your left hand. Command and signal your dogs to stay and step directly in front. I will then tell you to "prepare to down your dogs." You will kneel in front of your dogs and put two fingers of the left hand, palm facing down, through the collar, under the dog's chin. When I say "down your dogs" you will raise your right arm and with your left hand apply pressure back and down, as you say "down." **PRAISE** as soon as he is down.

The explanation tells the students what they are about to do and it creates a mental picture of how to do it. But if we were to stop there, few students, if any, would be able to complete the maneuver. So, we

Demonstrate

Demonstrations can be done with a trained dog or with one of the students' dogs. If you use assistants, have one demonstrate while you do the commentary—it's easier than doing both at the same time.

We demonstrate from two different angles, so everyone in the class has a good view. During the demonstration, we point out the specific areas that the students tend to overlook. In the example above, it would be the pressure *back* and down. After that

Instruct

The students are now given the specific instructions we want them to follow. It would sound something like this:

Everybody ready? All dogs sitting at heel. Neatly fold the leash into your left hand. Leave your dogs. Prepare to down your dogs—kneel down, put two fingers of your left hand, palm facing down, through the collar under the dog's muzzle. Down your dogs—raise your right arm and apply pressure back and down with your left hand. **PRAISE.** Very good. Now let's try it again. Pivot back to your dogs. Sit your dogs . . . .

Even though this is now the third time the students have heard this litany, there is a difference between hearing it and doing it, and most of them will leave out one or more of the instructions on the first try. This brings us to the next step of EDICT which is

Correct

It is at this step that the instructor uses his skills of observing his *students.*

John, the action with your left hand is **back** and down. If you pull forward and down, you will cause your dog to come towards you. Mary, turn your left hand over so that your palm faces down. Jim, praise your dog when he is down.

As each omission is spotted, it is pointed out to the student. It is pointed out in a positive way, as a form of constructive criticism. And, those students who made the same mistake, but were not "caught" by the instructor, have a chance to correct themselves.

92

Assistant demonstrates with student's dog, first one way . . .

then the other.

93

Assistant corrects student.

After three repetitions, everybody usually has it right.

The **correct** step of EDICT is the most critical. Unless the student does it correctly in class, he will not be able to practice correctly at home. The "he'll get it right at home" approach is patently false. He definitely will not, and every effort should be made to ensure he gets it right in class.

What about the student who for one reason or another simply can't get it right? How much class time can be devoted to that individual before moving on?

In every class there will be one or two students who will require extra help. It cannot, however, be given at the expense of the other students. The majority of the students in the class dictate whether the instructor can move on or whether more time needs to be spent on a particular exercise.

Extra help can be given by an assistant or after class.

A Point to Remember

The end does not justify the means. Regardless of the results, the means must be critiqued. Although the dog did lie down, the student's method was incorrect—he pointed to the ground.

First, because the student did not do it correctly, he will not reach his ultimate goal, that is, a dog that lies down on command, without additional visual cues. Secondly, if the handler runs into a problem at home, he will have no recourse. If he did not do it correctly in class, he will not be able to do it correctly at home.

Train

The student is now in a position to practice at home the exercises he has been taught in class. The homework sheet serves to refresh his recollection, as well as giving him the specific goal for every exercise.

STRATEGIES FOR SUCCESS

An awareness and understanding of direction, location, order, instructor position and applied psychology will help the instructor to conduct an effective class, so necessary for the students' success.

All at Once

The students are told to wait for the instructor's command before attempting the exercise with their dogs. If a student is trying to execute instructions while they are being given, he can't pay attention to the entire explanation. The instructions would be, "When I say sit your dogs, you will sit your dogs."

Another reason for insisting the class perform the exercise in unison is that it is easier for the instructor and assistants to spot and correct errors than when the students are doing it randomly on their own.

Direction

The direction in which a particular exercise is done will have a direct bearing on how easy or difficult it is for the student. For example, when heeling is introduced, the dogs are on the outside—handler and dog moving clockwise. Heeling in that direction makes it relatively easy for the handler to keep the dog in position. When the dog is on the outside, he tends to be less distracted by the other dogs. He also has to work that much harder to stay in heel position, which tends to eliminate forging.

Another example is the Stand. There are several ways in which this exercise can be done in class. The dogs and handlers can be placed in a straight line or they can be placed in a circle with each dog facing the rear of the dog in front. In both examples, the dogs will experience some apprehension about the dogs next to them, the dog behind, or the ones they cannot see. In the circle they will also be tempted to sniff the dog in front. The exercise becomes needlessly difficult because the dogs will want to move.

The instructor can make this exercise easy for his students by arranging the dogs in a circle facing the center. This direction eliminates apprehension because all the dogs are in full view of each other, and the temptation to move is reduced.

Teaching the Stand in a circle with the dogs facing the center of the training area.

The direction in which an exercise is done
  has a direct bearing on how easy or difficult it is

The Stand for Examination in a line encourages dogs to break

The Stand for Examination in a circle facing each other
  reduces the urge to break.

Direction of exercises.

The location in the training area where an exercise is done will have an impact on the ease or difficulty with which the handler can teach his dog. For example, in a beginner class the Down Stay is done in a different location from the Sit Stay. Beginner dogs have a tendency to be extra helpful and if the stays are routinely practiced in the same place many dogs will lie down on the Sit Stay. The dog is not breaking the Sit Stay as much as anticipating the Down Stay, which can be avoided by changing locations.

Another example is the effect on the dog of a location where he had a particularly unpleasant experience, such as a severe check. When the dog gets back to that spot, he will try to avoid it—jump to the side, rush ahead, or go behind the handler. How long he will remember that spot will depend on the impact of the experience. More compulsion is not the answer. The dog is encouraged and gently guided over the spot until he realizes nothing disagreeable will happen to him.

Order of Exercises

Exercises fall into three basic categories: action, control, and those that have elements of both. Action exercises tend to excite the dogs while control exercises calm them down. Heeling is an example of an action exercise, the Sit Stay is an example of a control exercise and the Finish is an example of one that has elements of both.

The main purpose of the beginner class is for the student to get control over his dog. The order in which the exercises are arranged can have a positive or a negative influence on this goal. The more action exercises, the more excited the dogs become. But, by alternating between action and control exercises and adjusting the amount of time spent on each, the instructor regulates the level of excitability in the class. For example, during the first few weeks, heeling is kept to a minimum and the control exercises are emphasized. In later weeks, when the handlers have more control, the number and duration of action exercises are increased.

Control exercises tend to have a depressing affect on the dog's psyche and thus can have an adverse impact on his willingness to learn. By instructing several control exercises in succession, the dogs will view training as unpleasant and depressing and will look thoroughly miserable, as though they've been beaten. Their motivation to learn can be maintained by alternating control and action exercises in a logical manner.

Another aspect of order relates to exercises that should not precede other exercises. The Down and the Stand, for example, have a particularly depressing effect on the dog. They are therefore not done immediately

The more action exercises, the more excited the dogs become...

but, by instructing too many control exercises in succession the dog will become depressed and look thoroughly miserable.

By alternating between action and control exercises the level of excitability is regulated.

Alternating action and control exercises.

Getting ready for the Recall.

Calling the dog.

Dog comes.

before the Recall or off leash heeling which are exercises requiring maximum voluntary cooperation from the dog. To do so in all likelihood will result in a slow response to the Recall, or lagging during the off leash heeling.

Finally, there are those exercises that *should be* practiced immediately before another exercise. The Automatic Sit, for example, is reviewed and reinforced several times before doing off leash heeling. Practicing Automatic Sits focuses the dog's attention on the handler and sets the stage for successful off leash heeling.

Instructor Position

Where the instructor stands determines how much of the class he can see at one time. If he stands in the middle of a circle, his back is to half the class. If he stands outside the circle, he has the entire class in view.

Applied Psychology

The application of canine psychology is the cornerstone for teaching the dog to *want* to respond to a command. For example, the foundation for teaching the dog to come off leash, is described in our book **TRAINING YOUR DOG—The Step-by-Step Manual.** The dog is left on a Sit Stay and the handler walks 15 feet forward, turns to face his dog, counts to five, kneels down, counts to five, places his hands, palms up on his thighs, smiles and calls his dog.

This same procedure is followed in class. The students are lined up and one at a time, a handler will heel his dog straight forward for 15 feet, turn and face the line-up. He will remove his leash, leave his dog on a Sit Stay and return to the line-up. He will turn to face his dog for a count of five, kneel sitting on his heels for a count of five, place his hands, palms up, on his thighs, smile and call his dog. The handler is instructed to maintain this posture and, specifically, keep his hands on his thighs, letting the dog come to him. When the dog gets there, he is to praise and pet him for one full minute.

The psychology behind this procedure is:

1. The dog is taken out of the line-up, which constitutes the pack.
2. The dog is left in isolation where he is uncomfortable and wants to re-join the pack.
3. Handler reduces body posture and thereby makes himself as inviting and as non-threatening as possible.
4. When called, all the dog has to do is to retrace his steps; he is not required to walk across unfamiliar territory the first time he does the exercise.

5. The handler's posture remains inviting, making no threatening gestures such as reaching or grabbing for the dog.
6. The dog re-joins the pack where he is received with positive reinforcement.
7. The exercise is taught off leash, because that is how the dog is expected to respond.

In our experience, we have seen few dogs who did not go directly to the handler the first time this exercise was done. The psychology is such that the dog will want to come to the handler.

CONCLUSION

In this chapter we have outlined those instructing techniques that have worked for us. These techniques can be used successfully regardless of the particular method or approach to training used by the instructor.

6

Student Motivation

INTRODUCTION

In 1978 Jack participated in a workshop sponsored by the National Association of Dog Obedience Instructors. Also on the program was Dr. Ted Clevenger, Dean of the Department of Psychology of the University of Florida. The topic was motivation—Jack speaking about dogs, Dr. Clevenger about people.

Dr. Clevenger clearly and concisely explained the requirements for motivating people. Motivation can be viewed from four different perspectives: the psychologist, the teacher, the salesman and the individual. In this chapter we will describe the elements of motivation from the teacher's perspective and how they are applied to an obedience training class.

FACTORS INFLUENCING MOTIVATION

Organization

From his first contact through graduation, the student's motivation to train his dog will be affected by his perception of the instructor's commitment to imparting quality instruction. Much of what influences him is organizational—being prepared, starting and ending the sessions on time, having enough equipment, handouts and personnel for the class. For example, a group of 35 beginners needs more than one instructor. Aside from these commonsense observations, other organizational aspects play an important role in student motivation.

The Initial Inquiry

When an individual calls a training organization to inquire about classes, he is demonstrating initiative and motivation. It is up to the person answering the call to convert this initiative into a desire to become a student. To do so requires skill and tact. Some callers, for example, want an immediate resolution, over the phone, of whatever problem they are experiencing. Since this is rarely possible, the caller's thinking has to be steered in the direction of becoming a student, something he may not have considered. Most of the callers, however, seek information on what is involved in attending a dog training class, the length of the course and the cost.

The caller is treated in a positive and pleasant manner. To the extent possible, questions on training or raising the dog are answered. The purpose of the training class is explained—many people think that the **instructor** will train the dog for them when they bring it to class.

It is made clear the **student** has to train the dog and that if he expects to get anything out of the course, he has to be prepared to train the dog five times a week. This point is emphasized so the caller knows what he is getting himself into.

Individuals who enroll thinking the instructor will train the dog or that they have to train the dog only during class are marked for failure.

The caller is then informed of the length of the program, the length of each session, the time and day of the week the class meets, the location, the fee for the course and what the fee includes. In our case, for example, the fee includes a training leash and collar, and weekly homework sheets. The reason for including these is by no means philanthropic. It ensures that right from the start every student has the equipment we want him or her to have.

The goal of the course is outlined, namely what the dog is expected to be able to do upon its completion, so the caller knows what the objectives are and what he will get out of it.

Finally, the caller's name and address are taken to send him written information about the classes. What is sent need not be elaborate, just enough to tell the potential student something about the organization's or instructor's credentials, the particulars about the next series of classes, and the location. We include a registration form and encourage preregistration to reduce the amount of administrative detail that has to be handled the first session.

A large group of beginners needs more than one instructor.

Make it clear that . . .

the student has to train the dog.

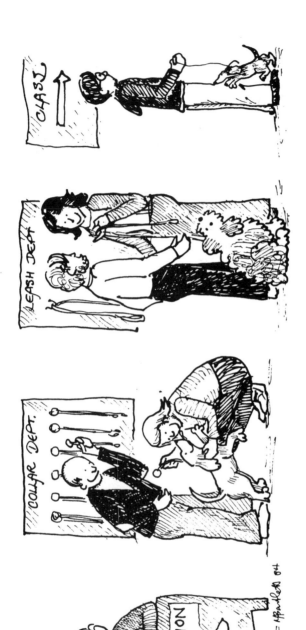

Organizing the first session.

To sum up:

1. Listen to what the caller is trying to tell you and exhibit interest in him and his dog.
2. Be courteous and friendly.
3. Explain the purpose of the class.
4. Give the length, date, time, location and fee of the class.
5. Describe what the fee includes.
6. Outline the goal of the course and what the student will get out of it.
7. Get the caller's name and address.
8. Send follow-up information with registration form.

The First Session

There are two schools of thought concerning the format of the first session. One teaches that it should be conducted without dogs, the other with dogs.

For the majority of students, the motivation to train will be at its peak for the first week. Think about it. The last time you purchased a new TV, or a stereo or camera, did you read the instructions before trying to use it? We bet you were so anxious to start that you did not bother reading the directions. The same thing happens when a student enrolls in a class—he wants to get started right away. To capitalize on that initial motivation, to maintain and even enhance it, the first session includes dogs. After a brief introduction, we start instructing and the student begins the training of his dog.

Whichever way you ultimately choose to go, make the first session a positive experience for the owner. Have enough staff available so that late registrations can be handled quickly and efficiently. Students who have pre-registered will become irritable standing around waiting for the class to begin. Since we start instructing during that class, this is of particular importance. Collars are fitted individually, leashes issued and late registrations handled, requiring time and personnel. Our aim is to get under way no later than 10 minutes after the announced start of the class. If you don't have enough help to do this, allow more time for the first class.

Homework Sheets

Upon the conclusion of each session we give out homework sheets as a reminder to the students of what to practice and how. Homework sheets permit the students to concentrate on what they are doing in class rather than having to worry about remembering all that is being taught. They are able to relax instead of being anxious.

107

The homework sheets are goal-oriented so that everyone progresses at about the same rate. For example, the goal for heeling for the first week is 10 paces without having to touch the leash. For the owner of a Wire Fox Terrier this may mean practicing 30 minutes a day, while the owner of the Border Collie will reach the goal in only two minutes. But when they come to Lesson 2, both are ready to progress.

Absentees

During the course, one or more of your students will have to miss a class, maybe even two. How such an absence is handled will have a direct bearing on the individual's motivation. If he is left to his own devices and no effort is made to give him the instructions he has missed he will fall behind the rest of the class, become discouraged and drop out. Providing make-up classes can avoid this.

How make-up sessions are set up will depend on the instructor's schedule. The best time is either at the end of the regular class, if the student knows he will miss the next session, or before the next class, if he missed the previous one. In either case, the student will be able to keep up and will not become discouraged. The material covered in a make-up class is limited to new instructions and can be covered in about fifteen minutes.

What about the student who misses a class without letting you know? He is a potential drop-out and deserves a friendly call to find out why. Often there is a valid reason why he can't continue the course. Just as often, however, he is discouraged and your interest may motivate him to continue.

Repeating the Course

Not every student will be able to graduate. If the instructor has done his job, it does not really matter why and the student will know the reason. What does matter is how it is handled. We offer the individual the opportunity to repeat the course free of charge. If the student has not put in the time and effort to work with his dog, he will probably not take us up on this offer. He knows why he did not graduate and he also knows that he will not put the necessary time and effort into training the second time around.

The offer to repeat the course is a gesture of good will and takes some of the sting out of not graduating.

The student who has honestly tried, but somehow just couldn't reach the required level of proficiency, will be motivated by this offer to try again. He will graduate the next time, which will have made it all worthwhile. In our experience, many of these students go on to further training and often become active in the sport.

Length of Program

Many programs consist of 10 or 12 weeks. We have also seen programs of as few as 5 weeks. In terms of student motivation the ideal program consists of 8 weeks.

A 5-week course is too short to reach a meaningful level of proficiency. A 12-week program is too long for many students. Few people are willing to commit that much time. It is also difficult to maintain their interest for three months, which increases the risk of drop-outs. Finally, it encourages an "I have plenty of time" attitude among some students who then fall hopelessly behind because the meat of the program is taught during the first four weeks.

An 8-week program, on the other hand, is long enough for the owner to obtain control. Yet it is not so long that the student feels he is able to coast for the first few weeks. Our experience with programs of varying lengths has shown that for maintaining student motivation and accomplishment, an 8-week program is the best.

Number of Students

The number of students required to create the feeling of a class and provide group identity is ten or more. If there are fewer students, say eight, and one of them drops out, a snowballing effect may develop. One drop-out from among eight is more noticeable than one from among 12, and can destroy the feeling of group cohesiveness and undermine motivation. For this reason, we will not start a class of fewer than ten.

There is also an optimum number of students per class, which is 15. A larger number is difficult to manage and to provide with the required individual attention necessary to maintain motivation.

Graduation

The manner of handling graduations has a direct bearing on the students' motivation to complete the course, attend graduation, and possibly continue training. How graduations are handled varies from very informal to a mock trial, replete with judge and placings.

Let's take a look at graduations from the student's point of view. The student enrolled in the course to train his dog. When he has achieved the requisite level of proficiency set by the organization as necessary to graduate, he is entitled to do so. Should this depend on how well he and his dog do at graduation? In the context of student motivation the answer is no. Assigning that much importance to the graduation will have the tendency to discourage students—they are beginners, they are unsure of how they and their dogs will react and they fear failure. As a result, many will avoid the situation by not attending graduation and not completing the course.

Another way of handling it is to tell the student, privately, a week before graduation that he will not graduate, the decision having been made on the basis of the instructor's observations of his achievements. Having eliminated the uncertainty of who will pass, it no longer matters what actually takes place at graduation.

We do not make a big fuss over graduation. We conduct an abbreviated class and then have a party to which the students are encouraged to bring family and friends. The atmosphere is friendly and relaxed. Those who are continuing their training are full of anticipation of what the next course will bring and the others will say their good-byes. A nice way to end a new experience.

Variety

Variety maintains interest, provided it is **meaningful.** Variations are achieved not only by teaching different exercises each session, but also with the progressions or sequences for each exercise. Each new progression is different from the previous one, which provides variety and brings the student closer to his goal.

Meaningful variety is also created by teaching the students different ways to practice the same exercise. Hand signals in addition to verbal commands are an example. Incorporating signals also increases the number of times an exercise is practiced, thereby accelerating the learning process.

In motivational terms, hand signals are a nice bonus. They enable the student to show off his training to the inquisitive neighbor who can't believe that one has to take a dog to school to teach it to lie down. Being able to demonstrate this feat with a hand signal makes a believer out of the neighbor and convinces the student that his efforts are worthwhile.

Pace

To be motivational, the tempo or pace of the class must be fast— almost too fast. As instructors, we must avoid dwelling on a subject or an exercise. The dictionary definition of to "dwell" is to "make dull."

Unless he carefully guards against it, the well-meaning instructor will try to make sure **everybody** fully understands **everything** being covered. He will spend the extra time with Mrs. Smith's little Konrad or perhaps expound at great lengths on some esoteric point. In the meantime half the

Hand Signals . . .

provide meaningful variety.

111

Showing off Hand Signals.

class is bored to tears. His good intentions are counterproductive, causing a part of the class to lose some of its motivation.

Move the class along briskly by keeping lectures to a minimum and relying on written handouts, such as orientation material and homework sheets. If extra time is necessary for a particular student, it can be given after class.

Climate

A friendly and helpful attitude by the instructor creates an atmosphere which makes the student want to attend class. The drill sergeant approach will not motivate people either to train or to come to class. People do not like to be embarrassed or ridiculed. By treating students the way you would want to be treated as a student, you will not have any problems creating the type of climate which makes everybody look forward to coming to class.

Positive vs. Negative Instructions

Instructions can be given in two ways: positively or negatively. For example, the instructor can say, "Keep your left hand in Control Position," or "Don't swing your left arm."

Positive instructions are more motivational than negative instructions. Negative instructions leave room for further error. "Don't swing your left arm" could mean place your left arm behind your back, or on top of your head. Positive instructions give specific directions, leaving no room for misinterpretation.

Negative instructions tend to cause resentment; positive instructions foster a willingness to comply. Although it is not always possible to avoid starting with "don't . . .," we make a conscious effort to couch instructions in "do . . .," or "try. . . ." Saying it with a smile will make the student try that much harder. "Don'ts" sound like nagging, no matter how well-meaning, and are not motivational.

"The Difficult Exercise"

Every instructor knows that some exercises are more difficult than others. He is not, however, doing his students a favor when he begins by saying, "Now, this is a difficult exercise." Such a preface creates a defeatist attitude. The student says to himself, "If my *instructor* thinks this is a difficult exercise, surely I will not be able to do it."

The best policy is to avoid characterizing exercises as "difficult" and to adopt a positive attitude.

In some cases this involves stretching the truth. "Teaching your dog to

Positive instructions are more motivational . . .

than negative instructions.

stand still is easy" or "all dogs like to retrieve." While not exactly the truth, at least the student is not predestined to failure.

Irrelevancies

Talking about topics that have no immediate relevance to the students is a waste of time and may cause confusion. Confusion causes apprehension and apprehension is not motivational. It would be irrelevant to tell students during the first session that someday they may become interested in AKC competition. With one or two exceptions, they will not know what that is. It would be equally pointless to refer to training errors in trial jargon such as "if you ever do that in the ring, you could lose a leg," conjuring up horrific visions of losing one of the lower extremities.

On the other hand, it is the instructor's responsibility to the sport of obedience to encourage students to consider further training and competitive events. This responsibility can be fulfilled toward the conclusion of the course, when the students' dogs are performing at a level where they can see that the requirements of a C.D. would not be beyond their capabilities.

Contacts

Another important influence on motivation is the opportunity for social interaction. Time is made available either before or after class when students can talk to each other, if they so desire. By comparing notes, they realize that the difficulties they may be experiencing are not unique. This awareness has a motivating effect—it creates group identity and a sense of belonging. It also allows for the making of friendships, something many of our students have done.

Attention

Individual attention is highly motivational and can be given in two ways. First, call each student by name. Learning the students' names so that you can address them correctly demonstrates that you care and is infinitely better than "hey you, with the big mutt."

Name tags with the student's name and the name of his dog are a great help. These can be of the plastic pin-on variety which are given out at the beginning of every class and collected again at the end. Combined with calling the roll out loud each week, you will quickly learn everyone's name and the name of his dog.

Second, whenever we can, we use a student's dog to demonstrate—it is motivational for the student and the rest of the class. Students like to watch their own dogs being used for a demonstration and the class sees that the particular exercise can be performed by an untrained dog.

Demonstrations with a trained dog, especially the instructor's dog, have little, if any, impact. They don't show the students how it can be done with an untrained dog.

We demonstrate with a trained dog only when the finished product has to be shown. For example, the first time the Finish is introduced, the end product is demonstrated with a trained dog so that the students can see the entire exercise.

MAINTAINING STUDENT MOTIVATION

The two key ingredients to maintaining motivation are **EARLY SUCCESS** and **FREQUENT SUCCESS.** Early means almost immediate and frequent means repeated success. Promises of how well the dog will do in the future if the student sticks with it do not meet this requirement.

Early success is achieved when we give our students a training collar and leash and show them Control Position. They immediately have more control over their dogs than they did before. The first exercises we instruct are the Sit, the Stand and the Down, thereby putting the student in a position of having more success. Although insignificant in comparison to what the student will eventually learn, these are the first steps in the right direction.

To maintain student motivation, success must be *frequent,* which is achieved with **small bites** and **clear goals.** The exercises are divided into small components which can readily be mastered by the student and his dog. At the same time, the student is given a specific goal to aim for during the week. In the case of heeling, for example, the first week homework assignment is to practice until the dog will heel for ten paces without any tension on the leash. The goal is clear and it can be reached, which means success and **success** is still the best motivator of them all.

Student motivation is further enhanced through the *structure of the organization,* that is, a recognizable unit with a clear chain of command. The students should be able to tell the coaches from the players which can be done with uniforms, common dress or club patches.

Student motivation is maintained through meaningful praise for a job well done. People, just like dogs, respond to positive reinforcement so long as it is sincere. With the particularly awkward or clumsy student this sometimes requires special efforts, but it still needs to be done.

Finally, there are several motivators which apply specifically to dog obedience training classes. These are telling the students about the learning plateaus their dogs will go through and giving them a preview of the next class.

The two key ingredients to maintaining motivation are EARLY SUCCESS . . .

and FREQUENT SUCCESS.

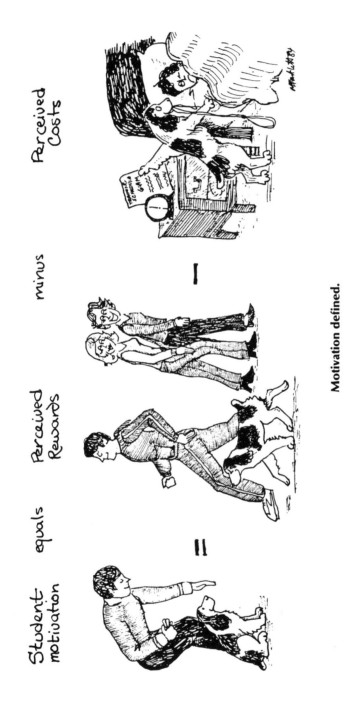

Student   equals   Perceived   minus   Perceived
motivation   Rewards   Costs

Motivation defined.

Learning Plateaus

Sometime between the 35th and 42nd day of training, the dog goes through a brief regression which generally lasts no more than several days. During this time the dog will appear to have forgotten what he has learned. While the experienced trainer is familiar with this phenomenon, it is devastating to the beginner. After having spent five weeks training his dog, he can't believe what is happening—he was doing ever so well, and now this! Many beginners give up at this point in utter disgust and training organizations often experience the highest drop-out rate between the sixth and seventh week of training.

We refer to this phenomenon as a "learning plateau" and instead of letting it destroy our students' motivation, we use it to increase it. We tell them that it *will* happen and when. It is amazing how many students will then make it a point to tell us that we were absolutely right. Once having recognized it, they are able to laugh it off. It now motivates them to continue, whereas it could have caused them to drop out.

Preview of the Next Class

We find it useful to tell the class what we will teach the following session. We do not recite the entire lesson plan, but pick out one exercise we believe is of particular interest to the students. For instance, upon conclusion of the second week's session we tell the class that next week we are going to teach the Recall. Since most of the students are enrolled to teach their dogs this one exercise, everyone will make a special effort to attend. Examples of other previewed exercises are the Stay, the first hand signal, and off leash heeling.

CONCLUSION

In this chapter we have described the elements of student motivation—the factors that influence it and how to maintain it. These elements are specific and are based on scientific research. Their effectiveness has been proven over time and provides the instructor with a workable formula for answering the question we are asked most frequently—"How do I motivate my students?"

PART III

The Obedience Class

"Success is a journey, not a destination."

7

Anatomy of an Instructing Program

INTRODUCTION

This Chapter deals with the main elements that need to be considered in establishing an instructing program. These include the criteria for the selection of training techniques and equipment, and how to devise a program that permits the inexperienced handler to successfully teach his dog in a structured and orderly way.

Instructing techniques are different from training techniques that might be used by an experienced trainer. Obedience classes consist of inexperienced handlers, beginners with varying degrees of aptitude who have neither the skill nor the intuition of the experienced trainer. Their dogs, too, vary widely, both in age and in willingness. Therefore, a training technique which works for a particular trainer and his dog may not be suitable as an instructing technique.

CRITERIA FOR SELECTING TECHNIQUES

Handler Aptitude

For anyone who has trained dogs for some time, it is difficult to

The major criterion for an instructing technique is whether the majority of <u>beginners</u> can do it successfully...

<u>not</u> whether an agile, experienced trainer can do it.

Selecting techniques for beginners.

remember back to the days when he or she started out—all thumbs, two left feet and without the foggiest idea what to do with that bouncy creature on the end of the leash. What is obvious now, was pure Greek then, and what is a reflex now, had to be studiously learned. The ability to read a dog and modify techniques to suit his temperament did not come overnight, but was developed over time.

The beginner is in the same position. When selecting instructing techniques, this lack of skill is taken into account, and the main criterion is whether the **majority** of students in the class can use it successfully with their dogs.

The instructor who takes his responsibility seriously, that is, putting his students in a position where they can achieve their goals, selects techniques that do not place a premium on timing or athletic ability. Techniques must be simple and the articulations precise. "Place your right hand against your dog's chest, and your left hand on top of the withers. Then I want you to . . . etc." Only with specific instructions that he can follow can the beginner do what is necessary to achieve the desired result.

Handler Acceptance

Handlers will use only techniques which they accept. Since beginners are not sufficiently well-versed in how the dog learns and often view their pets as furry little people on four legs, they frequently refuse to accept that some degree of compulsion may be necessary in the training of the dog. In teaching heeling, for example, we used to encounter a great deal of resistance when we tried to explain the so-called "correction," why it was necessary and how it had to be done. The beginner either did not think his dog needed it, did not want to use it with his dog, or both.

To overcome this problem, we adopted a different strategy. We eliminated intellectualizing the "correction" and instead began instructing "the leash over the shoulder" technique. The student is only permitted to touch the leash to bring the dog back to heel position and immediately lets go again.

As a result, we no longer have any second-guessing by the student about what he has to do and how. Since he cannot restrain his dog with the leash (hands off), it becomes readily apparent that his dog will in fact leave his side, demonstrating to the student that he has to do something. By continuously reminding him to let go of the leash, the student learns the beginnings of a check, exactly what we want. The student learns the mechanics without first having to wrestle with the theory of how the dog learns.

To sum up, techniques that place primary reliance on timing and

Leash over the shoulder technique.

Avoid techniques that produce needless anxiety or stress for the dog.

Techniques to avoid!

aptitude, and those that are highly compulsive, are ill-suited for beginners. Unless the student accepts the technique being instructed, he will either drop out or he will not use it.

Impact on the Dog

Finally, even though a technique may meet the first two criteria, it still may not be a good instructing technique because of its adverse effect on the psyche of the dog. We avoid techniques that produce anxiety or stress for the dog since anxiety impedes learning. All learning is stressful, but the amount of stress is kept to a level where learning can still take place.

Teaching the Recall is a good example. We first teach the dog what we want him to do, that is, respond to the come command. Then we teach him exactly where we want him to wind up—sitting directly in front. Lastly, we teach him that we want him to perform the exercise briskly. Attempting to teach two or more elements of the exercise at the same time would cause unnecessary stress, which in turn would significantly slow down the learning process. Instead of being faster, trying to teach two or more things at the same time is actually slower.

Picture yourself sitting at a computer terminal for the first time with the instructor leaning over your shoulder exhorting, "Faster, you have to do this much faster!" We doubt you could learn very much under those circumstances. You would not be able to increase your speed until you knew which keys to press. The same principle applies to dog training, both for the student **and** the dog.

All the techniques we instruct have been evaluated using these criteria, which is why we refer to them as "instructing techniques," rather than "training techniques."

CRITERIA FOR SELECTING EQUIPMENT

The Leash

The selection of equipment is largely dictated by the techniques being instructed. For example, we use the leash over the shoulder to teach heeling, which requires a 6' leash. We also teach folding the leash into one hand, and a technique called the Slip Release to get the dogs started on off leash heeling. These maneuvers require a light weight leash and that is what we use—a 6' by ⅜" to ⅝" canvas web or nylon leash, depending on the size of the dog.

The Collar

Many of the instructing techniques we use rely on getting a response to the check, that is, they depend on the dog's sense of touch. If the dog does not feel the check, the technique for the exercise where it is used will not work. The leash and the collar are used not to restrain, but to train the dog. Put another way, the purpose of the leash is not to physically move the dog from point A to point B, but to issue a check to provide the dog with the stimulus to move **himself** from point A to point B.

The type of collar used will depend on the aptitude of the handler and the touch sensitivity of the dog. The collar we issue to our beginners is a snap-around nylon collar which is measured for every dog. This collar is used because it is snapped around the dog's neck, rather than having to go over his head. Its advantage over a slip-on collar is that it can be fitted to stay on any part of the dog's neck. The stronger the dog in relation to the handler, the higher on the neck the collar is fitted.

The strongest and most muscular part of the dog's body is where the neck joins the shoulders; the weakest part is behind the ears. By placing the collar high on the neck, the odds between the novice trainer and the dog are somewhat equalized so that even an ineffective check will get some response.

Even with the snap-around collar, however, there will be times when the student is physically outclassed by his dog. The dog is either extremely touch insensitive and does not feel the check as a more sensitive dog would, or, as is not uncommon with Newfoundlands and Saint Bernards, the dog outweighs the handler, which tends to put the beginner at an enormous disadvantage.

When this happens we recommend the use of a pinch collar. Although an experienced instructor can usually tell by the end of the first session which handlers need this tool, we make it a practice to wait until the fourth week of training before we suggest its use. We want the handler to reach a certain level of frustration, such as when he comes to class panting and out of breath saying: "I just can't go on. I practiced every day this week and it's not working. I'm not getting anywhere and I just don't know what to do anymore. I'm at my wit's end!"

It is then, at the "teachable moment," that we introduce him to the pinch collar. We do it without fanfare by saying, "Here, this will help." As one of our students put it after she tried it, "Oh, it's like power steering."

Although the pinch collar looks like a medieval instrument of torture, its effect on the touch insensitive dog is far less than its appearance might suggest.

A Word of Caution

Pinch collars are **NOT** used with an aggressive dog. Since it is self-

To control the large, touch insensitive dog...

it is advisable to introduce the pinch collar at the right
teachable moment.

Selecting the right equipment.

129

limiting, like a Martingale collar, the handler, be it the owner or the instructor, has no protection against the dog that tries to bite.

THE THREE PHASES OF TRAINING

In the development of our instructing program we have divided the training of the dog into three phases—the teaching, the practicing and the testing phases. While all three overlap, each contains its own objectives and its own techniques for achieving the trainer's ultimate goal—an enthusiastic, reliable and precise response on the part of the dog.

The Teaching Phase

The principal objective of the teaching phase is to teach the dog whatever response he has to learn. The quickest method for the dog to learn, and the easiest for the beginner to master, is to avoid putting the dog in a position where he can make a mistake. Each exercise is broken down into small components and each component is designed so that both student and dog almost cannot help but perform correctly.

For example, with the Automatic Sit, first we teach the dog to respond to the sit command. Next, we teach him where we want him to sit, and lastly, we teach him to do it briskly. But there is more.

The Volhard/Fisher Model

For each exercise we follow a **model** to teach the dog, which is:

1. Place/show
2. Induce
3. Induce/compel
4. If necessary, compel

1. Place/show—during the first step of any exercise we show the dog exactly what it is we want. Let's take the example of teaching the dog to lie down on command. The dog is placed into the down position with the command "down." The dog will not learn from this to go down on command, but he *does* learn that his handler can place him in that position, thereby laying the foundation for the next step.

2. Induce—next, we elicit a voluntary response from the dog to the command "down." We take an object to which the dog is attracted, such as a ball, his favorite toy, or a tempting morsel of food, and we show it to the dog. We say "down" and lower the object to the ground, enticing the dog to lie down. Some dogs will learn to lie down on command at this step. Most, however, learn it at the next step, which is

130

1. Place and show

2. Induce

3. Induce/compel

4. If necessary, compel

The Volhard/Fisher Model.

3. Induce/compel—where we lay the foundation for compulsion, should it become necessary. Again, we induce the dog with the object, this time combining the command "down" with downward pressure on the collar. If, after this step, the dog will not lie down on command, we go to

4. Compel—we say "down" and, if the dog does not respond, we check straight down.

We follow this model for every exercise. The dog has a chance to learn without creating needless anxiety, and the student can accept the techniques being taught, as well as reach his goal.

Tiers of Learning

During the teaching phase, the dog is also conditioned to respond in different locations and in the presence of distractions. Some of these distractions can be created by the student himself, but for most of them he will have to take the dog to different locations.

In her book *Lads Before the Wind,* Karen Pryor describes how she had painstakingly trained a number of porpoises to perform a variety of feats in the training tank, only to find that the animals became confused and unreliable when asked to perform in the show tank. The same thing happens to dogs when asked to respond in unfamiliar locations or locations with distractions. To ensure that the dog will be reliable under all circumstances, he is trained in a variety of locations.

The guidelines we give our students are as follows:

1. In the beginning, train your dog in an area familiar to him, such as your own backyard, and without distractions so you are the center of attention and he can concentrate on his lesson.
2. Once he has some familiarity with what you have taught him, train him in an unfamiliar location without distractions, such as the neighbor's backyard.
3. Bringing him to class each week provides him with a familiar location with distractions.
4. Finally, take him to unfamiliar locations with distraction, such as a supermarket parking lot or ball park.

Following this regimen is just one of the steps in conditioning the dog, in an orderly way, to become a reliable companion.

The Practicing Phase

The practicing phase is the most exciting part of training and the one that rounds out the dog's education. During the teaching phase we carefully avoid putting the dog in a position where he could make a mistake. Now we solidify his learning by systematically inviting him to make mistakes. It is done by means of distractions, the key word being "systematically."

The distractions we use are:

1. First degree (visual)—an object or person.
2. Second degree (auditory and visual)—a person clapping and calling "here, puppy, puppy," trying to entice the dog to come to him.
3. Third degree (sensory and tactile)—offering the dog a treat or touching him to try and distract him.

Distractions are introduced in Level 2, after the dog has been in training for eight weeks. For example, the Recall with first degree distraction is introduced the fourth week of Level 2. It is done by having the distractor, who can be an assistant, the instructor or another student, crouch 2′ from the line the dog will travel. As the dog approaches, the distractor will smile at the dog. If the dog goes to the distractor, his handler then shows the dog what is expected from him. He quietly walks up to the dog, puts both hands through the dog's collar under the chin, palms up, and trots backward to the point where he called the dog. He sits the dog, takes his hands out of the collar and then praises the dog. The exercise is then repeated. Rarely does it take more than three repetitions for the dog to understand that he is to ignore the distractor.

The following week, second degree distractions are introduced and the week after that, third degree distractions.

When using this approach, there are two points to remember. First, if the dog becomes distracted, we go back to step 1 of the Model—we **show** the dog what we want. By adding a distraction the exercise has been changed, at least for the dog, from the Recall he has learned so far. It has become a **new** exercise and no assumptions as to the dog's understanding can be made. It is for this reason that we go back to the beginning. It would be unfair to the dog to use compulsion at this point. Should the dog persist, however, in permitting himself to become distracted, then compulsion may have to be introduced. The second point is that the handler is not to repeat the command or try to verbally encourage the dog. The dog has to learn to respond to the first command.

The Instructing Models describe in detail how and when in the program the various distractions are incorporated. Neither the dog nor the student will experience difficulties in handling distractions provided they are presented in a logical and orderly way.

An Important Note

Distraction training is a powerful technique to teach the dog to respond reliably under all circumstances, but it does require the application of common sense. The dogs are **gradually** introduced to increasingly greater distractions. During the process, the instructor monitors the dogs' responses to make sure that problems are not inadvertently created. The shy dog, in particular, has to be handled gently and with compassion so as not to frighten him. By the same token, it is the shy dog who will benefit most from distraction training—he learns that he **can** do it, which builds his confidence.

Other dogs may become confused, even after having been shown several times what to do. For example, when practicing Recalls with distractions, after several repetitions, the dog may just sit there and not come. When this happens, the student is instructed to use one of the inducive progressions for the exercise, such as using a treat or crouching as he calls, to help the dog over this hurdle.

By being alert to possible negative effects of distraction training and by carefully instructing the students who act as distractors what they can and cannot do, the instructor avoids potential pitfalls.

The most exciting part of distraction training is seeing the dogs learning to "think" and getting to what behaviorists call the "aha" response. The dog, in effect, says, "Now I've got it." Giving him the opportunity to figure it out by himself makes him ever so pleased with himself when he does and intensifies his response.

Number of Repetitions

How many times an exercise is repeated depends on who is doing it. If the handler does it for or with the dog, the exercise can be repeated several times. If the dog does it by himself, the handler stops after the first correct response. For example, once the dog has finished correctly by himself, the handler goes on to something else. Trying it once more "just to see whether he will do it again" encourages the dog to become inventive.

The Testing Phase

During this phase the dog's response to what he has been taught is tested. The principal distinctions between this and the other two phases is that when the dog is tested no effort is made to deal with incorrect responses. They are merely noted and then dealt with during practice.

There are times when a student is having a training problem. Whatever he tries and no matter how diligently he is applying himself, it is just not working and the dog is not responding as expected. When this happens, as it will, the first order of business is to identify the source of the problem. Once it is **identified,** it can be **isolated** so as to **improve** the dog's performance.

There are two reasons a trained dog fails to respond—the dog can't or the dog won't.

The Dog Can't

At the top of the list of reasons why a dog is unable to do what he is asked is an underlying physical problem. The dog may be ill and not feeling well. An ear infection causes pain when the dog is checked and to avoid the pain he climbs up on the leash. Impacted anal glands make it painful to stay in the sitting position so he tries not to. Hip dysplasia may make it difficult for the dog to sit quickly. These are some of the more obvious causes of training problems.

Other ailments which adversely affect the dog are more subtle, such as low grade infections or dietary deficiencies.

In Chapter 1 we described the dog's growth stages during which some dogs experience growing pains or structural imbalances for brief periods, affecting their ability to change position. Osteochondritis dissecans, fragmentation of joint cartilage during growth, which can last for months, will cause the dog to limp and make even walking painful.

It has been our experience that most of the so-called training problems, including aggression, are caused by some physical problem. Once it has been cured, the dog will respond again as expected. It is for this reason that in our classes we make it a practice to recommend a veterinary check-up when confronted with a training problem. Under no circumstances would we deal with a sick dog by applying compulsion.

The second most common reason for a training problem is confusion on the part of the dog; he simply does not understand what it is we want. Confusion can be caused by the lack of a proper foundation, the incorrect application of the technique being taught, or the technique does not work for that handler and his dog. Having identified the cause and having made the appropriate modifications, either on the part of the student or the instructor, the problem will be overcome.

Finally, the dog may lack confidence or be afraid in certain situations. Again, compulsion is not the answer here; instead, the dog is worked through these difficulties with understanding and kindness.

Physical problems

Confusion

Fear

Three reasons why the dog can't.

The Dog Won't

Some training problems are caused by the dog being unwilling—he says, "No, I don't want to and you can't make me." This means one of two things. Either the dog is "bucking for a promotion"—he is challenging his handler for pack leadership, or he already is the pack leader and is taking control.

How this situation is handled will depend on the dog and the handler. Before instructing a disciplinary approach, we first make the handler aware of what is happening by asking him to observe the dog at home: who goes up and down the stairs first; who goes through the door first; does the dog get out of your way; does he tell **you** when he wants to be petted? We then instruct the student to review the Long Down five times a week and begin on a program of making the dog understand who is in charge, which includes petting the dog *only* after he has responded to a command and then no longer than five seconds; no food treats unless he first obeys a command; making him get out of the way; and no charging up or down stairs or through doorways.

Consistently followed, such a program will resolve the dominance issue in most cases. If it does not, disciplinary measures may become necessary.

Some dominant dogs have learned that by *acting* submissive the owner will stop what they do not want him to do, including training. This type of "submission" is not confusion although its signs are almost identical, and the dog is worked like any other dominant dog.

CONCLUSION

With a little foresight and understanding, a sound instructing program is developed which meets the needs of the beginner trainer, as well as those of the dog. The blueprint we have described provides the necessary guidance for developing such a program.

8

The Evolution of an Instructing Program

INTRODUCTION

When we started instructing, a program was already in place and all we had to do was follow what had been done before. It was not until much later that we began to ask ourselves questions like, "Is this program meeting the needs of the majority of students? How can we find out whether it is or is not? If it is not, how do we make it responsive to their needs?"

The answers to these questions are found in this chapter.

STARTING A PROGRAM

Setting Goals

Goals can be viewed from three different perspectives—the organization's, the instructor's and the student's.

138

1. The organization.

The main reason for its existence will determine the priority of its goals. As an obedience club, its chief objectives may be to further the sport of dog obedience training by putting on an annual obedience trial, to educate the public in all matters pertaining to pure-bred dogs and to sponsor training classes. It would include the obtaining of obedience titles by its members. To finance all these endeavors requires money, so that, too, would be one of the goals. A training school, on the other hand, may be interested only peripherally in the sport of obedience and its chief goal may be monetary. The primary objective of an adult education program would be to provide a public service.

2. The instructor.

For the vast majority of instructors the main motivation is the desire to see their students succeed. What success means to the individual instructor varies, but the sincerity is the same. Certainly for many, financial gain is an important consideration. But if it is the instructor's only reward, we doubt he will be in the field very long.

3. The student.

It may appear, at first glance, that when students enroll in an obedience class, their goals are as diverse as they are. Mrs. Smith, along with several others, wants her dog to come when called. Mr. Jones has a chewing problem. Mr. Brown's dog barks too much. Miss Case does not want her dog to jump on people. Mrs. White wants to be able to take her dog for a walk without being pulled off her feet. Dr. Mason does not want the dog to chase cars. And the list goes on. Are these divergent goals incompatible with a program that meets the needs of the students? Not at all!

Reconciling Goals

Different people, ourselves included, have spent countless hours trying to devise a program that addresses these problems individually, in a class setting, without the need for the traditional obedience exercises of heel, stay and come. Perhaps it can be done, but we have not found the way.

There is, however, one common denominator, one word, which sums up all these problems, and that is **CONTROL.**

The one thing all the students have in common is the inability to control a specific behavior of the dog which they consider objectionable. The particular problem is merely symptomatic of an inability to **communicate** with the dog. Unless and until the student learns this skill, he will not be able to solve his problem.

The purpose of a training class is to teach the student the skill of communicating with another species, a dog. Just like learning a foreign language, it is done systematically. The traditional obedience exercises are used as a means to this end. They can be viewed as the rules of grammar which then enable us to use the words we have learned correctly. Once he has learned to communicate with his dog and now understands **his dog's** language, the student can resolve whatever problem he has on his own.

The student's primary goal, regardless of how he may initially view it, is control. But what of his expectations when he signs up for class? Consider the example of Mrs. Smith whose dog will not come when called. Her goal, and what she expects from attending the classes, is to have a dog that will come when called. Does this mean on leash? Certainly not!

If we were to tell Mrs. Smith that at the end of the course she will be able to put her dog on leash, tell it to stay, go to the end of the leash, call her dog and he will come, she would tell us, "I can do that right now, after I catch him!" And she is right. Control implies responding off leash, and that is the beginner's goal.

Viewed in this light, the goals of the organization, the instructor and the student are no longer as incompatible as they at first appeared. If, for example, one of the organization's objectives is to further the sport of obedience by having students obtain obedience titles, this can be achieved if the students have control over their dogs. Certainly, anyone who has control over his dog can get a Companion Dog title.

Designing a Program

The first decision that has to be made is the overall purpose of a training class. It can be either to train under the supervision of the instructor or to impart instructions so that the student can practice at home. To train under the supervision of the instructor is a slow and tedious task which is not very motivational. A more efficient use of time is to use the weekly class session to briefly review last week's lesson and then instruct the new material. More information can be covered that way in the same time span and the student is able to achieve his goal that much more quickly.

The next items to consider are how to reach these goals. These include the following:

1. The selection of exercises to be taught;
2. The specific techniques that are to be used;
3. The selection of training equipment;
4. The number of progressions for each exercise;
5. When each progression is introduced;

Traditional obedience exercises are used . . .

to teach students how to communicate with their dogs.

6. The order in which the exercises will be done;
7. The length of each session; and
8. The length of the course.

We have previously described the criteria we apply to each of these points and the thought processes that led us to designing the program we now use.

EVALUATING A PROGRAM

Class Evaluation

To help us evaluate our instructing program, we go to those whom we instruct—our students. Upon conclusion of the seventh lesson we ask our students to complete the **Class Evaluation** reproduced on the following pages. It was formulated by Olive Point in 1977 and is now used by many training organizations.

The evaluation is designed to pinpoint those portions and exercises of the program which were the most difficult for the student. The responses will tell the instructor where adjustments or changes will have to be made. For example, if a student with a Siberian Husky answers "heeling" to "What was the most difficult exercise in this class for you and your dog?" that would be understandable. But if several students, including those with Shelties and Poodles, had this difficulty, it would call for an evaluation of how the exercise was taught.

Any exercise that students mention consistently as being the most difficult needs to be examined to see whether the way in which it is taught can be improved. Our own instructing program was largely shaped by reviewing the responses we received to the Class Evaluation and then making the necessary modifications so that our students could be successful.

The evaluation is weighted, in that it first ascertains what the student put into the training. The student, for example, who missed three classes and then says he had difficulty with heeling or the stays would not be a cause for any concern. We would expect him to have those difficulties.

The evaluation will also tell the instructor how he or she did in presenting the subject matter, in giving individual attention and in relating the training to practical applications. His or her weaknesses will be pointed out objectively and constructively so that the necessary improvements can be made.

We consider the Class Evaluation an invaluable tool in shaping our instructing procedures and in letting us know whether the program meets the needs of our students.

CLASS EVALUATION

1. Have you attended all training sessions?   ( ) Yes   ( ) No

2. How Many times were you absent?   (Check one)   (1)   (2)   (3)   (4)

3. Approximately how many days a week did you train at home?
Check one   (7)   (6)   (5)   (4)   (3)   (2)   (1)

4. Do you think you received the necessary individual attention?   ( ) Yes   ( ) No

5. Is this the type of training you expected?   ( ) Yes   ( ) No

6. Have you noticed improvement in your dog's behavior?   ( ) Yes   ( ) No

7. Do you plan to continue your training with us?   ( ) Yes   ( ) No

8. Will you recommend these classes to a friend?   ( ) Yes   ( ) No

9. Are you interested in earning AKC obedience titles on your dog?   ( ) Yes   ( ) No

10. What is the greatest benefit you derived from the classes?

_____

11. What was the most difficult exercise in this class for you and your dog?

_____

12. What did you like most about the training program?

_____

13. What is your overall evaluation of this course?
( ) Excellent   ( ) Good   ( ) Fair   ( ) Poor

14. Comments, criticisms, suggestions, etc. _____

_____

_____

It is not necessary to sign your name unless you wish to do so. We will value your comments and will use them as a guide to improve our instruction and methods of holding classes. Thank you.

Name _____

Date _____

Our instructing program was largely shaped . . .

CLASS EVALUATION
Part 2

Please **circle the appropriate number** at the right of each statement in order to help us evaluate our instruction techniques. The numbers have the following significance:

4 = VERY GOOD 3 = GOOD 2 = FAIR 1 = POOR

15. The organization of the subject material by the instructor.   4 3 2 1

16. The instructor's preparation for the class.   4 3 2 1

17. The presentation of the subject matter.   4 3 2 1

18. The degree to which you were motivated or stimulated by the instructor.   4 3 2 1

19. The general attitude exhibited by the instructor toward the students.   4 3 2 1

20. The attitude exhibited by the assistants or others who helped with the class.   4 3 2 1

21. The instructor's willingness and availability to give individual help, if needed.   4 3 2 1

22. The clarity with which the instructor presented the subject.   4 3 2 1

23. The extent to which you feel the class time was well spent.   4 3 2 1

24. The instructor's ability to relate the training to practical application.   4 3 2 1

25. The instructor's ability to answer questions not directly related to training matters.   4 3 2 1

26. The degree to which YOU were adequately prepared when you attended the class.   4 3 2 1

27. In order of importance, list ways you feel instruction in this course could be improved:

_____

_____

_____

28. What was the most interesting aspect of the whole course?

_____

29. What was the least interesting part of the course?

_____

by the responses to the Class Evaluation.

Another way of evaluating a program is by the number of students who drop out before completing the course. There will invariably be a few students who cannot continue their training. Moving, a change in job hours, the dog getting run over by a car, the dog becoming ill, all are legitimate reasons for dropping out. But what about those who just do not come back? Why do they not come back?

It is often assumed that the main reason people do not finish the program is because they have achieved what they came for and no longer see the need to continue. Experience has shown this argument to be false. It is just the opposite—students drop out because they are **not** getting what they came for.

When we first began to concern ourselves with this question, we kept statistics to find out whether there is a specific time during the course when people are likely to drop out. We discovered that the highest drop-out rate occurred between the sixth and seventh week of training which coincides with the first learning plateau. After five to six weeks of training, the dog appears to have forgotten everything he has been taught and the owner, who has no idea what has happened, gives up in disgust. Once we realized that this phenomenon contributed to our drop-out rate, we made a slight modification in our instructions. We began to tell the students about the learning plateau at the beginning of the course, and later reminded them of it. We assured them that it was normal, that it would last for only a few days, and that they should not become discouraged.

With this explanation we have been able to circumvent the potential problem of the first learning plateau. Now when it happens to our students, instead of becoming frustrated, they delight in telling us that we were absolutely right—last week little Fido did nothing.

A drop-out rate in excess of 10% requires an evaluation of the program to see why the students are dissatisfied.

Here are some things to look for. If there is a significant drop-out rate during the first half of the course, examine

1. Instructor/assistant to student ratio. A 1 to 5 ratio is ideal. It is virtually impossible to provide the necessary individual attention if the instructor has to watch more than 10 students himself.
2. Student acceptance of training techniques used.
3. Is the student able to use the techniques taught?
4. Is the student experiencing immediate success?

If there is a significant drop-out rate during the second half of the course, examine

A legitimate reason for missing class.

Explaining the learning plateau prevents drop outs.

1. Variety and progressions of exercises—is the students' interest being maintained?
2. Tempo of the class—are the students kept busy?
3. Is there too much talk about AKC events?
4. Is the atmosphere friendly and inviting so that students want to come to class?

In addition to these points, examine the program in light of Chapter 6, Student Motivation. The lesson to remember about drop-outs is that no matter how brilliant you are as an instructor, if the student does not come to class, you cannot teach him.

Successful Course Completion

The final step in the evaluation of an instructing program is to monitor how many students successfully complete the course. To some extent this would depend on the program's initial objectives. Our expectations are that upon completion of the course the student's dog will walk on a loose leash, come when called off leash, and stay when told.

No matter what the program's objectives are, if less than 85% of the students are able to complete it successfully, the program needs to be examined. Are the expectations too high? Are the techniques too difficult? Are the techniques effective for beginners? Whatever the reason may be, changes need to be made.

CHANGING A PROGRAM

Progress requires change. An unwillingness to change denies those who need it the most benefit of the "better mousetrap."

There are, however, some ground rules that need to be followed when making changes.

1. Make changes only for a specific reason and with a clear understanding of what the change is expected to accomplish. Change for the sake of change is a waste of time and effort.
2. Change no more than one or two items at a time so the effectiveness of the change can be evaluated. Avoid wholesale changes because they will only lead to confusion.
3. When changing a training technique, subject it to the appropriate criteria for inclusion in an instructing program.
4. When dealing with a group of instructors, listen to the *least* experienced member. He or she will be most able to relate to the students and their abilities.

There is a delicate balance between not enough change . . .

and too much change all at once.

Dog training and instructing are not a religion.

There is a delicate balance between not enough change and too much change all at once. During our seminars we admonish the participants to make changes slowly and gradually, to gain experience with the new and different, and evaluate its impact on the program. Training techniques, in particular, require a germination period before they become second nature.

There are, of course, program changes that can be made without altering the training techniques that are already being used. We refer to these as changes in the mechanics of the program. Examples are the Long Down and Sit, the order in which the exercises are taught, the location of the exercises, and matters pertaining to student motivation and the mechanics of instructing. These apply to any program, no matter what the techniques being taught.

UNIFORMITY

When two or more instructors teach for the same organization, a consensus among them is necessary as to when what is to be taught and the specific techniques that are to be taught. The benefits of a uniform approach are two-fold.

First, if an instructor is unable to teach a class because of illness or some other reason, someone else in the organization can readily take over without any loss in continuity.

Second, students who continue are not subjected to having to learn varying methods under different instructors.

CONCLUSION

We have described in this chapter the road we have taken in the development of our instructing program. We do not consider the task finished by any means or that our program is cast in concrete. It is an **evolving** approach to instructing dog obedience training. Any time we come across a concept or an idea that we think will make it easier for the student to train his dog and for the dog to learn, we will try it. If it proves itself, we incorporate it into our program. Dog training and instructing are not a religion. It is permissible and advisable, as new insights are gained, to make changes.

9

Administrative
Details

_____

INTRODUCTION

The obedience instructor who is setting up his own classes or classes for a training club has a number of organizational details to consider. In this chapter we will discuss what to do before starting classes, administering staff and supplemental materials.

GETTING STARTED

Training Site

The weather dictates whether classes can be held indoors or out. If you live in a climate that lends itself to outdoor classes, the training site can be a yard, playing field, park or parking lot. If the area is surrounded by fencing, off leash exercises will pose no danger to the participants.

To run indoor classes, the training site can be any area where dogs are permitted—generally where no food is served. Halls such as VFW and Elks, gymnasiums (if you provide mats), recreation departments, churches, square dance halls, schools and the like are good places for the instructor to make contacts. When approaching any organization to run dog classes, the instructor emphasizes the responsibility of the training organization. Clean-up will include sweeping and picking up after the dogs, if necessary. It is helpful for the instructor to emphasize that dog training boosts responsible pet ownership.

The number of classes run per week will determine if the site will be rented on a part-time basis, or if the organization will need a permanent training location.

Rent

The amount of rent a training organization can afford to pay will be determined by use, number of classes and what is charged.

Insurance

The training organization carries its own insurance to cover personal injury, including dog bites, and professional liability to cover the instructing staff.

Liability

We have our students sign a *Waiver, Assumption of Risk and Agreement to Hold Harmless* agreement (see Supplemental Material, below). While this would not prevent legal action in the event of an injury, it does make the student aware of his responsibility with his own dog.

Advertising

Posting notices in veterinarian's offices, pet shops, grooming parlors and supermarket bulletin boards is one way of notifying the public about your classes. Classified advertisements in local newspapers is another.

Advertising includes what, when, where and who to contact for further information.

Local newspapers are constantly looking for human interest stories about residents. By sending news releases about such topics as graduation with a list of the graduates, and including information about when the next session of classes will begin, an instructor receives free advertising.

Equipment

We order our equipment from the following sources: Collars and leashes from Handcraft Collars, 3517 Victoria Road, Birmingham, Alabama 35223. Pinch collars from J & J Dog Supplies, P.O. Box 1517, Galesburg, Illinois 61402.

ADMINISTRATIVE STAFF

Assistants

As discussed earlier, assistants and apprentice instructors are trained in regular meetings or workshops. In addition, written instructions are helpful. The following is a sample instruction sheet for assistants:

ASSISTANTS GENERAL INSTRUCTIONS

(1) Your job is to make sure that each student is getting the most out of class time. Class is for the purpose of teaching the *people*. The dogs will learn at home. Consequently, if the students are not performing an exercise correctly in class, they will not be able to practice it correctly.

(2) Occasionally a student will be difficult—either the person or the dog. Help the difficult student, but don't become bogged down with him while the rest of the class goes without your attention.

(3) When re-explaining an instruction, use the *exact same articulation* as the instructor. If you feel a change in technique is necessary for one student, bring it to the attention of the instructor.

(4) When the instructor is talking to the class, *stop talking,* even if you are in the middle of a sentence. The student must be able to listen to the instructor. Finish your instructions later.

(5) Keep talking to a minimum. Frequently a gesture can correct the student's actions more quickly than a speech would.

(6) No social talking among yourselves during class. Spread out around the room for maximum coverage of the entire class.

(7) If anything unusual happens, bring it to the instructor's attention *during* class.

(8) Familiarize yourself with the lesson plan prior to class. There will be a de-briefing after class to discuss the class and answer any questions you may have.

(9) Wear your name tag each week. Wear the club uniform and appropriate footwear.

(10) Please be available one half hour before class starts for setting up and greeting students, and to help answer questions.

Telephone Committee

As discussed in Chapter 6, Student Motivation, the person answering the telephone has an important role in enlisting potential students. The following is a sample instruction sheet for the telephone committee:

(1) Be polite and friendly. A smile on your face transmits across the telephone lines.

(2) Be informative and answer questions. If you are unsure of an answer, don't make up information. Refer the caller to _____.

(3) Take the caller's name and address to send them our registration packet. Even if they are unsure about wanting to attend, they may read our information and decide to take the classes.

(4) Be positive about our training classes. Your enthusiasm will convince many people to attend.

(5) Inquire as to whether or not the dog has been on leash. If it has not, send the leash training instructions with the information packet.

(6) Inform the caller that the purpose of the class is to teach *him* to train the dog. He will need to set aside time five days a week for training. The amount of time will vary, but will generally be about a half hour a day.

(7) Tell the caller specifically what the goal of the class is.

(8) Tell him the location, including directions, the length of the class, the time of the next session, and number of weeks.

(9) Tell the caller what the class fee is and what it includes.

(10) Ask how he heard about our classes, and keep a record of calls.

(11) Send follow-up information with a registration form.

SUPPLEMENTAL MATERIAL

In every class, there will be questions on housetraining, crate training, chewing, barking, breeding, nutrition and so on. Since these questions come up again and again, the instructor saves himself much time by using written material dealing with these topics. When asked a question about a particular topic, he simply gives the student the appropriate handout.

The following describe the handouts we use to supplement our classes.

Point of Contact Brochure

Following the initial phone inquiry, the written information sent to the caller includes something about the instructor's or organization's credentials, what the course includes, the particulars about the next series of classes, the location, directions and a map, if necessary.

We include the following registration form and release:

154

REGISTRATION FORM

Class Beginning_____

Name of Owner
or Person Training Dog_____

Address _____ City_____ Zip_____

Occupation _____ Spouse's Occupation_____

Home Phone_____Business Phone _____

Call Name of Dog _____ Breed_____ Age_____

Sex_____ Spayed/Neutered?_____ Age when spayed/neutered_____

Age obtained?_____ From where? _____

Have you owned a dog before?_____ Breed(s) _____

Have you trained a dog before?_____ When?_____ Where?_____

State briefly the problems that brought you to class.

Please be specific _____

_____

What do you hope to accomplish? _____

_____

Do you have any hearing or other physical handicaps? _____

Does your dog have any physical problems or disabilities which may affect

his training?_____

If your dog has had any illness or skin disorder in the last 6 months, state

the nature of the problem and whether treated by a veterinarian _____

_____

Name of veterinarian_____ Date of last Distemper & Parvovirus innoculation___

What kind of dog food do you feed your dog? Please state *exact* brand,

canned, dry, etc. _____

How did you hear about our classes?_____

I understand that attendance of a dog obedience training class is not without risk to myself, members of my family or guests who may attend, or my dog, because some of the dogs to which I (we) will be exposed may be difficult to control and may be the cause of injury even when handled with the greatest amount of care.

I hereby waive and release XYZ Training School, its employees, owners and agents from any and all liability of any nature, for injury or damage which I or my dog may suffer, including specifically, but not without limitation, any injury or damage resulting from the action of any dog, and I expressly assume the risk of any such damage or injury while attending any training session or other function of the School, or while on the training grounds or the surrounding area thereto.

In consideration of and as inducement to the acceptance of my application for training membership in this obedience training class, I hereby agree to indemnify and hold harmless this School, its employees, owners and agents from any and all claims, or claims by any member of my family or any other person accompanying me to any training session or function of the School or while on the grounds or the surrounding area thereto as a result of any action by any dog, including my own.

Signature of Owner or Authorized Agent _____

Date_____

General Information

Along with the registration form, we include a sheet of General Instructions. This information is important for the student to know prior to coming to class to work with his dog:

┌───┐
│ GENERAL INSTRUCTIONS   │
└───┘

WHEN & WHERE TO TRAIN AT HOME—Choose a quiet area to work with your dog so that *you* can be the center of attention. Don't work your dog directly after feeding him. Two short training sessions are better than one long one.

In addition to setting aside specific times to train your dog, you will want to start making him obey you with the training techniques you are learning. Use the training methods we show you **whenever** you want your dog to behave *with* or *without* a training collar and leash. That's what training is all about!

156

Dogs learn by repetition. In order to be successful you have to practice with your dog five days a week. It is practice at *home* that will bring success. Class time is to teach *you* what to teach your dog at home.

SAFETY RULES—Many dogs react unfavorably to alcohol and some medications; therefore, no one is permitted to train in class if there is evidence of using alcohol. Smoking is prohibited when on the training floor during sessions. We strongly recommend that you not smoke or use alcohol when training at home.

BOOKS & ADVICE—Well-meaning friends can give you the wrong advice about training. To get the most from this program, use the techniques and procedures you will be shown in class. If you have any difficulty, call us right away.

If you are interested in a book on dog training, **TRAINING YOUR DOG—The Step-by-Step Manual** by Joachim Volhard and Gail Fisher (Howell Book House, 1983) gives you comprehensive information about the training approach used in our classes. This method of training works for most handlers and dogs; however, if you need special assistance, the experience and education of your instructor and assistants enables us to select the right approach for your dog.

ATTENDANCE IN CLASS—To get the most from the program, class attendance is important. If you must miss a class, please call your instructor or an assistant. You are permitted one free make-up class. Additional make-up sessions may be arranged with your instructor at a nominal fee. Do not bring a female in season to class. During her absence the owner attends to keep up with the class, and continues to work with the dog at home.

EXERCISE & FEED—Be sure to exercise your dog before class. If an accident happens, we will clean it up for you. We ask only that you stand in one place.

Do not work your dog for at least two hours after a meal. This means bringing him to class as well. Give him a small snack before training, so he is not working on an empty stomach.

CLOTHING—Comfortable clothing is best for training. You will have to get down on the floor with your dog. The best shoes for training are low heels with rubber soles. Sneakers are ideal. Dr. Scholl's sandals or platform shoes are inappropriate.

WHO SHOULD TRAIN—The same handler trains the dog in class and at home. Switching handlers can be confusing to a beginning dog. But *all* members of the family can be instructed how to give commands and have the dog obey, and all must be consistent and learn to praise the dog.

157

EQUIPMENT—You will be issued the proper equipment for your dog. Replacements may be purchased at a nominal fee. We exchange collars which the dog outgrows if they are in good condition and clean. When you complete the training, the equipment belongs to you. Please do not use chlorine bleach when washing the collar and leash. Frequent washings will keep the equipment in good condition.

SPECTATORS—Visitors are welcome, but must remain quiet during class. We always welcome spectators and we hope you will tell your friends and relatives about our classes.

CANCELLATIONS—In case of inclement weather or if driving conditions are poor, we will cancel class. Cancellations will be broadcast on WXYZ-AM and WXYZ-FM after 3 p.m. on the day of the class (for evening classes), or you can call your Instructor or the Director of Training.

STARTING TIME—All classes begin promptly. We appreciate your being on time as we run several classes during the evening.

Much of this information is repeated in the orientation pamphlet issued the first night of class.

Leash Training

Students whose dogs have never been on a leash are sent the following schedule of introduction:

LEASH TRAINING

STEP 1—Place a buckle collar on your dog or puppy until he becomes used to it. Allow a few days for this.

STEP 2—Attach a lightweight cloth or leather leash, or a piece of lightweight cord about twice the length of your dog to his collar, and let your dog drag it around. Keep an eye on him to make sure the leash doesn't wrap around a chair leg or a tree. Don't leave it on when you aren't supervising.

STEP 3—Once your dog is ignoring the line or leash, pick up the end and hold it. Do not apply any pressure. Follow your dog, keeping the line slack. Work for a total of ten minutes on this.

STEP 4—After your dog is used to being on the end of the leash while you hold it, the final step is for you to coax him in the direction you wish to go. Do not allow the leash to tighten without immediately loosening up again, and tell your pup how well he is doing when he is walking with you.

158

Depending on the amount of time the instructor wants to spend on orientation, it can be given orally or in written form. Since our classes start with dogs present the first session, the bulk of the general information the student needs is contained in the pamphlet "Teaching You to Train Your Dog" written by Jack in 1975 and available from Arner Publications (see Bibliography).

The pamphlet is a written orientation. It tells the students, in a general way, the object of the course, what to wear, the importance of class attendance and punctuality, and the need to practice at home the lessons they have learned in class. Items that are specific to the class are imparted orally or as a part of the first week homework sheet.

Housetraining

Since questions about housetraining are asked frequently, we use the following one-page handout:

HOUSETRAINING HINTS

(1) Feed at set times. Do not vary your schedule, even on weekends. If you feed at 7:00 a.m. on a weekday, feed at that same time on Saturday and Sunday, at least until he is housetrained.

(2) Feed one diet and do not vary it. Do not feed table scraps or treats during the housetraining period.

(3) Watch your puppy's stools—if they are loose, you may be overfeeding.

(4) Have your veterinarian do a stool check for worms.

(5) Take your puppy out on a regular schedule, stay out with him, and praise him when he goes. Take your puppy out after he has eaten or drunk, after he wakes from a nap, after he has played or when he begins to sniff in a circling motion.

(6) When you take him out, go straight to the spot you want to make his toilet area and stand there. Do not walk with him. Teach him that this is the time and place to relieve himself.

(7) Clean accidents with a cleaner designed for urine odor, or with white vinegar and water. Do not use an ammonia-based cleaner. Urine contains ammonia and such a cleaner would attract your dog to that spot again.

(8) If you catch your puppy in the act of relieving himself in the house, say **"STOP!"** Pick him up, carry him directly outside to his toilet area, wait with him until he goes there and then praise.

(9) Keep a chart of exactly what the puppy does at what time, including accidents. You will notice a pattern and be better able to plan his schedule.

(10) Under no circumstances drag your puppy over to an accident to show it to him and scold him, or worst of all, rub his nose in it. If you don't catch him in the act, say nothing. Put him in another area and clean it up.

Crate Training

Questions concerning crate training usually do not require lengthy answers, but those who are having difficulties we refer to our training book which contains a section spelling out in detail the mechanics of crate training a dog. We also recommend crate training to facilitate house-training.

Neutering

Questions about spaying females are generally limited to how old the dog should be.

It is rare that we are asked about neutering a male. Far more frequently it is we who suggest that in the interest of the dog and the handler the dog be neutered. Since this can be a touchy subject and one that will consume a great deal of time, we accompany our recommendation with a reprint of an article Gail wrote on the subject (see Bibliography). After the student has read the article, we repeat the suggestion and answer any other questions the student may have.

If you wish further information on how to answer questions owners may have relating to neutering, Gail wrote an article entitled "Castration, Convincing Owners" which will be helpful to you (see Bibliography).

Obedience Titles

When students begin to ask about obedience titles we give them the pamphlet "All About Obedience Trials" written by Jack and Olive Point in 1977 and available from Arner Publications (see Bibliography). It answers the most frequently asked questions about showing, what the various initials stand for, how to enter trials and matches, and includes a glossary of terms.

We also give them a copy of the Obedience Regulations, available from the American Kennel Club (see Bibliography).

A ready source for a variety of educational materials are the pamphlets distributed by dog food companies, often free of charge. These pamphlets deal with grooming, feeding, parasites, handling emergencies, vaccinations and other topics instructors are often asked about. The American Kennel Club has educational materials as well.

PART IV

Problem Solving

"A behavioral analysis acknowledges the importance of physiological research. What an organism does will eventually be seen to be due to what it is, at the moment it behaves, and the physiologist will someday give us all the details. He will tell us how it has arrived at that condition as a result of its previous exposure to the environment as a member of the species and as an individual."

B. F. Skinner
About Behaviorism

10

Instructing
Challenges

INTRODUCTION

Any instructor, regardless of the subject being taught, has had to deal with the challenging or problem student. In a dog obedience class, this student might be canine or human. In this chapter, we will discuss instructing challenges related to **people.**

INSTRUCTING PROBLEMS

The instructor's responsibility is to offer instruction to each student enrolled in the class. As long as the teaching is unbiased, the instructor's opinions about his students are immaterial.

Occasionally there will be a problem dealing with the personalities of individuals. How the instructor deals with these problems will affect not only the difficult student, but in many cases, the rest of the class as well. Problem students can interfere with the instructor's ability to teach effectively, undermine his or her self-confidence and reduce motivation.

We view instructing problems as a challenge to our ingenuity and abilities to deal with people. The students who are difficult in class are often people with problems, and it is beyond our capabilities, our professional training, and our responsibility to sort out the causes and cures.

Following are some of the more common reasons for instructing problems:

Incompatibility

The student's success in an obedience class is in part related to the temperament and personality of the student himself, and to his perception of the instructor. Respect for the instructor's knowledge and ability to teach is important. It is also helpful, but not essential, if the student likes the instructor personally.

For the majority of students, personal regard for the instructor is unimportant in terms of their goal. We have had students in our classes who seemed not to like us, at least as far as we could tell.

It is not necessary for all students to appreciate your personality. It is, however, necessary for the students to learn from you in order for them to be successful. For some students, incompatibility with the instructor will interfere with their ability to learn. When the student's personal feelings about the instructor hinder his ability to take instruction, the student then has a problem. Whatever it may be, it can only be resolved by the student himself.

Few students will approach the instructor with their feelings. Most will simply drop out of class.

Sometimes the student will be motivated to try to deal with this incompatibility. This happened with a student who was competition oriented, wanted to remain in our classes, but had a personality conflict with her instructor. When evaluations were done, this student wrote on her form that she had had difficulty relating to one of the instructors, and stated her reasons. After talking to the student, a nice friendship developed, and she has since put two Utility titles on her dogs.

This is the rare instance. In most cases, if there is incompatibility between the student and the instructor, it is the student's responsibility to resolve it by either swallowing their dislike of the instructor and learning anyway, or taking their dog to another class.

Age Differences

Beyond the occasional instance of personal incompatibility, there are predictable problems that arise between age groups. A young instructor may have a problem establishing his or her credibility with an older student. Again, this is the student's problem to work out.

166

A young instructor may have a problem with an older student.

Some students cannot deal with the instructor.

In addition to the age problem, there will be difficulties resulting from the sex of the instructor. For example, a young woman instructor may have difficulty teaching a young or a middle-aged man. Often these men are unable to take instruction from a woman they view as less than a peer, much less as someone who knows more than they do.

We once observed a class which a very capable young woman was instructing. After explaining the Down exercise, she instructed the class to down their dogs. A young man wearing a leather jacket, decorated with studs and chains, could not get his Doberman to go down. The instructor went over to help him, and in a quiet and businesslike manner, showed him how to down his dog. The young man never returned.

What happened? This particular student could not deal with a woman being able to handle his dog better than he could. What should she have done? There really is nothing that she could have or should have done differently. If a student has difficulty relating to the instructor, he will either have to learn to deal with his feelings, or find another class taught by someone better suited to his temperament. But it is *his* problem, not the instructor's.

PROBLEM STUDENTS

A problem student is one who has the potential to take more class time than he is entitled to, either by requiring special attention, or by upsetting the class or the instructor in some way. Anyone who has ever taught an obedience class has dealt with this student. There are four categories of problem students: Belligerent, Demanding, Helpless and Alcoholic.

The Belligerent Personality

The Belligerent personality complains about the method or the equipment or the facility or something else that isn't to his liking. He may do this under his breath, but usually loud enough for the instructor to hear him. There is only one way to deal with this type of student—refund his money and ask him to leave. In spite of our no refund policy, this person is given his money back to ensure he will not return to class.

The Belligerent has a problem, but it is not your responsibility, nor within your training as an obedience instructor to solve it. If he's unhappy in the world in which he lives, let him find another one in which to vent his frustrations, but not your obedience class.

The rest of the class will be relieved to have him leave. The majority of the students are sincerely interested in training their dogs, and they don't want their own efforts undermined by someone moaning and groaning all the time.

The Demanding Student

The Demanding student actively solicits attention from either the instructor or an assistant. This student asks for special attention by saying, "I don't think I'm doing this quite right. Would you watch me." While there will be occasions when a non-demanding student would say that, the Demanding student does it repeatedly, on almost every exercise. This student also is the first one to ask questions, even before you have solicited any. The Demanding student is an exhibitionist. He or she wants to be watched. He or she will solicit unruly behavior from the dog, for example, encouraging the dog to jump up and then loudly admonishing him or making a joke of it.

The best way to handle a Demanding type is to ignore him. Give him his share of attention, i.e., 1/15th in a class of 15 students. If you give any more attention, even disapproval, it positively reinforces the demanding behavior. **Any reinforcement** encourages this behavior.

The Helpless Student

This is the student who stands there waiting for his or her neighbor to comply with an instruction, and then watches to see what he should do. He is the one who calls you over and, thrusting the leash at you, says, "I can't do this. You do it."

Helpless students are demanding and should be treated the same as demanding students—give them their share of the attention, then ignore them. When challenged by a Helpless student to perform the exercise with the dog, politely explain that we know **we** can do it; our task in class is to see that **he** can do it. Why doesn't he try again while we watch. The instructor or assistant watches to correct any errors the student may be making, praises briefly when he does it correctly, and immediately walks away. Spending extra time with a Helpless student encourages and reinforces his helplessness. It is amazing how being ignored will turn a helpless student into a capable student.

The Alcoholic

The final category of problem students is the one who comes to class drunk. In spite of the fact that our General Instructions Sheet includes an admonition that students not drink before training their dogs, some will come to class after having had a few drinks.

Belligerent student.

Demanding student.

Helpless student.

The Alcoholic student is usually disruptive, and lacks patience with his dog and the ability to follow instructions. He often fits into another category, such as being belligerent or helpless.

Jack has his own way of dealing with students who come to class drunk. He once had a woman student who had had so much to drink before class that all the personnel were getting a contact high from breathing the fumes surrounding her. He instructed her to go off to one side of the training room and practice the Figure 8. After two repetitions, she rushed out of the room, never to be seen again.

The Nightmare Class

Anyone who has been instructing obedience classes for any length of time has had the class with all the above types. This Nightmare Class has no shining stars to assure you that you are speaking English. It is as if the entire class is brain damaged.

When you get such a class, our advice is, be friendly and helpful to the individuals and don't be concerned if you cannot stick to your class outline. We've had classes where we have had to re-instruct each instruction every week—there was no recall memory from one week to another. The seventh week of class our instructions were the same that we used the second week.

This class is usually having a good time, even though they are not learning at the rate the instructor expects. We had one such class, filled with nice, albeit slow learners, one of whom at graduation brought a dish of German Potato Salad with sausages, only to neglect to bring a serving utensil, plates or forks. It seemed a fitting end to that session.

SPECIAL NEEDS STUDENTS

There is another category of students who, while they present challenges to an instructor, are not problem students. They fall into two categories: the physically challenged and those who have difficulty learning from oral instructions.

The Physically Challenged

The physically challenged student may have a hearing difficulty, a debilitating condition such as arthritis or Multiple Sclerosis, or a functional handicap such as blindness, deafness, paraplegia, loss of a limb or innumerable others.

The manner in which a physically challenged student is treated in class will affect not only his success or failure in training his dog, but his dignity as well. By not making a big fuss over the handicap or the handicapped

The nightmare class.

person, the class can be run with the other students often not even aware that there was a special needs student in the class. We have had deaf students whom we have trained successfully simply by always facing them when we gave instructions. The rest of the class was not even aware that the person was deaf.

A student with arthritis can put his dog on a table for the exercises requiring students to bend or kneel in order to sit or down their dogs. Students with MS work at their own pace, taking time to rest if they need it.

Students in a wheelchair can be taken in a class if the training area is wheelchair accessible, and if the student has a helper to work the chair while he is working the dog. Alternative techniques may be required, but the student will usually be able to figure out what is needed. As a blind student once said to us, "We've been involved with our handicaps a lot longer than you have. Tell us what we need to do, and we'll figure out a way to do it."

If an instructor is interested in running a class for the physically challenged, this is certainly a worthwhile endeavor. We prefer to mainstream the physically challenged student into a regular class, if possible. If the class or training area is not adequate for a special needs person, the instructor may want to work with the student privately, or suggest private lessons with someone else.

Orally Challenged

The other category of special needs students is the one who has difficulty translating oral instructions into physical responses. He is not stupid. To the contrary, he is often very bright. Because he has difficulty distinguishing left from right, up from down or a turn from a straight line, he might be mistaken for a slow learner.

This student requires a little extra time from the instructor or assistant, and it is usually time well spent. It is this student who most often benefits from repeating a class, or from the little extra time that may be spent helping him to follow the instructions correctly. This may mean physically taking his or her hands and placing them in the proper position, or guiding him by the shoulders through a turn to indicate the proper direction. He is not incapable of learning, but has difficulty learning from *oral* instructions.

INSTRUCTOR'S STATURE

The class instructor is the pack leader. He or she walks around the class area with impunity—infringing on everyone else's territory when

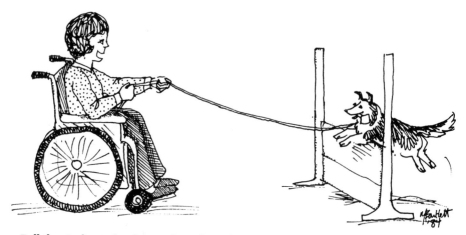

Tell the student what he needs to do and he'll figure out a way to do it.

The orally challenged student.

174

ALPHA
EARS

DOMINANT
SNOOT POSITION

DRESS FOR SUCCESS
PENCIL

DOMINANT
TAIL POSITION

The instructor as pack leader.

necessary, and giving commands to all involved. This status is not unnoticed by the dogs, who often behave quite meekly for the instructor, only to become unruly again when handed back to the non-pack-leader owner. Neither is this status unnoticed by the students—even though they wouldn't articulate their feelings about the instructor in such a manner.

We were aware of the impact the pack leadership status the instructor has on the dogs in the class, but less aware of its effect on the human students until Gail had an accident and severely sprained her ankle. It was the third week of an eight-week course when she arrived on crutches and ran the class sitting on a chair in the corner with her leg elevated.

The first class after the accident was uneventful, although the class did not go as well as it might have. We chalked this up to Gail's being in pain and not in top form. The second week after the accident, the demeanor of the entire class changed. Gail, still on crutches, again conducted class from a chair. But this session, the fourth week of class, did not go as most fourth weeks do. Several members of the class were belligerent, asking questions in a less than friendly tone of voice, and arguing with answers. We found this interesting, from a psychological point of view. Was it that the class, the pack, sensed weakness in the leader? Were these students attacking the downed leader?

We learned the answers to these questions in the next two weeks. The following week, the fifth week of class, Gail was still on crutches and still having to keep her leg elevated, although part of the time she was on her feet, not sitting in the chair. The class remained just as hostile as it had the previous week.

The sixth week, Gail was mobile again and was able to conduct the class standing up and moving around. The class, which had previously been hostile, was fine again, with no hostility or belligerence.

We found this an interesting study in human nature. The message here is not that an instructor has to be able to walk. On the contrary, an instructor in a wheelchair or on crutches would be perfectly acceptable, as long as the class accepted this stature from the beginning. The decline in the attitude of this class was due to perceived weakness, much the way a pack of animals will perceive weakness in the pack leader.

CONCLUSION

The instructor's relationship with the students in an obedience class determines their success with their dogs. Understanding personality problems and special needs enables the instructor to be a successful teacher. To paraphrase Abraham Lincoln: It is true that you may teach all the people some of the time; you can even teach some of the people all the time; but you can't teach all of the people all the time.

11

Analyzing Problems

INTRODUCTION

Few students come to class for the first time because they are interested in learning how to train a dog or in obtaining obedience titles. The majority come because they are unable to live with the dog or because they envision the day when the dog may be a problem unless he is trained.

In some cases obedience training, by creating a positive relationship between owner and dog, will be sufficient to eliminate any difficulties that may have existed. There will be those dogs, however, who, while responding well to the training, continue to be a problem in other areas.

For example, Fido will come when called, but he still destroys the house when left alone. Rover does a wonderful Sit Stay, but he continues to use the Oriental as his bathroom. The children can now walk Rosie without her pulling them down the street, but her howling when left alone is enough to wake the dead.

For the owners of these dogs, obedience class has not been enough. They need help with these behavior problems, and look to the instructor for guidance.

Exactly what constitutes a behavior problem? Most often, problem behavior is normal behavior occurring at the wrong time. The dog's conduct is not unacceptable unless and until it interferes with his relationship with his owner. For example, going to the bathroom is normal behavior. Going to the bathroom in the living room is inappropriate; however, if the dog is a young puppy, most people would consider it a normal consequence of housetraining. But for the one-year-old dog, it is considered a behavior problem.

In this chapter, we will discuss the analysis of problem behavior. In the following chapter, we will give specific information for solving many of the problems our students have presented to us over the years. To find the right solution, however, it is important to understand the underlying cause.

BEHAVIOR PROBLEM MODEL

To analyze problem behavior, we use a ten point Behavior Problem Model. These ten points are:

1. Temperament
2. Instinctive Behavior
3. Exercise & Attention
4. Mental Stimulation
5. Established Routine
6. Nutrition
7. Physical Problems
8. Environment
9. Spay/Neuter
10. Training

Temperament

Temperament is defined as the dog's suitability for a specific task or function. There are no good or bad temperaments; there are suitable and unsuitable temperaments.

For example, a particular dog may be unsuitable as a pet because he is too active and aggressive; however, he would be perfectly acceptable as a patrol dog in a used car lot. An older couple desiring a quiet dog to share their walks in the woods would be unhappy with a dog with a temperament best suited for an active family with teenage children.

There are a variety of definitions used to describe temperament:

Aggressive

An aggressive dog is combative. This is a dog who will bite. Dogs may be dog aggressive, people aggressive or both. A dog aggressive dog is difficult to handle in an obedience class. For specific techniques to deal with this dog, see Chapter 12, Behavior Problems.

A people aggressive dog may be trained in class, provided the members of the class are not in danger. Aggression to people is often a result of lack of socialization, and obedience class can temper this. If he is biting his own handler, refer to Chapter 12, Behavior Problems, for information you can use to help the handler.

Self-Confident

An assertive or self-confident dog has a strong sense of self and his abilities. He is bold and self-assured. While this dog makes an excellent pet when he is under control, this type of temperament can lead to behavior problems if the dog is not trained.

Dominant

The dominant dog strives to be pack leader. The more dominant he is, the more important it is to him to be the leader. Rarely will a dog be so dominant that it cannot accept human leadership, but this does happen occasionally. The degree of dominance a dog exhibits will have a direct bearing on the ease with which he will take to training. The more dominant the dog, the more important that he have a consistent trainer who understands how to be the pack leader. The obedience instructor can help the handler reach leadership status over the dominant dog through various exercises such as the Long Down and Safety exercises (see Appendix I).

Submissive

The submissive dog, on the other hand, accepts human leadership readily. He has no desire to be in control, and is generally willing to please and to do as bidden. This is not to be confused with "wimpy." A submissive dog can be a good protector of the home, even though he is willing to submit to the control of a master. This makes him an excellent pet and companion, and a willing worker for the average family and handler.

Shyness

Submissiveness is not to be confused with shyness. Shyness can be due to lack of socialization or may be an inherent response to sight and sound stimuli. The shy dog is sensitive to noise and movement, responding fearfully. In a situation where a submissive dog will lower his body posture and assume a submissive attitude, a shy dog will leave the scene or even bite if cornered or forced to do something it fears. This is the "fear biter." Training helps to build the shy dog's confidence, and makes him more comfortable. Some shy behaviors, such as fear of people, can be desensitized through obedience class (see Chapter 12, Behavior Problems).

Independence

An independent dog is one that neither needs nor wants guidance from others. He is self-directed and self-reliant. He is not affectionate, and needs no affection from others. This dog does not care about praise or pleasing his handler.

Activity Level

The final aspect of temperament is the dog's activity level, ranging from extremely active to lethargic. A quick, active dog requires the handler to think ahead more than he would need to with a lethargic dog. For example, as the handler of a fast-moving dog is coming to a halt, he will need to physically prepare himself to sit the dog prior to stopping. Whereas the handler of a slow-moving dog may be able to stop, and *then* begin to think about placing his hands in position for the Automatic Sit.

Instinctive Behavior

As discussed in Chapter 3, Influences on Learning, individual breed characteristics affect the ease or difficulty with which a dog learns. Breed characteristics affect his behavior as well, and sometimes create problems.

There are six activities which are frequently related to breed characteristics and instincts. These are:

1. Herding
2. Hunting
3. Guarding
4. Sex
5. Barking
6. Digging

The first four most often result from instincts, whereas the last two, barking and digging, may be related to breed instincts or may be related to boredom. We will discuss this under Environment.

Without having an understanding of breed characteristics, an owner may not recognize that, for example, a Collie who nips at the heels of the children as they cavort and run around is doing what he was bred to do.

Scampering children elicit his herding instinct—he is trying to establish order among his keep. His owner, however, may perceive this as aggressive behavior and be concerned that his dog is going to attack the children. Once he understands the basis of the behavior, the owner is now in a position to train the dog to be under control without worrying that his dog is going to "turn bad."

A Basset Hound on the trail of a rabbit will not come when called. On the other hand, a breed with a less highly developed hunting instinct, for instance a Pekingese, would not be as likely to disregard the command in the same circumstances. It is not that the Basset is less responsive to his owner than the Peke, he is simply following his instincts. The Basset's owner, once he recognizes the precedence that his dog's nose takes over almost everything else in his life, can now proceed with training, understanding that he will have to work harder to achieve his goal than does the Peke's owner.

On the first night of class, we instruct our students to learn about their breeds, finding out any tasks that might be in harmony with, or contrary to the dog's instincts. Having some idea of what their breed was selectively bred for, they now have a basis for understanding some behavior problems. If, for example, the problem is a terrier that digs holes in the garden, the owner now understands that this is instinctive behavior, not that the dog is being ornery or spiteful.

Whether or not instinctive behavior can be modified depends on the owner's commitment to resolve the problem. The stronger the instinct, the greater the commitment required to modify the behavior. In many cases the solution is to change the environment and avoid putting the dog in a position of inappropriately exercising his instincts—for example, fencing an area for the terrier where he can dig as much as he likes and not interfere with the garden.

It often becomes necessary to give a dog an outlet for his instinctive behaviors. The expression of his instincts creates a healthy psychology which helps the dog to concentrate on those tasks which are non-instinctive. For example, teaching a Basset to track, or taking him on walks where he can use his nose, facilitates concentration on an exercise which is less instinctive, such as heeling or retrieving.

This does not mean that a family with a Collie has to keep sheep, but they need to find an outlet for the energy which the Collie would instinctively expend on herding. For instance, he is given regular exercise chasing a ball.

Paying attention to the instinctive needs of a dog eliminates many behavior problems.

Providing the dog with an outlet for instinctive behavior.

Many behavior problems, such as door crashing, stem from lack of exercise.

Exercise

One of the first questions we ask our students when they come to us with a behavior problem is, "How much exercise does your dog get?" The more active the breed, the more exercise it requires. Too little exercise will result in a behavior problem.

For example, a Labrador Retriever requires a great deal of exercise on a regular basis. If this is not attended to, behavior problems such as destroying the house, not considered socially acceptable, may result.

Another behavior problem resulting from lack of exercise is running away. A dog of a breed requiring exercise, who does not have an opportunity to run on a regular basis, will take a mistakenly offered opportunity, that is the door left slightly ajar, and be off. This is an example of an *action specific energy* behavior, one which is related to the energy being released. Action specific energy can be responsible for other behaviors as well, such as chewing (see Chapter 12).

If the dog is not getting enough exercise, the solution is to exercise him. By giving him regular, daily exercise (at least 15 minutes a day), the behavior problem probably will be eliminated. Fifteen minutes of retrieving not only exercises him, but provides an outlet for his instinctive behavior as well. A fifteen-minute walk provides exercise as well as presenting an opportunity to investigate, which is instinctive.

If the owner claims that without a fenced yard the dog will run away, he has several options: First, fence the yard; second, train the dog sufficiently so he won't run away; third, play with him on a long line so he is exercised while under physical control; fourth, visit a friend with a fenced yard. There is one final option, which some people prefer to confinement— giving the dog away or euthanizing it. It stems from the notion that it is cruel not to give a dog his freedom and leads to a perverted sense of justice: let him play in traffic; let him scour the neighborhood and get into rat poison; or just put him down.

All dogs, regardless of breed, require a minimum of 15 minutes of exercise a day. By giving a dog this outlet for his energies, not only is he less likely to have a behavior problem, but he will be healthier.

Attention

Lack of meaningful attention can have a direct bearing on problem behavior. Meaningful attention is grooming, training and playing with the dog. To be meaningful, the dog has to be the sole focus of the owner's attention, which does not include mindless petting while watching TV.

Mental Stimulation

Mental Stimulation means allowing the dog to interact with and explore his environment, in short, **letting the dog be a dog.**

Dogs investigate and learn about the world through the sense of smell, much the way we investigate and learn through our eyesight. In order to be psychologically healthy and well adjusted, the dog needs to exercise his investigative abilities—he needs to sniff.

Behavior problems can arise if the dog is rarely, if ever, given an opportunity for mental stimulation. A dog owner who is frightened of germs, for instance, and doesn't allow his dog to sniff the fire hydrants or trees is creating psychological frustrations which will surface as a behavior problem.

Behavior problems resulting from lack of mental stimulation are easily solved by letting the dog be a dog. If, along with his 15 minutes of daily exercise, the owner allows the dog to investigate and explore his environment, his mental health will be intact.

Established Routine

Dogs thrive on monotony. They are secure knowing that the master will wake up and let them out every day at the same time; that they can expect their meals at a specific time; and that they will receive exercise and training at about the same time every day. In the absence of a routine, dogs live in a constant state of anxiety: Is it mealtime soon? Will I get to go out shortly? Am I going to get exercise today?

Lack of a regular routine might cause a dog to relieve himself in the house since he isn't sure when he'll be let out. Not knowing whether or not he's going to get something to eat, he might rummage through the garbage, or eat a non-food item. Not knowing if he's going to get exercise, he might release his excess energies through engaging in an activity such as destructive chewing.

Lack of a consistent schedule can cause such anxiety in a dog that it leads to neurotic behavior. The remedy is simple: the dog is put on a regular routine.

Nutrition

We are what we eat, and so are our dogs. One of the questions we ask our students with behavior problems is, "What do you feed your dog?"

Behavior problems commonly caused by diet are: housetraining, lethargy, hyperactivity, aggression and "rage syndrome."

Allow the dog to be a dog and let him interact with his environment.

Lack of meaningful attention, such as grooming and training, indicates an owner who doesn't care for his dog.

Housetraining

The type of diet a dog is fed can greatly affect the housetraining effort. The semi-moist varieties of dog food contain great amounts of salt as a preservative. Salt causes the dog to drink a lot of water, which creates a concurrent need to eliminate.

Some dog foods contain greater amounts of filler than others. Filler is generally non-digestible and nutritionally non-utilizable; however, once the dog has eaten it, it must be eliminated. Some dogs have difficulty controlling their bowel movements when they are fed a high bulk diet. When analyzing a housetraining problem, if the volume of the dog's stool seems equal to, or even greater than the amount of food he has consumed, chances are his diet is high in bulk. By switching the dog to a high density, highly digestible dog food, housetraining is facilitated.

Lethargy, Hyperactivity, Aggression & "Rage Syndrome"

Research has established a correlation between artificial additives, sugar, salt and many preservatives in food and behavior problems in people. The same holds true for dogs. Sugar is a major cause of obesity, which would cause lethargy, and also of hyperactivity.

Many aggressive dogs, including those with "Rage Syndrome," have been cured with the help of a nutritional program.

Physical Problems

Over the years, we have made note of the number of behavior problems we are presented with in class which were caused by a physical difficulty. In our experience, over 90% of aggression is caused by physical discomfort, pain or illness. With this in mind, the first thing we recommend to a person with a behavior problem dog, especially if it is a change in behavior of recent onset, is a veterinary checkup.

Following are some examples of dogs with physical problems which created behavioral changes:

Tiger is a four-year-old Airedale who is a wonderful representative of his breed. His temperament and personality are definitive of the King of Terriers. He is bold, outgoing, and supremely self-confident. His obedience work is quick and accurate, and he is delightful to have in class.

One day Tiger came to class a changed dog. He was timid, lacking in self-confidence, was frightened of the other dogs in class and was sensitive to noise. We recommended a veterinary checkup, which showed nothing out of the ordinary. Several weeks went by with no discernible change in Tiger's attitude. Then Tiger was groomed, and as part of the grooming

186

In the absence of routine, dogs live in a constant state of anxiety which may lead to undesirable behavior.

Before treating abnormal behavior as a training problem, first rule out the possibility of a physical problem.

procedure, his anal glands were expressed. Immediately upon getting off the grooming table, Tiger rushed up to a crated dog and started to fence fight—exhibiting the behavior we had all come to know as Tiger's. He was himself again. Impacted anal glands had been the cause of his change in personality.

Brandy was a five-month-old Cocker Spaniel who had started training with us when she was about three and a half months old. Her training had gone uneventfully, until one day she bit her owner during the Down on Command exercise. As Brandy had shown no prior inclination to bite, we recommended a veterinary checkup. The veterinarian found a low-grade throat infection, and put Brandy on antibiotics.

By the time of the next class, Brandy's biting problem was gone. Even a low-grade throat infection can cause sufficient discomfort to create a behavior problem.

Sherman is a lovely working Golden Retriever who, with two legs toward his Utility Title, suddenly started refusing the Go Out. As Sherman is an extremely willing worker who had been well trained, we chose to check out the possibility of a physical problem before treating it as a training problem. We recommended a veterinary checkup, including x-rays of his front end. The x-rays showed elbow dysplasia. Sherman had refused the Go Out because the return over the jumps was painful to him. Unfortunately, the solution in this case was to retire Sherman from competition.

Bruiser is a Springer Spaniel who began training with us at the age of 8 weeks. He is a huge specimen of the breed, and we would laugh about his extreme lethargy, saying that it was because he was growing so fast. We had ruled out diet or a physical ailment as a possible cause for his lethargy, and chalked it up to this particular dog's low activity level.

After 10 months of training, when Bruiser was almost one year old with no discernible difference in his energy, we noticed one night in class that he was blinking a lot, and his eyes were watering. We recommended a veterinary checkup. The next week Bruiser came to class with sutures in his eyelids from entropion surgery.

That week in class we saw Bruiser trot. He was not a speedy demon, but he moved above a slow stroll for the first time in his training. His painful eyes had caused his extreme lethargy.

Other physical conditions which can cause behavioral changes are ear infections, skin infections, flea allergies, epilepsy, structural problems such as luxated patella, hip dysplasia, arthritis, osteochondritis dessecans, eosinophilic panosteitis, and poor grooming such as matting and long toenails.

A veterinary examination includes the following areas:

1. Overall condition (including skin and coat, heart, lungs, abdomen).
2. Eyes
3. Ears
4. Throat
5. Anal glands
6. Feet and nails
7. Fecal examination

If the presenting complaint necessitates, the veterinarian will do diagnostic work including such things as x-rays or a blood work-up.

Before treating any abnormal behavior as a training or behavior problem, we first rule out the possibility that it is physical. If there is nothing physically wrong, or if the behavior persists even once the physical problem has been cleared up, then it is addressed through training or behavior modification.

Environment

The environment affects the dog in two ways: first, how he is kept and second, the environment of the household itself.

The Dog's Environment

If a dog is tied out isolated in the back yard for most of his life, it is likely that he will develop a number of behavior problems such as barking, digging, uncontrollable behavior when brought in the house, and often biting. Because these behaviors tend not to endear a dog to his family, they become self-perpetuating. The family feels justified in keeping the dog in isolation because he is "bad."

Dogs that are kept tied, even by well-meaning people who provide what they feel is sufficient room for exercise by putting the dog on a 40' pulley system, are subject to the same frustrations as being tied on a two-foot tether. To the dog, being tied causes tension and frustration. Once these build up, they will be expressed in a variety of ways, none of which are socially acceptable. In addition, this frustration often causes problems even when the dog is free. For example, tether frustration may cause a dog to lunge out at another dog or a person, and if the tether snaps, the dog may then bite.

We recommend a fenced area for the dog, but with common sense precautions. Barrier frustration behind a fence can lead to the same behavior problems. If the dog does not receive sufficient exercise, training and attention, being kept penned up all the time is little better than being kept tied all day.

Dogs are social creatures, and they need interaction with their families. If the dog is too unruly to have in the house, training will get the dog under sufficient control to be a contributing member of the household. Once the vicious cycle of keeping the "bad dog" isolated is broken by allowing the dog to be part of the family, he will continue to improve.

The Family's Environment

The environment of the household has a great effect on the dog. If it is noisy and chaotic, the dog will reflect this. To a dog, the noise that emanates from our mouths is the equivalent of barking. If we yell a lot, the dog may bark a lot in response. This is a touchy area for the obedience instructor. It is not really his place to tell people that they are loud and unruly, and that is why their dog is behaving in a like fashion.

A change in the atmosphere of a household can also affect the dog. For example, if one of the providers loses his or her job, and there is tension and fighting over money, the dog may develop behavior problems resulting from this tension. Divorce or separation, death, illness, the birth of a child, moving, change in job hours, and the like can affect the dog's behavior. Advice to students in these situations is to give the dog as much positive and meaningful attention as is possible through obedience training.

Spay & Neuter

Spaying

We recommend spaying a female as a matter of routine, unless the handler plans to breed or show her in conformation. The care and maintenance of a female is easier when she has been spayed. Owners do not have to put up with the discharge, the attraction of all the neighborhood males to camp out and fight on the front lawn, and the threat of unwanted pregnancy. Spaying is also advisable for reasons of overall health. A veterinarian can answer any questions your student has about this surgery.

From a behavioral point of view, the hormones accompanying the estrus cycle often cause personality changes in females. These can range from slight depression to flaky behavior to a pseudo pregnancy including milk production and nesting. Spaying eliminates behavioral changes.

Neutering

We recommend neutering a dog who is not going to be used for breeding or be shown in conformation. Most students are unwilling to neuter their dogs unless there is a reason to do so. There are three behavioral situations in which neutering is recommended:

If the dog is too unruly to be in the house . . .

train him and make him a part of the family.

1. For the dog who is more assertive than the owner can handle or for the owner who has difficulty resolving the dominance issue.
2. For the dog whose sex drive materially interferes with training and control. This is the dog who, when coming in proximity with a female in season, is oblivious to everything but the desire to breed.
3. For the dog who exhibits other behaviors related to sex drive: roaming, mounting, frequent erection, inappropriate marking behavior (leg lifting in the house), overprotectiveness and dog fighting.

Neutering will not make a male less territorially protective. He will still bark at intruders. If the male is hunted, neutering will not affect his hunting ability. On the contrary, he will be better able to concentrate on the task at hand. Females who could not be hunted during their season will be able to work through the entire hunting season.

Contrary to popular belief, spaying and neutering will not cause obesity. Overfeeding causes obesity. Spaying and neutering may cause a reduction in the dog's activity level, which in turn means that he or she will require less food to maintain optimal weight.

For further information on convincing your students as to the advisability of spaying and neutering, refer to the Bibliography.

Training

Obedience training frequently eliminates problem behavior. Commonly students who have enrolled in class because of a behavior problem tell us several weeks later that the problem had disappeared without having had to be addressed directly.

There are five aspects to training which promote a harmonious relationship, thereby eliminating problem behavior. These are:

1. Establishing communication and understanding
2. Teaching the dog to work for the master
3. Giving the dog a job to do
4. Providing a tool to circumvent problem behavior
5. Laying the foundation for solving behavior problems.

1. Establishing Communication and Understanding

Through training, the owner and dog establish a line of communication and understanding. The dog learns the spoken language of the owner in the form of commands, praise and disciplinary words. The owner learns to use language, including body language, so that the dog understands what he is being told.

Many people mistakenly believe that dogs are born understanding English. This is no more true for a dog than for a person. Babies are taught who Mommy and Daddy are just as dogs are taught what "sit" and "come" mean, through repetition and association.

2. Teaching the Dog to Work for the Master

The dog learns to respond to commands, or to work for his master. In canine society, he or she who must be obeyed is the top dog. Therefore, teaching the dog to respond to the owner's commands teaches the dog who is the pack leader.

3. Giving the Dog a Job

Obedience training gives the dog a job to do. It is rarely sufficient for a dog to have as his function to be ornamental. He needs to have a reason for being. Something as simple as sitting on command, staying when told, and being rewarded with a word of praise for a job well done provides him with a function.

4. Providing a Tool for Circumventing Problem Behavior

Training provides a tool to circumvent problem behavior. For example, a dog that jumps on people is told to sit and stay. When he is sitting, he is unable to jump. No disciplinary measures are necessary. He just sits. Not only that, but he gets praised for sitting instead of being yelled at for jumping.

Another example of training circumventing problem behavior is for a dog who begs at the table. He is trained to do a Long Down.

5. Laying the Foundation for Solving Behavior Problems

If training has not been sufficient to solve the behavior problem, a foundation has been laid through communication, giving the dog a function, teaching him who the pack leader is, and putting him in a position to be praised for positive responses instead of always being reprimanded for negative ones. If behavior modification is needed, there is a sound basis for it to work.

CONCLUSION

The Behavior Problem Model gives the instructor a structured view of behavior problems. Most often the solution is found in one of these seven areas. Becoming aware that the dog is not being "spiteful," "willful" or "bad," many owners are motivated to finding solutions to the causes of the problem.

Viewing problem behavior from this perspective, it eliminates the concept of "blame." It is not the dog's fault that his behavior is unacceptable, and it is not the person's fault either. Problems result from circumstances that can be adjusted to eliminate the underlying cause of the problem. Rarely do we view behavior problems in a disciplinary context.

12

Behavior Problems

INTRODUCTION

As mentioned earlier, there are two purposes to dog training: the first is to teach the dog *to do* something he would not do on his own on command, and the second is to teach the dog to refrain from doing something he would do on his own. In the context of teaching him to stop objectionable behavior, people consider they have a behavior problem; however, in the context of teaching him to respond to commands, most problems are cured.

Therefore, all of our cures for behavioral ills are based on training combined with behavior modification. When training has not brought about a change, behavior modification will.

SIX ASPECTS

There are six aspects to a behavior problem which, when understood, dictate a behavior modification program. These are:

1. The dog's reward
2. The owner's objection
3. The owner's perception of the situation
4. The dog's perception of the situation
5. Avenues for prevention
6. The cure.

Remember, most often a behavior problem is normal behavior occurring at an inappropriate time or place. For example, eating is normal behavior. Eating garbage is objectionable. To illustrate the six aspects of a behavior problem, let's examine garbage eating: Konrad's reward is that he gets to eat tasty (to him) leftovers. His owner objects because cleaning up after Konrad is messy, and if there are bones in the garbage, Konrad is in danger. He perceives that Konrad should know better because he's given his own food and because he gets yelled at for having strewn garbage all over the place. Konrad's perception is that garbage tastes good, and if given an opportunity to do so, he'll eat it again. Prevention in this case is putting the garbage out of reach of the dog. That eliminates the need for a cure.

In this chapter we will examine these six elements of viewing a behavior problem. Using this as a basis for understanding, we will then address some specific problem areas.

The Dog's Reward

Every behavior the dog exhibits involves some sort of reward for him.

Konrad is not chewing the couch every day because he's mad at Mom for leaving him alone while she's at work. His destructiveness is not to punish his owners for anything they did or did not do. Frequently behavior such as destructiveness is a tension-releasing action. The dog may be stressed or bored. Since dogs do not hold in their negative feelings, tension-releasing behavior involves a reward system comparable to our blowing off steam.

When examining the dog's behavior, keep in mind that he is telling you something is wrong.

In problem evaluation, the rewards involved in each behavior must be understood. In many cases, eliminating the reward is enough to eliminate the problem behavior. In others, some remedial training or behavior modification may be required.

The Owner's Objection

There are no hard and fast rules for what constitutes acceptable behavior. **If the owner views it as a problem, it is a problem.** Some people like dogs sleeping on the bed with them; for others this is objectionable.

In some cases the owner has an idealized view of what the dog's behavior should be, and if the dog doesn't measure up, the owner thinks he has a problem. We call these *non*-problems. For example, some people find a dog's method of greeting another dog to be objectionable. They are offended that a dog will sniff the genitals of another dog. When they understand that this is normal greeting behavior, that this is how dogs assess each other's status and stature, the behavior becomes a non-problem.

First, examine what the owner finds objectionable and whether or not his objections are reasonable. A student, objecting that his German Shepherd Dog sheds too much and is angry at him for it, is unrealistic.

Sometimes an owner may object to a certain behavior at some times and not at others. For instance, when the owner is wearing jeans, he may not mind if the dog jumps on him, but if he's dressed up, he does mind. Or, as long as the dog's feet are clean it's okay, but not when it's raining and his feet are muddy.

Inconsistencies such as this are enough to drive a sane dog crazy. How is the dog to know which clothes are for going to the office and which are for cleaning the house? An owner must make up his mind that either he doesn't object to the behavior, or he does. Not sometimes, all the time.

The Owner's Perception

For behavior modification to be successful, the owner must abandon the idea that the dog "knows better." If the dog knew better, he would discontinue the behavior that gets him in trouble.

Many dog owners have difficulty absorbing this concept. They perceive the dog as "understanding every word I say," interpreting Konrad's submissive body posture as "guilt."

The Dog's Perception of the Situation

How does Konrad view the situation? If he doesn't know better, what is he learning from his discipline? Let's examine, for example, Konrad's lying on the couch.

Konrad knows that lying on the couch is comfortable. This comfort, no matter how brief, is his reward every time he gets up on the furniture. His owner finds this behavior objectionable, and every time he discovers Konrad on the couch, he yells at him. So Konrad has learned through repetition that every time his owner enters the living room, and he is on the couch, he gets yelled at. Konrad, being no dummy, learns that when he hears his owner coming, he can quickly get off the couch and not get yelled at.

Avenues for Prevention

Problems can be avoided if owners use a little common sense and learn to think ahead. For instance, if a chicken carcass from last night's dinner is in the garbage, the owner can put the garbage out of reach.

196

The dog's perception of the situation and that of the owner are not always the same.

It's unrealistic to be angry at the dog for shedding.

For curing most problems, it is far more fair to the dog, and far more pleasant for dog and owner alike, to use a positive approach. Our cures may involve some behavior modification of both the owner's behavior and of the situation that is causing the problem. In some cases changes in the environment may be required. This approach neither blames poor Konrad, nor "punishes" him for behavior he didn't know was wrong.

Some solutions refer to specific training techniques. In those cases, the owner will first have to train the dog.

Behavior problems do not develop overnight, and the solutions to these problems are not magical. Some will take several weeks, or even months before the owner will be satisfied with his dog's behavior. Often, part of the solution will involve some of the aspects of the Behavior Problem Model discussed in the last chapter, such as changing the diet, giving the dog more exercise, providing an outlet for mental stimulation, and spaying or neutering.

The following problem-solving techniques will help the owner achieve a harmonious relationship with his dog.

SOLUTIONS

Begging

Begging food from the dinner table is easy to teach a dog, and, once learned, is a hard habit to break. Konrad's training to beg begins when he is a young, adorable puppy. "Oh, he's such a cute thing. This little piece of fat won't hurt just this once." Few repetitions are required before Konrad learns that he gets fed from the table by begging. Then Konrad sits by his owner's chair while he is eating and stares at him. Occasionally he'll get up on his hind legs and paw at or nudge his owner's arm to remind him he's waiting. And he drools. He looks as though he's never been fed. So, of course, his owner gives him a little tidbit each time. Who can resist those pleading eyes?

The Dog's Reward is obvious. Konrad gets treats for begging at the table.

The Owner's Objection doesn't usually occur until he first tries to end Konrad's begging. When Konrad becomes a little more persistent—he nudges and paws—and the owner gives in, the behavior is reinforced. This is the first step in the owner's teaching Konrad to persist.

The second step occurs when the owner decides "This is it! I've had it! No more of this!" So he ignores Konrad's nudging, and Konrad's pawing, and Konrad's harder pawing. Then Konrad tries something new. He whines, then barks, and barks again. To get some peace, the owner gives Konrad his reward. From this Konrad learns an important human axiom: "If at first you don't succeed, try try again." At this point the owner strongly objects.

The Owner's Perception is that Konrad should know that the begging behavior is unacceptable. After all, he gets yelled at and ignored, doesn't he? He may even be isolated during dinner for a few days, only to return to the undesirable behavior as soon as he's given access to the dining room again—the ingrate.

The Dog's Perception is different. "If I'm really persistent, I get rewarded."

Avenues for Prevention in this case are simple. Don't feed the dog from the table—*ever*.

The Cure for a begging problem involves using training. The dog is taught the Down on Command, and Long Down. He is placed on a Long Down by his owner's side at the dinner table. The owner must be prepared for many interruptions initially, to reinforce Konrad's Long Down each time he gets up.

Once he has made up his mind that he doesn't want Konrad to beg anymore, Konrad will soon become resigned to the fact that the party is over, at least at the dinner table.

Before long, the owner is eating dinner in the company of a well-trained, well-behaved dog lying quietly in the corner.

To cure a begging problem, the owner:

(1) No longer feeds the dog from the table.
(2) Uses the Long Down by his chair, being prepared to reinforce the command.
(3) As Konrad becomes steadier on the Long Down, teaches him to remain in his place during dinner.
(4) Releases him at the end of the meal with lots of praise.

Jumping

Dogs jump on people as a form of greeting, in an attempt to get close to the person's mouth. One of the ways in which dogs greet each other is by licking the lips and mouth of a returning family member.

Another reason is play. Many owners encourage jumping on them during roughhousing, chase games or retrieving. If this is the case, and the owners are objecting to the behavior at other times, they must be consistent in discouraging jumping.

The Dog's Reward is threefold. First, he is greeting the returning pack member, his owner, or a visitor, by getting close to the mouth. Secondly, and more rewarding for the dog is that in the process of putting him back down on the floor, his owner is petting him and giving him lots of physical contact. His tone may be angry, but his hands are petting and rewarding. Finally, if the jumping is encouraged in play, then it is fun for the dog and is a learned behavior.

The Owner's Objection is often only in the event that he is wearing good clothes. As we mentioned earlier, this inconsistency is confusing to Konrad. Some owners don't mind the dog jumping on *them,* but get embarrassed when he jumps on visitors. Others have cured Konrad from jumping on *them,* but not on others.

The Owner's Perception. The owner is unaware of the rewards involved for the dog. He can't understand why the dog doesn't learn—he's tried "everything."

The Dog's Perception is that he's excited and happy to see his owner, and he wants to get up to the mouth for the proper greeting ritual.

Avenues for Prevention of jumping are to crouch down in greeting, especially with a young puppy, which prevents him from learning to jump up. If, from the beginning, the owner teaches the puppy to sit for his greeting, greets and strokes him briefly—no more than five seconds—the puppy will not develop a jumping problem.

The Cure. There are two aspects to the cure. The first is to teach Konrad not to jump on his owner, and the second is to teach him not to jump on other people. Both require training.

To stop Konrad from jumping on his owner, the owner:

(1) Ignores Konrad when he first arrives home. He walks past the dog, saying nothing to him, even if he's jumping.

(2) When he is out of the entry area, he greets Konrad by having him sit. Konrad may initially have to be placed into a sit which is done with a minimum of touching. When Konrad is sitting, the owner crouches down to pet him for **five seconds only.**

(3) After five seconds of greeting, the owner stands up and goes on about his business, ignoring Konrad a little longer. Then the owner interacts with him on a normal basis.

To stop Konrad from jumping on other people, the owner:

(1) Sits Konrad before letting people in the door. Initially he will have to put on Konrad's leash and collar to reinforce the command.

(2) Has the visitors ignore Konrad, walk in and sit down.

(3) Heels Konrad into the room and has him do a Long Down for 15

minutes. If he is quiet, he may be released. Otherwise, he is kept on a Long Down until he is quiet.

(4) Repeats the exercise a number of times. The more it is repeated, the easier it will become. This cure requires practice and repetition.

We recommend to our students that they spend a weekend setting up a training situation to teach the dog not to jump on people anymore. They plan it as a day-long party, asking friends and relatives to come at scheduled, staggered times during the day. They offer food and drink in return for help in training. After several repetitions with different people, the dog will easily sit when people come to visit.

Chewing

There are a variety of reasons dogs chew. One is a physiological need associated with teething. When puppies reach a certain age, they *must* chew. If they don't have anything to chew on, they'll find something—even doors and walls. This need peaks between six and ten months of age.

Another possible cause of chewing is due to a nutritional deficiency. We had a student whose dog would chew rocks. This wasn't so terrible except that occasionally he'd swallow one. After his dog had undergone two surgical procedures for rock removal, the student had an analysis done of the rocks. He discovered they were high in some minerals, which, when added to his dog's diet, ended the rock eating.

Chewing can also be an *action specific energy* behavior. When the dog eats, the behavior specific to eating is released. If his diet is highly concentrated, the amount of time spent eating may not be sufficient to expend this energy. The left over energy results in chewing after eating. The remedy is to provide the dog with a marrow bone.

The main reason dogs chew is because of boredom, frustration or lack of exercise. A dog left to his own devices all day may find unacceptable ways to amuse himself. Remember, if a dog is feeling tense and frustrated, he will not hold these feelings in—chewing is one release.

The Dog's Reward is dependent upon the cause of the chewing. If Konrad is teething, he is exercising his teeth and jaw. That feels good. If it is nutritional, he's trying to replace whatever nutrient he needs. If it's a release of tension, frustration or excess energy, then that is his reward.

The Owner's Objection is obvious. Chewing is an expensive problem, and when a problem hits the pocketbook, it is taken seriously.

The Owner's Perception is usually that he has tried "everything" to get Konrad to stop chewing. He's lost his temper, showed him his destruction and hollered, and hit him. But Konrad doesn't learn. Is he stupid?

The Dog's Perception. Konrad doesn't learn because he doesn't understand what the yelling and hitting is all about. To him it is removed from the destructive chewing. Here is the probable scenario: Mom leaves for work at eight o'clock, after having checked most of the family's possessions to make sure they are put away or out of Konrad's reach. Just before she closes the door, she admonishes Konrad not to touch anything—to be good. She uses her firmest, most threatening voice, and Konrad, who doesn't understand the language, is left alone with the feeling that something is very wrong. This immediately creates tension for him.

Now Mom is gone. Konrad, who likes to imitate his owner, goes around the house and checks things out, as Mom did. Then he finds something that feels particularly good to him, an overlooked shoe, and he sets about playing with it.

Five o'clock arrives, and Mom returns from work. Konrad is very happy to see her, but while he is greeting her she spies her shoe. At least she *thinks* it's her shoe. She grabs the happy Konrad by the collar, pushes his face into the shoe, yells and even hits him to let him know how awful she thinks he is for chewing her shoe.

Did she convince Konrad by this punishment that chewing her shoe was terrible? It *wasn't* terrible. It was a great deal of fun. What is bad in this scene was not his chewing the shoe, but Mom's coming home.

What Mom did by chastising Konrad was to make her homecoming unpleasant and frightening. It will not stop him from chewing shoes, or anything else in the future, but it will make him fear his owner.

Avenues for Prevention and The Cure are to confine the dog when he is left alone. Confinement puts the dog in an environment where he can do no wrong. He can have a toy, such as a marrow bone, to fulfill his physiological need to chew, but he will not have access to anything else that he can destroy.

Confinement may be in a small, well-ventilated room such as a bathroom or utility room. If, however, a chewing problem already exists, this will be too large an area.

We advocate crating dogs. For information on crate training, refer to our book **TRAINING YOUR DOG—The Step-by-Step Manual,** page 44.

To solve a chewing problem, the owner:

(1) Provides him with one chewable toy of his own.
(2) Gives him no more than one toy. That one is his, the rest are not.
(3) Keeps chewable objects out of the dog's reach.
(4) Confines him in a small area, preferably a crate, when he is unable to keep any eye on him.
(5) Trains him on a regular basis, thereby giving him a function and

Dogs are _not_ spiteful. Destructiveness is a tension releasing action which tells the owner something is wrong.

A little common sense will prevent a lot of frustration.

making him a contributing member of the household.

(6) Exercises him regularly.

Once the dog is past the chewing stage and has become accustomed to chewing his one toy, the owner may want to give the dog more freedom. He can do this as long as he observes the following rules:

(1) He keeps all chewable objects out of the dog's reach.
(2) He does not rush around the house just before leaving in a frantic effort to stash things away. This kind of manic behavior causes anxiety or excitement in the dog. Also, he may mimic the owner's behavior when he's alone.
(3) Prior to leaving the house, the owner sits down quietly for five minutes. He may read the paper, listen to the radio, have a cup of coffee, but pays no attention to his dog.
(4) When it is time to leave, he gets up and leaves. He is unemotional— no teary goodbyes. No "Daddy will miss you, but he'll be back soon." No admonitions to "be good." He simply leaves.
(5) Should the dog regress, the owner returns him to confinement for a short time while the possible causes of the relapse are examined. Is there a crisis in the family? Did he lose his job? Has he failed to follow advice?

Aggression

Aggression is divided into three categories: dog aggression, people aggression and other-animal aggression, all of which can be caused by improper socialization during the critical periods of development, dominance or a bad experience.

The Owner's Objection depends on the type of aggression and the personality of the owner. Some owners like their dogs to be aggressive, and even encourage it. A dog owner who does not perceive his dog's aggression as a behavior problem will not seek help.

The majority of dog owners do not like owning an aggressive dog. Not only is an aggressive dog a danger to their health or the health of others, but he may be responsible for a law suit.

The Owner's Perception of biting behavior is specific to the act itself.

The Dog's Perception is also specific to the situation. Discipline for aggression is almost always done *after the fact,* therefore, in the dog's mind, the discipline is unrelated to the act.

Avenues for Prevention of an aggression problem begin early. As we discussed in Chapter 1, attempts at leadership usually begin at around 13 weeks of age, during the Seniority Classification Period. This is when the puppy first attempts to dominate his handler, and, if handled properly, may end there.

At this age, not before, when a puppy tries to bite his handler, even in play, or takes the leash in his mouth during training, the owner deals with it immediately and firmly. The puppy perceives the leash as an extension of the handler's arm, therefore biting the leash is discouraged. During training, when the pup takes the leash in his mouth, the handler uses his right hand to quickly and firmly pull it through his mouth in a firm check to the right and says, "Stop it!" in a firm, stern tone. The check will cause the snap of the leash to knock against the puppy's mouth which is unpleasant. The handler follows this with a direct command, such as "heel," starts to walk and praises the puppy for his response. If the puppy takes the leash again, the check is repeated while the handler continues walking. After several repetitions, the puppy will stop trying to take the leash—for the moment. That doesn't mean his attempt to test for leadership is over, but it will usually end temporarily.

If the puppy tries to bite the handler rather than the leash, it is dealt with by the handler taking the loop end of the leash and smacking him across the top of his muzzle with "stop it!" This is not followed with praise.

In addition to dealing with overt attempts to dominate, the handler includes in his training special emphasis on the exercise designed to teach the dog who is pack leader: the Long Down. With an especially dominant puppy, one who tries to get up repeatedly, the handler does **five** Long Downs each week instead of the three we recommend for most people.

The Cure for an aggression problem depends on what type aggression it is.

Curing other-animal aggression involves training the dog to be under control, and then controlling him. A dog who is permitted to run free, and in so doing kills the neighbor's chickens, must be restrained. This can be accomplished by the owner either fencing him or supervising his recreation, preventing him from leaving the handler's sight.

Many trainers have used remote control electronic collars for curing such problems. If you desire to do so, consult with a trainer who is familiar with their use and has used them successfully. Improper use can worsen the problem.

Curing dog aggression is accomplished in several ways. First, neutering is recommended. Second, train to get the dog under control, and to teach response to commands.

In an obedience class, aggression to other dogs can be dealt with by the instructor. The instructor takes the dog from the handler, and uses the loop end of the leash across his muzzle when the dog is **THINKING** about aggressing. If the dog so much as *looks* at another dog, he is disciplined. If

205

Aggression often results when the dog's perception is that the owner is challenging the *real* pack leader.

the instructor does not feel capable of handling the dog, the owner is referred to a private trainer. A dog aggressive dog in an obedience class is either dealt with or is sent elsewhere.

The cure for a people aggression problem depends on whether the aggression is to other people or to the handler. If the aggression is to people other than the handler, the dog is desensitized as follows: The dog is put on a Sit Stay with the handler remaining at his side. The instructor and assistants walk by the dog's left side, and offer the dog food with their left hands. They do not make eye contact with the dog. It is the offer of food that is important, not whether or not the dog takes it. Initially, depending on the dog's level of aggression, they will not walk close to the dog, but as the weeks go by, they will move closer and closer. Using this technique, we have often, after a few weeks, been able to examine dogs who came to class aggressive to people.

A dog who is aggressive to his owner is dealt with differently. In this case the owner goes through a training and behavior modification program designed to convince the dog that it is the person, not the dog, who is pack leader. As people are ill-equipped to deal with a physical challenge on the dog's level, our recommendations for convincing Konrad he is no longer pack leader are subtle and non-physical, but they work.

The following rules must be adhered to by the dog's owner at all times:

(1) Train on a regular basis. This teaches the dog in a positive manner that the owner is in control.

(2) Absolutely no food treats unless the dog has worked for it—to perform a function or obey a command such as Sit or Down. He is given no between meal snacks except those he earns.

(3) The dog is petted for only five seconds at a time, and only after he has been made to respond to a command such as "sit." He is not mindlessly stroked for minutes on end.

(4) When the dog nudges his owner's arm to be petted, he is given a command such as "sit" before the owner pets him. He is then petted for up to five seconds, no longer.

(5) At the end of five seconds, the owner says "no more" or "enough" or some other command word used consistently, folds his arms and ignores the dog. He never resumes petting once he has said "no more" until after a lapse of ten minutes or more.

(6) The dog is not permitted to precede the handler through doorways or up or down stairs. The handler uses the door to stop the dog's rushing through. This exercise, called Safety, is included in the Level 1 Model in the Appendix.

(7) The dog is given only one toy to play with. Everything else is the owner's.

(8) The only game played with the dog is fetch. No tug o'war, wrestling or chase games. Physical games encourage the dog to pit his strength against the handler's. Additionally, games such as tug o'war encourage growling, and usually end with the owner getting tired of the game and giving up the rag. This teaches the dog to persevere until he wins. Fetch, on the other hand, teaches the dog to work for the owner. He is, however, made to bring the object back to the handler, and release it on command. Initially this may mean playing with the dog on a long line.

(9) Once the training program is completed, the owner continues to work with the dog on a regular basis, at least two times a week. The sessions need not be long—five or ten minutes is sufficient to put the dog through his paces and praise him for his responses.

(10) Initially, the handler will do five Long Downs each week. Once the dog is trained, the handler will continue to do three Long Downs each week, incorporating them into his regular schedule, such as during dinner.

(11) The dog is required to stand, sit or lie still during grooming. Initially the owner may have to work for short periods to enforce this.

(12) The owner is instructed that when he vacuums or sweeps the floor, or if the dog is lying in front of a cabinet door or doorway to which the owner needs access, or if he is sleeping in the owner's direct line of travel across the room, the dog is made to move. The owner does not work around the dog. As the pack leader, the owner has the right to go anywhere in the territory. The other pack members must get out of the way.

(13) Neuter the dog.

This approach to curing aggression by taking over pack leadership does not involve the owner confronting his dog in any physical battles or using force to "show him who's boss." Dogs are willing to relinquish pack leadership to another pack member who deserves it.

Barking

To approach a solution to a barking problem, the owner must have an understanding of the cause of the dog's barking. Is he being a good watchdog? Is there a strange dog on his property? Is he tied up in the yard and ignored, and is barking out of boredom? Does he bark to get attention in the house? Is he a herding dog who is barking at his "flock" as they run around?

The Dog's Reward varies, depending on the reason for the barking.

Some dogs bark for attention, so the problem is self-perpetuating. The owner can't ignore that piercing bark, yet to pay attention to it is to reward the behavior.

The most common reason for dogs barking continuously is boredom and frustration. Barking is their outlet, and the reward is the release of tension. When a dog is isolated and begins barking, the result is that the owner comes running out of the house to scold him. For just a moment, the dog is not alone. To a dog left alone too much, the owner's presence, even when angry, is a reward.

The Owner's Objection is quite understandable. Persistent, uncontrollable barking is not only a nuisance to him, but to his neighbors as well.

The Owner's Perception is again related to the discipline administered. Going out and hitting the dog should be enough to teach him the lesson.

The Dog's Perception is that he would rather put up with a little scolding than be alone.

Avenues for Prevention are to not put the dog in the frustrating position of being left alone in the yard too long. In addition, regular obedience training puts the dog in a position of working for the owner, gives him meaningful attention and makes him better able to cope with periods of isolation. Exercise plays an important role in this preventative program.

The Cure includes the recommendations for prevention. If the owner has a barking problem, obedience training will give him a job to do and the owner can make him an integral part of the family by bringing him in the house.

If the dog is not welcome in the house because of other problems, help the owner solve them. Dogs who bark because of isolation, and dogs who dig for the same reason (see next section), cannot be cured by any magical cure. If the problem results from his frustration, the only cure involves the owner spending some meaningful, quality time with his dog and making him a member of the family.

In the case of the dog who is doing his duty as a watchdog by barking to alert the owner, barking is commendable behavior. But when he keeps it up longer than necessary, the owner wants to be able to stop him. To teach the dog to quiet down once he has alerted the owner, we use a positive approach to modify the behavior as follows:

(1) Obedience training must include response to the command "come."

(2) Once he is responding, the owner uses this command when the dog is barking. The owner calls the dog to him, rewards him with food and praise, and takes control.

Teaching the dog to alert the owner.

210

(3) Taking control includes thanking the dog for letting him know someone or something is out there. He gives the dog a down command, praises him and leaves him on a Down Stay.

(4) He then goes to the window/door to look for himself, returns to his dog, praises him for staying and releases him. If the window/door the dog was barking at is in a different room, he takes the dog to that room, puts him on a Down Stay and proceeds as above.

(5) If the dog immediately runs back to resume his barking after being released, the owner calls him again, repeats the procedure, then does a Long Down for ten minutes.

The owner is teaching the dog that alerting his owner when there is danger is good, that he should go to him and tell him about it, but then his owner takes over. The owner is in control of both the situation and the dog. Konrad learns that his job is done once he has alerted Dad.

Barking in the Crate

Dogs confined in a crate may begin barking to be let out. If the dog is let out when he starts barking, he is being rewarded for the behavior.

To stop the dog from barking in the crate, and to teach him to respond to the command "quiet," instruct the owner to take half a glass of water and toss the water directly in the dog's face as he says "quiet." His tone of voice should be a normal command tone, not yelling. After the dog has been quiet, he is let out of the crate. The owner gradually increases the length of time the dog must remain quiet before being let out. Initially, it may only be a second or two, but after several repetitions, he will be able to have quiet for a minute or more before letting the dog out of the crate. After a few repetitions with the water, just saying "quiet" and leaving the water glass in sight of the dog will be enough to have him stop barking.

Digging

Digging is a behavior problem with many possible causes.

The Dog's Rewards in most cases are apparent, once there is an understanding of the reasons behind the digging.

As we discussed in the last chapter, digging is instinctive for some dogs. Instinctive digging can occur for several reasons:

1. Terriers and terrier mixes have been bred for generations to dig. This is instinctive behavior and the reward is the satisfaction of that instinct.

2. Pregnant females will dig to make a nest in which to have their puppies. If she is provided with a whelping box with rags or

newspapers to tear up and dig into, this behavior can be channelled so it is not destructive.

3. Dogs will dig to bury bones. This is instinctive caching behavior.
4. Dogs dig when they are hot. A dog will find a nice shady spot and dig down to some damp earth to lie on. He is making himself cooler, and that is rewarding.
5. Many dogs like to mimic their owners, called *allelomimetic behavior*. When they watch their owners garden, they want to try it too. This is instinctive behavior, and is rewarding to the dog.
6. Some dogs that are penned up, try to dig out of the pen. A male may smell a female in season, or a rabbit, and dig to get to the source. This, too, is instinctive, and his freedom is his reward.

The most common causes of digging are non-instinctive—boredom, frustration and loneliness. If a dog is isolated in the yard for hours on end, he releases his frustrations in any way he can. This often means digging— usually near the house, by the stairs, or around the foundation. The reward in this case is the release of tension.

The Owner's Objection is that holes are unsightly and dangerous.

The Owner's Perception is the same as for barking or chewing. He cannot understand why the dog doesn't learn not to dig. After all, he shoves the dog's nose in the hole and yells and scolds. But Konrad doesn't learn.

The Dog's Perception is that, even when caught in the act of digging, the rewards for instinctive digging are so strong they will probably override his awareness of his owner's displeasure. He is not digging out of spite or to teach his owner a lesson.

Avenues for Prevention depend on the reason for the digging. If he is digging to cache bones, the owner can prevent this by not giving him bones. If it is to find coolness, a kiddy pool or hosing off will help. If the female is making a nest, providing her with her own place to nest is sufficient. If the dog is imitating his owners in the garden, the owner can leave him in the house when gardening. If he is a terrier digging to find a rabbit or chipmunk, the owner would do best to provide him with an area to exercise his instincts, where holes won't be a problem.

If the cause of the problem is boredom or frustration due to isolation, then the prevention and cure are for the owner to stop putting the dog in a position of being isolated and ignored. The problem is prevented by making him part of the family, giving him a function and teaching him to be a contributing member of the household. Obedience training, exercise and attention will go a long way toward preventing digging.

Showing the dog the hole and chastising him will neither prevent nor cure the problem. Konrad will make no association between the hole, his responsibility for it, and the owner's anger.

A common reason for digging is boredom.

Teaching the dog to retrieve, encourages the dominant dog to work *for* the owner.

The Cure is as follows:

(1) Identify the underlying cause of the problem.
(2) Instruct the owners not to keep the dog isolated in the yard.
(3) Include obedience training as part of the solution.
(4) Have the owners make the dog a contributing member of the household and give him a function.

Other Problems

Shyness

As discussed earlier, a shy dog responds fearfully to sight and sound stimuli. The owner of a shy dog is instructed as follows:

(1) Train the dog to build self-confidence. It also gives the dog a job to do in a situation that may be fear producing. For example, the owner of a shy dog, when faced with a situation in which he knows his dog will respond fearfully, gives his dog a command such as "sit." The dog, upon hearing this command, knows what to do in response, and that when he does sit, he gets praised. Therefore, rather than respond out of fear to the situation, he responds out of confidence to the command.
(2) Shyness to or fear of people is dealt with through desensitization in class. The dog is placed on a Sit Stay by the handler's side, and the instructor and assistants pass to the dog's left, holding food in their left hand. The food is offered to the dog. The people will walk as close to the dog as they can without his moving out of position. They do not make eye contact. Gradually, over time, they will be able to move closer to the dog, and eventually to offer the food directly to him. Whether or not he takes the food is not important. It is the offer that counts. Eventually, this is done with the entire class passing the dog.
(3) The handler is instructed not to praise or pet the dog when he is frightened. Physical or verbal reinforcement unintentionally teaches the dog that Mommy likes it when he is frightened. Neither is the dog picked up when he is frightened.
(4) Once trained, take the dog to new places and new situations and use his obedience training there. This will build his self-confidence.

Fear Biting

A fear biter does not attack and bites only as a last resort. If he is unable to get away, he will bite and try to run. In obedience class, the fear biter is discernable the first night of class when equipment is fitted. The instructor or assistant is unable to measure the dog's neck, so the owner is instructed how to do so.

The fear biter will not bite someone familiar, such as his owner, but only someone he is frightened of. The desensitization process is the same as for a shy dog.

Kennel Dog Syndrome

Kennel Dog Syndrome is lack of socialization. It is not necessary for a dog to be raised in a kennel to suffer from Kennel Dog Syndrome. If, during the critical socialization periods, and thereafter, a dog is not exposed to people and new situations, he may develop this syndrome. It is not hereditary shyness, but the responses are similar. In the extreme, he may exhibit fear biting responses.

The desensitization process for a dog suffering from lack of socialization is the same as for the shy dog and fear biter.

To reiterate, with a dog with temperament problems, the handler:

(1) Trains the dog to build his self-confidence.
(2) Uses food to desensitize him to people.
(3) Avoids reinforcement of the undesirable behavior by petting or talking in soothing tones.
(4) Once trained, takes the dog to new places to build self-confidence.

Housetraining

There are two aspects to housetraining: training the puppy, and training the older dog.

Puppy Housetraining

Housetraining the puppy does not constitute a behavior problem. Instructors can facilitate housetraining by giving the handout in Chapter 9 to their students.

Housetraining the Older Dog

Housetraining an older dog constitutes a behavior problem, and the aspects of the behavioral analysis need to be examined. In many cases, diet is a contributing factor. Some dog foods contain large amounts of filler, nondigestible additives which do nothing for the dog but increase the amount of bulk that must be eliminated. Semi-moist foods, which contain large amounts of salt, cause the dog to drink a great deal of water, undermining a housetraining effort. In general, if the dog is eliminating as much as he is eating, he is not digesting enough of his dog food. Refer to the section on Nutrition in Chapter 11.

The Dog's Reward is that he is doing what comes naturally. In some instances, the dog is making a social statement. For example, a dog who regularly uses his owner's shoes as his bathroom is indicating that the relationship is not that of the human as the pack leader and the dog as the pack member. In such a case, the relationship needs addressing, not just the housetraining problem.

The male dog who lifts his leg in the house is marking territory. In many cases, neutering is the solution. Refer to Spaying and Neutering in Chapter 11.

The Owner's Objection depends on the owner. Many people do not object to the dog using the interior for a bathroom. These people usually think they have a problem only when the dog begins going somewhere that they don't want him to. For example, they don't mind him using the spare bedroom, but not the master bedroom. Most owners, however, do not want the dog to go to the bathroom in the house.

The Owner's Perception is that they have tried "everything." They have rubbed his nose in it; isolated him in the basement; yelled; hit; and lectured.

Some owners believe that breeding their male dog will stop his marking in the house. On the contrary, if breeding has an impact on leg lifting, it is to make it worse.

We occasionally talk with dog owners who tell us that their dog is "mostly housetrained." Being mostly housetrained is like being a little pregnant—you either are or you're not. A dog either goes to the bathroom in the house on occasion, in which case he is not housetrained, or, barring illness, he never goes in the house, in which case he is housetrained.

The Dog's Perception of the discipline meted out for a housetraining problem has nothing to do with what the owner thinks it does. At the moment the dog is going to the bathroom, he is unaware of the consequences of his physical action. As soon as he is finished, he may turn around, see the puddle and remember that he gets yelled at when that's there, but that is after the fact. It is too late for him to do anything about it, even if he knew what to do.

Avenues for Prevention are to housetrain the puppy when he is still young.

The Cure is similar to the rules for training a puppy. With a grown dog or older puppy (five months or more), the owner keeps the dog confined in a crate when not under supervision. Everything else is the same as for the puppy: he is taken out, praised for going, accidents are ignored, he is fed on a regular schedule and the owner follows the advice spelled out in Chapter 9.

One Final Note

Many people confine a dog in a garage or basement in an attempt to housetrain. Because the dog goes to the bathroom there, they believe he is not housetrained. To the dog, the smell of the basement and the garage are similar to outdoors. They both smell damp and musty. Dogs confined in basements are difficult to housetrain.

Chasing

Car chasing is dangerous not only to the dog, but to the driver and to pedestrians.

The Dog's Reward is success. The automobile has invaded his territory. He chases it, and it leaves.

The Owner's Objection is that he is frightened his dog will be hurt or killed—and he's right.

The Owner's Perception is that the dog should know better—after all, he is chastized when he gets home.

The Dog's Perception is that the chastizing is related to the homecoming, not the car chasing.

Avenues for Prevention are to supervise the dog when he is outside, or confine him in an area where he cannot escape to chase cars.

The Cure is similar to the prevention. Car chasing is most easily prevented. Dogs who are allowed to run free and unsupervised, especially dogs with a history of chasing cars, are involved in a game of Russian Roulette—sooner or later they will be seriously injured or killed.

Obedience training can help cure a car chasing problem. Through training, the owner will establish control over his dog. When the owner is present, at least, the dog can be prevented from chasing cars by calling him **before** he starts to chase. This will not, however, stop the dog from chasing if he is left on his own.

Running Away

Running away is a behavior most dog owners find objectionable. There are many causes for running away. As discussed in Chapter 1, this behavior often begins during the Flight Instinct Period. When the dog returns from a romp, he is punished, so he stays away longer and longer.

Lack of exercise is also responsible for this behavior. The dog's action specific energy for running has not been expended. He **must** run and he **will** run until the available energy for the behavior has been exhausted.

Another reason for dogs running is if there is an attractive diversion in the neighborhood, such as a female in season.

The Dog's Reward is the release of the action specific energy for running, or in the case of a male finding a female in season, the rewards are obvious.

The Owner's Objection is that running without supervision is dangerous.

The Owner's Perception is that Konrad should know better.

The Dog's Perception is that he is punished when he gets home, so he stays away longer and longer.

Avenues for Prevention and The Cure are that the dog is confined when not under supervision and is given sufficient exercise often enough to expend his energy.

The dog is taught to come when called. For the dog who has learned that coming means a thrashing, a program of retraining rewarding the dog for coming combined with exercise eliminates this problem.

Coprophagy

Halitosis is one thing, but no one wants to be greeted by his canine companion who is in the habit of eating stools.

The most common causes of stool eating are dietary deficiencies—usually poor protein assimilation—the precise cause of which will have to be established by a veterinarian. Worms can cause stool eating, and again the veterinarian is consulted. Boredom is also responsible for coprophagia. If stool eating results from boredom, it can develop into an annoying habit. Some dogs take particular delight in eating frozen stools.

With proper treatment, the dog will stop by himself. If it has become a habit, the cure is simple, as demonstrated by the following incident:

> Mary had trained both her dogs with us. About a year after, she called to say, "My dogs are eating their stools. I have consulted my veterinarian, and the food supplements he prescribed did not help. I then went to a dog psychiatrist and he told me to sprinkle tabasco sauce on the stools. That stopped the dogs for a while, but now they have developed a taste for tabasco and are right back at it again. I don't know what to do anymore."
>
> We advised Mary that while she was out in the yard sprinkling tabasco, it would probably be just as easy to clean up after the dogs, thereby precluding the dogs from doing their cleaning up. Two weeks later she called again and excitedly exclaimed, "It works—they are no longer eating their stools!" Moral of the story: keep the yard cleaned.

218

Appendices

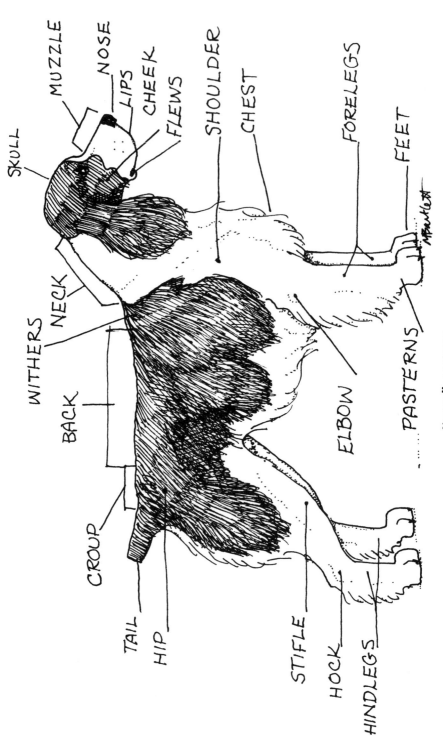

SKULL
MUZZLE
NOSE
LIPS
CHEEK
FLEWS
SHOULDER
CHEST
FORELEGS
FEET
WITHERS
NECK
BACK
CROUP
ELBOW
PASTERNS
TAIL
HIP
STIFLE
HOCK
HINDLEGS

Konrad's anatomy.

Appendix I

INSTRUCTING MODEL—LEVEL 1

INTRODUCTION

Level 1 is for the owners of untrained dogs and puppies. Class can be a mixture of ages, or can be split into age categories. Exercises taught in this class are to give handlers control of their dogs. In Level 1 the basis of communication between handler and dog is formed.

In addition to untrained dogs and handlers, Level 1 is for students with dogs who have been trained with a different methodology. The foundation training of this class is a prerequisite to further training.

The requirements for graduation from Level 1 are that the dog will heel on a loose leash, maintain a Sit, Stand and Down Stay, and come when called, off leash.

The following Weekly Sessions detail the Level 1 program. Because of grammatical difficulties pluralizing instructions, we refer to students in the singular. When we say "have the student . . ." we mean *all* the students. We refer to the student as "he" with no sexist intent. It is less cumbersome than "he or she."

WEEKLY SESSIONS

WEEK 1

(1) REGISTRATION:

Instructions: Complete registrations and check the innoculation certificates. Hand out name tags.

(2) EQUIPMENT:

Instructions: Measure and individually show each student how to put on the collar. Demonstrate leash handling and Control Position.

221

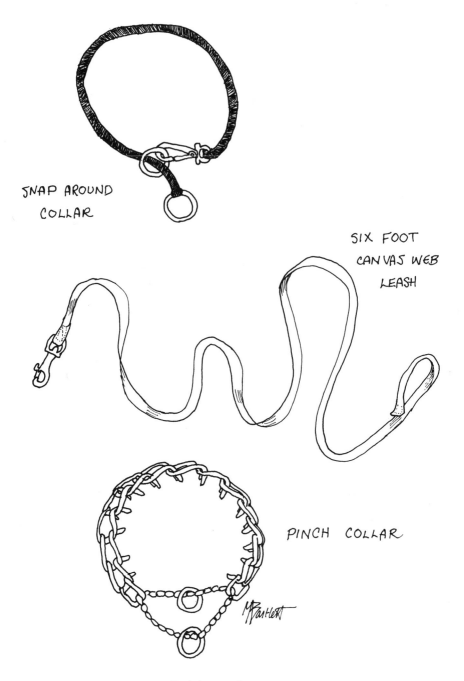

SNAP AROUND
COLLAR

SIX FOOT
CANVAS WEB
LEASH

PINCH COLLAR

Training equipment.

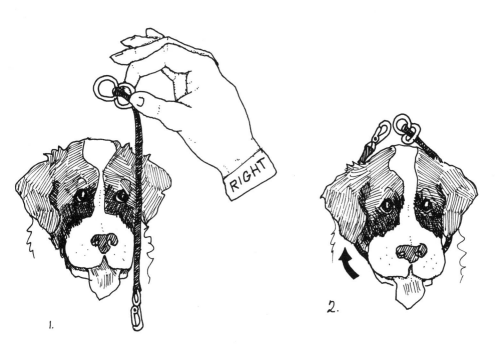

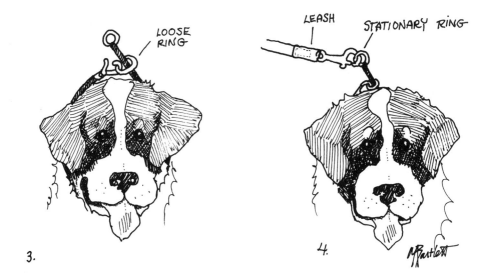

How to put on the training collar.

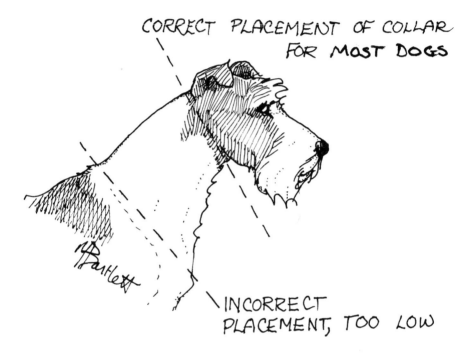

CORRECT PLACEMENT OF COLLAR FOR MOST DOGS

INCORRECT PLACEMENT, TOO LOW

Placement of the training collar.

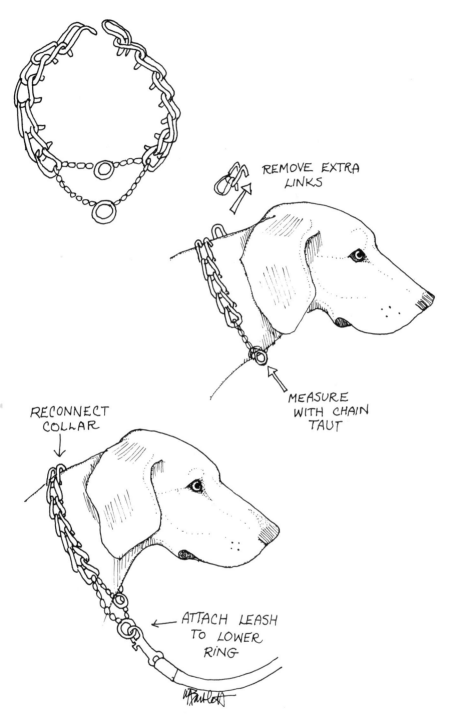

REMOVE EXTRA LINKS

MEASURE WITH CHAIN TAUT

RECONNECT COLLAR

ATTACH LEASH TO LOWER RING

How to put on a pinch collar.

(3) INTRODUCTION:

Instructions: Introduce yourself and the support staff. Then give a brief lecture:

1. Object of the Course: The object of the course is to make a well-mannered pet out of the dog by teaching him to walk at your left side without pulling, to come when called and to stay when told.

2. Homework: Practice at home is what brings success. Class is for the purpose of teaching you how to train. The dog will learn the lessons through the repetition of the exercises at home. To achieve success, five days of training are required. The amount of time required will vary depending on the dog and the exercise. Homework sheets are goal oriented. Work on each lesson until you achieve the specified goal.

3. Building Block Approach: Each week's work lays the foundation for the next week. In order to progress, the dog must be ready for the next lesson. This is accomplished through homework.

4. Absences: If you must miss a class, please let the instructor know beforehand, if possible. A make-up session will be arranged.

5. Questions: Ask questions whenever you are confused or need help. If you run into a problem during the week, call the instructor, whose phone number is on the homework sheet.

6. Patience & Tone of Voice: Dog training is the formation of communication between the owner and his dog. Since dogs don't understand our words until we teach them, the message they get from us comes from our demeanor and tone of voice. Training requires patience and different tones of voice to communicate with the dog. Praise tone is pleasant (demonstrate with "good"); command tone is matter of fact (demonstrate with "sit" and "down"); and reprimand tone is firm (demonstrate with "ah, ah" and "stop").

7. Praise versus Petting: "Praise your dog" means verbal praise, not petting. During the training sessions, do not pet your dog. This rule does not apply between training sessions.

8. House Rules: If your dog relieves himself in class, he is not the first, nor will he be the last. To prevent this, exercise the dog before bringing him into the training area; however, in case of an accident, **stand still.** An Assistant will clean it up, but do not create a 15' trail to be mopped. (Inform them of any other rules regarding the training facility. For example, where should they exercise their dogs before class?)

9. Learning Plateau: The first Learning Plateau takes place between the 35th and 42nd days of training (the 6th week). This is a time when your dog will seemingly have forgotten everything you've taught him for the past five weeks. This is normal. Be patient—it lasts for only a few days—but continue training.

10. Equipment: The training equipment that has been issued is yours to keep. If you need to exchange the collar you may do so. If you need replacement equipment, you may purchase it. Because this is a training collar, it is dangerous to leave it on the dog when he is not under supervision.

Demonstrate for the group how to put on the training collar.

Hints for Traffic Control: Have the students and their dogs sit on the floor in a semi-circle facing the instructor during this brief orientation.

(4) SIT—Sequence 1:

Object: "To teach you how to place your dog into a sit."

Instructions: Instruct Sequence 1. With the dog at the handler's left side, both facing the same direction, have handler kneel down, placing the leash under his knees. The handler places his right hand on the dog's chest, the left hand on the withers (explain where that is). He says "sit," then strokes down the dog's back, over the tail and tucks forward behind the knees. Equal pressure with both hands is applied in a squeezing motion. He praises, holding the dog in position without petting for the count of five.

Demonstration: Demonstrate emphasizing the right hand is on the *chest*, not throat, that the left hand starts at the withers, not the tail and that the tucking action is *forward*. Repeat the demonstration so the entire class can see both the rear view and the side view.

Articulation: "Let's all do this together at the same time. Wait for my commands. Kneel and place your leash under your knees. Place your right hand on the dog's chest, your left hand on his withers. On my command 'sit your dog,' say 'sit' then stroke down the back, over the tail and tuck forward with your left hand. Hold the dog in position for the count of five while you praise, and do not pet ... Sit your dogs ... Praise ... Don't pet!"

Watch for: The right hand is on the chest (or in the case of a really bouncy dog, in the collar at the back of his neck), and not on the throat. The left hand starts at the withers. The action is a tucking one, not applying pressure on the hips or croup. The tucking action of the left hand is *forward* not *downward*.

Listen for the command "sit" with no use of name and no repetition. Watch for petting.

227

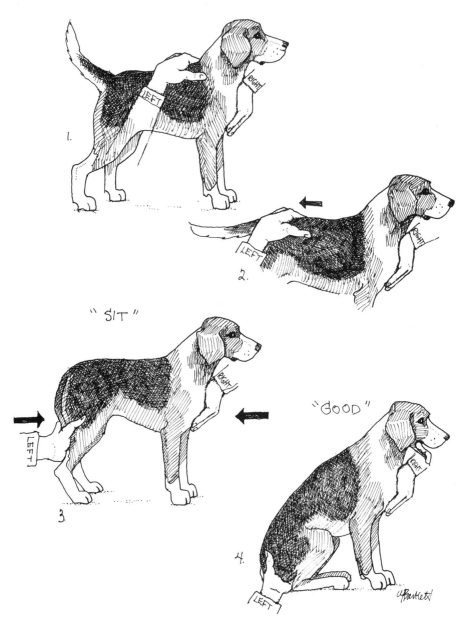

Placing the dog into a Sit.

Repetitions: Repeat 3 times. Handlers get their dogs up with no specific command.

Hints for Traffic Control: Handlers remain in the same semi-circle they were in for the lecture.

(5) STAND—Sequence 1:

Object: "To teach your dog to stand still so you can groom him and make it easier for your veterinarian to examine him."

Instructions: Instruct Sequence 1. With the handler on his knees, dog at his left facing the same direction, have the handler remove the leash and put it to the right and behind him, out of sight of the dog. The handler will place two fingers of his right hand in the collar, under the dog's chin, palm facing down. With "stand" he moves his right hand forward and parallel to the ground, bringing the dog forward into a stand, and places his left hand, palm forward, in front of the stifles (explain and demonstrate where that is) to stop his forward movement. He praises while holding the dog in position.

Demonstration: Demonstrate emphasizing the left hand position, and the dog's position standing facing straight forward at the demonstrator's left side. Face sideways to the group so everyone can see the left hand position.

Articulation: "Remove your leashes and put them to the right and behind you. Place two fingers of your right hand in the dog's collar under his chin, with your palm down. When I say 'stand your dogs' say 'stand' then pull straight forward and parallel to the ground with your right hand, bringing the dog into a stand. Place your left hand under the dog's belly, in front of his stifles or knees, palm facing forward. Hold him in position while you praise. . . . Stand your dogs."

Watch for: The movement with the right hand is forward and parallel to the ground, not upward. The left hand faces forward in front of the stifles, not pushing upward against the belly or backward against the legs. Petting during this exercise will cause the dog to move.

Repetitions: To repeat, the handler transfers the right hand to the dog's chest, left hand to the withers and on your command, sits his dog. He is then ready to repeat the Stand. Repeat 3 times.

Hints for Traffic Control: Handlers and dogs are in the same position as for the previous exercise.

Standing the dog.

230

(6) DOWN—Sequence 1:

Object: "To teach you how to place your dog in the down position."

Instructions: Instruct Sequence 1. Dog sitting at the handler's left side, both facing in the same direction, the handler kneels on the leash. The handler reaches over his dog's back with his left arm and drapes it across the dog's withers. He places his left hand, palm open behind the dog's left foreleg, just below the elbow, and his right hand, palm open behind the dog's right foreleg, just below the elbow. Keeping his hands open, and applying no pressure to the top of the dog's legs, the handler says "down," then *lifts* the dog's forelegs up and lowers him to the ground. He may have to apply downward pressure on the dog's withers with his left forearm. To discourage petting, have the handler hold this position while praising.

Demonstration: Demonstrate emphasizing the **lift** before lowering the dog down, and the position of the hands. Face toward the group for this demonstration.

Articulation: "Kneel and put your leash under your knees with your dog sitting at your left side facing the same direction you are facing. Drape your left arm across the dog's withers so your left hand is behind his left foreleg, just below the elbow. Place your right hand behind his right foreleg, just below the elbow. On my command 'down your dog' you will say 'down' then lift the dog's front end up so he is in a begging position. Then lower the front end to the ground, keep your hands in position and praise. . . . Down your dogs. . . . Praise. . . . Don't pet."

Repetitions: To repeat the Down, the handler sits his dog by placing two fingers of his left hand in the dog's collar at the back of his neck. With "sit" have him apply upward pressure to bring the dog into a sit, and praise. Repeat three times.

Watch for: Hands remaining open, with no pressure on the tops of the legs. Many dogs object to having pressure applied to their forelegs. This can cause such problems as fidgeting, pulling away, or even protest biting.

Lifting and lowering—if the handler pulls the dog's legs out from under him it may frighten him. It may also cause him to lift up his rear.

Hands just below the elbow and not further down on the leg. With hands close to the pastern, the handler has less leverage to lift the dog into the Down.

For the dog who is too tall for the handler to reach across his back, have the handler bring the rings of the collar to the back of the dog's neck, fold the leash into his left hand, and hold the leash snap with his left hand. The handler kneels next to the dog with him sitting at his left side and places

Placing . . .

the dog . . .

down.

his left forearm along the dog's spine. His right hand and forearm go behind both of the dog's front legs, with his palm facing away from the dog. With "down" he lifts or slides the front legs up and then lowers the dog to the ground. The handler maintains this position, and praises.

Hints for Traffic Control: Handlers and dogs are in the same position as for the previous exercises.

(7) LONG DOWN—Sequence 1 (Homework Assignment):

Object: "To teach your dog you are his master."

Instructions: Instruct Sequence 1. The handler sits on the floor, places the dog down at his left side as he just did, removes his hands and remains there for 30 minutes. During that time he is to keep his hands off the dog except to reposition him or prevent him from getting up. To prevent him from getting up, the handler applies downward pressure with the left hand on the withers, and immediately removes the hand. If the dog does get up, he replaces him down as instructed. Explain the need for patience throughout this exercise. At the end of the 30 minutes, the handler releases the dog with "OK!" If he has fallen asleep, wake him. The handler may watch TV or read during this exercise, but be aware of why he is there. If something interrupts this exercise, such as the telephone or someone coming to visit, the dog is released. This is not a play session. The dog is not given a toy to play with for 30 minutes. If he rolls over on his back, that is permissible, so long as he doesn't roll away, but do not rub his belly.

If the dog has not settled after 30 minutes, the handler continues the exercise until the dog has remained quiet for ten seconds before releasing him. (Releasing the dog *before* he has settled undermines the purpose of the exercise—the dog will have won!)

(8) TURNS IN PLACE (RIGHT & ABOUT)—Sequence 1:

Object: "To teach the dog heel position, where you want him to be when you take him for a walk."

Instructions: Explain heel position—the area from the dog's head to his shoulder is in line with the handler's left hip.

Demonstrate and explain Control Position—leash held in both hands, kept below the waist, palms facing body, with any excess folded accordion style into the right hand, coming out from under the little finger. There is no tension on the leash when the dog is in heel position and no more than $1/2''$ of slack.

Control Position.

Explain that for all heeling exercises the handler will use the dog's name before the command.

Instruct Right Turn Sequence 1 and About Turn Sequence 1.

Demonstration: For the Right Turn, emphasis is on the placement of the foot prior to giving the command, and that it is a *large* step to the right. Demonstrator has his back to the class to show the direction of the turn.

For the About Turn, emphasis is on two *full steps* forward, turn keeping feet together, and two *full steps* forward. Demonstrator moves sideways to the group for this demonstration.

Articulation: "Sit your dogs at your left side in heel position and hold the leash in Control Position. When I say 'prepare for a Right Turn,' place your right leg one large step to the right at a 90 degree angle to your left leg. When I say 'Right Turn,' say 'Dog's name, heel' and then close with your left leg. Guide your dog into position and sit him by placing your right hand on his chest, your left hand on his withers and tucking him into a sit with 'sit.' Hold him in position to the count of five while you praise, then stand up so we can do it again. . . . Prepare for a Right Turn . . . Right Turn . . . praise. Don't pet.

"For the About Turn in Place, say 'Dog's name, heel,' take two steps straight forward, turn in place away from your dog 180 degrees keeping your feet together, take two steps straight forward and tuck your dog into a sit with 'sit,' right hand on his chest, left on his withers. Hold him in position to the count of five while you praise, then stand up so we can do it again. . . . About Turn . . . Praise. Don't pet."

Repetitions: 4 times for each turn.

Watch for: Hands in Control Position throughout the exercise and not drifting back behind the body or out to the left.

For the Right Turn in Place, the right foot is placed **before** giving the command. Some students will wait for the dog to move before moving their left leg. It is the motion of the left leg that causes the dog to move.

Some handlers will turn more than a quarter turn. Tell them which wall they will be facing at the completion of the turn.

For the About Turn in Place, the student takes **two full steps** forward, then turns keeping his feet together, takes **two full steps** forward and sits the dog. If the student takes one and a half steps or only one step forward, the dog will not get to heel position. Or if the student completes the turn and sits the dog without taking two more steps forward, the dog does not have a chance to complete the turn and straighten out.

Some students will turn more than 180 degrees. Tell them which wall they will be facing at the completion of the turn.

Watch for sits in heel position. **The degree of precision has a direct**

Diagram for the Right Turn in Place.

correlation with the degree of control. Now is the time dogs are learning to sit at heel. Regardless of the dog's future in obedience training, it is just as easy to teach him to sit in proper heel position as to sit somewhere else.

Listen for the Command/Motion Sequence—the student gives the command **before** moving.

Hints for Traffic Control: Having the students lined up in one or two straight lines facing the same direction is helpful so the Instructor/ Assistants are able to see that everyone is turning either 90 degrees or 180 degrees. Allow sufficient room to walk around and assist those who need it, and to go to the opposite side to give further instructions, if necessary.

(9) HANDLERS' PACE:

Object: "To teach handlers to walk briskly to keep the dog's attention."

Instructions: Handlers walk once around the training area with leashes held in Control Position. Stop them and emphasize moving at a **brisk** pace. Repeat, encouraging faster movement until all are walking briskly. Then stop them for the next instructions.

Hints for Traffic Control: Face the handlers in a *clockwise* direction to circle the training area for this exercise.

(10) HEEL ON LEASH:

Object: "To teach you how to train your dog not to pull when taking him for a walk."

Instructions: Explain your commands: "Forward" means say the dog's name, "heel" and then start to move. "Halt" means stop and sit the dog as you did for Turns in Place. Explain leash over the shoulder.

Instruct heeling once around the room, then call a halt and instruct the About Turn in Motion.

Demonstration: A demonstration of the left hand action coordinated with the praise can be done with or without a dog as the instructor walks briskly around the room to show that he keeps walking and says nothing but "good" as he brings the real or imaginary dog back to heel position.

Articulation: "Take the full length of the leash and throw it over your right shoulder. On my command 'forward' say your dog's name and 'heel' and start to walk briskly. Keep your hands off the leash unless your dog strays from heel position. If he leaves heel position, grasp the leash in your *left* hand, quickly bring the dog back to your left side, and *immediately* remove

237

your hand from the leash. Act as if the leash is hot—very hot—and touching it hurts. Each time the dog is brought back to heel position, praise with 'good,' let go of the leash and place your hand into Control Position. When I say 'halt,' stop and sit your dog placing your right hand on his chest to stop his forward motion, place your left hand on his withers and tuck him into a sit with 'sit.'... Forward... [After the handlers have gone once around the room, call a halt and give instructions for the About Turn in Motion.] Halt.... Sit your dogs. When I say 'about turn,' call your dog's name, grasp the leash in your left hand, keep your feet together and turn away from the dog 180 degrees to face the opposite direction and let go of the leash. Move out briskly, and don't wait for your dog.... Forward... About turn . . ."

Repetitions: Repeat as necessary to give directions and go through the Correction portion of EDICT, with no more than 3 minutes spent on heeling.

Watch for: Handlers holding onto the leash. The purpose of the "hands off the leash" is to teach the handlers the mechanics of checking their dogs without intellectualizing to them what they are doing.

Handlers petting their dogs while moving. Instruct them to keep their hands off the dog. Verbal praise only.

Repetition of the "heel" command. The only word that is repeated is "good" each time the dog is brought back to heel position.

Slow movers. Remind them to keep moving briskly.

Stopping to wait for the dog on the About Turn, or stopping each time they use the leash. Handlers keep moving briskly throughout this exercise.

Hints for Traffic Control: A *clockwise* circle (dogs on the outside) to begin this exercise, followed by two About Turns in Motion.

(11) AUTOMATIC SIT—Sequence 1:

Object: "To teach you what to do with your dog when you come to a halt."

Instructions: Instruct the handler that when you say "... and ... halt," he will plant his left foot facing straight ahead, in front of the right foot, bend his knees, place his right hand on the dog's chest, left hand on the withers and tuck the dog into a sit with "sit."

Demonstration: Demonstrate emphasizing the left foot planted straight ahead so the dog is sitting in a straight line with the left thigh.

Articulation: "When I say 'and,' prepare to sit your dogs by placing your right hand on your dog's chest and planting your left foot facing straight ahead, in front of the right. When I say 'halt,' say 'sit' and tuck your dog into a sit, bending your knees."

Repetitions: Repeat 3-5 times, calling "Forward . . . and, halt" after 5 paces.

Watch for: Handlers who turn to face the dog to sit them or handlers who plant the right foot instead of the left. Planting the left foot ahead of the right prevents the handler from turning toward the dog to sit him, thereby moving himself out of heel position.

Hints for Traffic Control: The same clockwise circle in which they have been heeling.

(12) DEMONSTRATION:

Object: "This is what your dog will do after these 8 weeks."

Demonstration: Demonstrate heel on leash and automatic sit with a trained dog, preferably a student who has just graduated from Level 1.

Hints for Traffic Control: Have handlers and dogs line up along one side of training area to be able to see the demonstration.

(13) GRADUATION REQUIREMENTS:

"To graduate from Level 1, your dog must be able to walk on a loose leash at your left side, come when called and stay when told."

(14) REMINDERS:

"Never punish a dog when it comes when called, and never call a dog to punish him.
"Success can be achieved by working with your dog five times a week.
"Call your instructor if you are confused about something."
Answer questions.

(15) PREVIEW:

"Next week you will learn the first hand signal."

(16) COLLECT NAME TAGS & HAND OUT HOMEWORK SHEETS.

(1) CHECK COLLARS & HAND OUT NAME TAGS:

As students enter training area, the instructor/assistant hands out the name tags and checks the collars to see that they are on properly. If one is not, the student is re-instructed how to put on the collar correctly.

(2) CALL ROLL:

The instructor calls the roll out loud, including students' first and last names and the dogs' names. Students are instructed to respond when they hear their names. Calling the roll aids the instructor in becoming familiar with the students' names, and helps create a feeling of group cohesiveness.

(3) SIT & DOWN—Sequence 2:

Object: "To elicit a voluntary response from the dog to the commands."

Review: Review Sequence 1. For the Sit, right hand on the chest, left hand tucks. For the Down, left arm is placed over shoulder, left hand behind left foreleg, right hand behind right foreleg, lift and lower down.

Instructions: Instruct Sequence 2. Each handler is given an object of attraction, which can be a ball, a toy or a treat.

Demonstration: Demonstrate emphasizing the left hand on the dog's withers and the direction of movement. Place the dog sideways to the class to enable them to see this clearly.

Articulation: "Kneel and place your leash under your knees. Place your left hand on the dog's withers and hold the object in your right hand directly in front of the dog's face, above his eyes. When I say 'down your dog,' say 'down' and quickly motion with the object down and in front in a rounded 'L.' The object is within your dog's reach when he is lying down. When he is down, give him the object with praise, but don't pet. If he fails to go down, put the object on the floor, place him down, give him the object and praise. . . . Down your dog.

To sit your dog from the Down, place two fingers of your left hand in the collar at the back of the dog's neck. Hold the object in your right hand, just in front of the dog's face. On my command 'sit your dog,' motion upward and slightly behind your dog's head at a 45 degree angle as you say 'sit.' When he is sitting, give him the object and praise, but don't pet. If he fails to sit on his own, guide him up with your left hand, give him the object and praise. . . . Sit your dog."

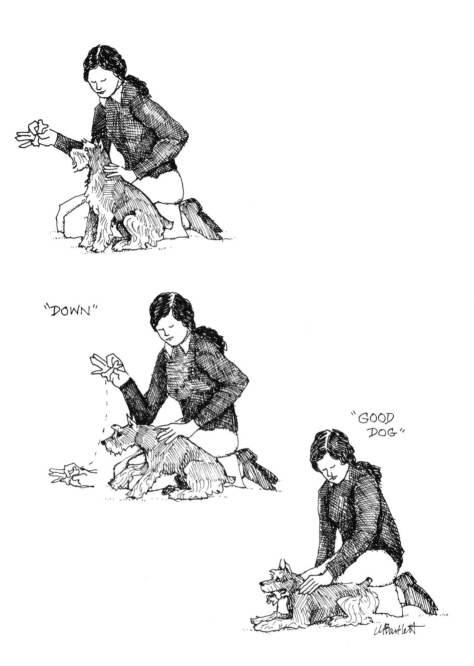

Down with Object of Attraction.

Repetitions: Repeat each 3 times.

Watch for: The left hand on the withers is to prevent the dog from getting up and walking toward the object. It is not there to push the dog down.

On the Down, the object is within the dog's reach when he is lying down. It is not so far way that the dog wants to get up to walk toward it. The dog is not given the object before he is fully lying down.

Handlers use the command words along with the motion. The purpose of this exercise is to teach the dogs to respond to the commands voluntarily.

Neither the motion nor the command is repeated if the dog fails to respond. After one command the dog is placed in position, given the object and praised.

Hints for Traffic Control: A semi-circle as last week for these exercises.

(4) HEEL ON LEASH:

Review: Briefly review heeling with leash over shoulder including two Automatic Sits (Sequence 1).

Articulation: "HANDS OFF THE LEASH!"

Repetitions: Two times around the training area.

Watch for: Handlers hanging onto the leash. Remind them to use the left hand to bring the dog back, **immediately** take the hand off the leash returning it to Control Position and praise.

Hints for Traffic Control: Begin with a clockwise circle, dogs on the outside.

(5) AUTOMATIC SIT—Sequence 2:

Object: "To teach the dog to sit by himself when you halt."

Instructions: Instruct Sequence 2.

Demonstration: Demonstrate the leash transfer facing toward the class. Then demonstrate the Automatic Sit facing sideways to the class, emphasizing the check with the right hand, the left hand starting at the withers, and the left foot position.

Articulation: "Bring the rings of the collar to the back of the dog's neck. Hold the leash in Control Position, left hand on the leash snap. On my command 'forward,' say your dog's name, 'heel' and start to walk. When I say 'and,' transfer the leash snap from your left hand to your right and prepare to stop. When I say 'halt,' plant your left foot straight ahead in front of the right, check with your right hand directly above the dog's head and tuck him into a sit with your left hand, starting at the withers, stroking down the back and tucking him into a sit as you have been doing all week. A check is a quick snap on the leash with an immediate release of tension. Hold him in a sit to the count of five. Praise, but don't pet."

Repetitions: Repeat 3 times.

Watch for: The direction of the check which is straight up, above the dog's head. The dog is facing straight in line with the handler's left thigh. The right hand grasps the leash at the snap. **The closer to the collar the right hand is positioned, the more control the handler has over the dog.**

Hints for Traffic Control: A clockwise circle.

(6) STAND—Sequence 2:

Review: Review Sequence 1. Handler removes leash, places it to the right and behind, and places two fingers of the right hand in the collar, palm down, under the chin. Pulling straight forward, parallel with the ground, he stands his dog. Left hand is in front of the stifles, palm forward.

Instructions: Instruct Sequence 2. The handler keeps his right hand in the collar under the dog's chin. The left hand is lowered so it is not touching the dog, but remains under the dog's belly to reposition the dog, if necessary. The assignment is to gradually work up to being able to stand next to the dog without the left hand being underneath the dog. The right hand remains in the collar.

Demonstration: Demonstrate standing next to the dog, right hand in the collar, left hand at the dog's side, preparing to reposition the dog, if he should move. Demonstrator's position is at the edge of the circle so entire class can see him.

Repetitions: Keep the dogs standing for 1 minute.

Hints for Traffic Control: A circle, handlers and dogs facing the center.

(7) RETRIEVE OF BALL:

Object: "To teach you how to take something out of your dog's mouth."

Instructions: Instruct handler to transfer the leash snap to the dead ring of the collar. Each is handed a ball and instructed to spread out around the room facing a wall, and crouch down five feet from the wall. The handler gets his dog's attention on the ball, then rolls the ball toward the wall with

243

Sequence 2 of the Automatic Sit.

Sequence 2 of the Stand.

"take it." When the dog picks up the ball, he is praised, brought back to the handler, and the handler removes the ball from the dog's mouth with "give," and praises. To remove the ball, the handler places his left hand *under* the dog's jaw, fingers on one side, thumb on the other, at the back of his mouth where the jaw hinges. His right hand is on the ball. When he says "give," he applies pressure to the lips against the dog's teeth. As soon as the dog's mouth is open, he *immediately* releases pressure, takes the object and praises.

Demonstration: Select a natural retriever for this demonstration.

Repetitions: No more than 3 times. Then handlers replace the leash on the live ring.

Watch for: If a dog does not retrieve the ball, the handler can still practice the action of removing something from the dog's mouth. The left hand is *under* the jaw, not on top of the muzzle. Squeeze only hard enough to get the desired response.

Hints for Traffic Control: If the training area does not easily lend itself to this exercise, that is, with students spread out facing a blank wall, it can be done by having the students in a circle facing out. Each student gets his dog's attention on the ball, lets him have it briefly, and then removes it from his mouth.

(8) CIRCLES RIGHT AND LEFT:

Object: "To teach your dog to remain in heel position when you change direction."

Instructions: Instruct Circles Right and Left.

Demonstration: Demonstrate emphasizing the pace, the size of the circles and especially the position of the left hand against the thigh in Control Position.

Articulation: "Hold the leash in Control Position. When I say 'Circle Left,' you will say your dog's name and heel, take two steps straight forward, then make a circle to the left, 4' in diameter, walking **very** slowly. Complete one circle, stop and sit your dog with your right hand on the leash snap, left foot planted in front of the right, tucking with your left hand.

"When I say 'Circle Right,' you will say your dog's name and heel, take two steps straight forward, then make a circle to the right 4' in diameter, trotting with short, choppy steps. Keep your hands in front of your legs in

Control Position throughout both circles. Your left hand stays **glued** to your left leg. Complete one circle, stop and sit your dog."

Repetitions: Do 3 Circles Left, an about turn in place to face in the opposite direction and 3 Circles Right.

Watch for: The changes of pace. The Circle Left is done **very slowly,** holding the dog in heel position. The Circle Right is done at a trot, not a run. Short, choppy steps allow the dog to remain in heel position without fishtailing.

The left hand remains on the left thigh as if **glued** there.

Hints for Traffic Control: For the Circle Left, face the class in a counterclockwise direction, dogs on the inside. They will take two steps straight forward, then circle toward the center of the training area. After completing one circle, they will be back at the starting point. When you have completed the repetitions, call an About Turn in Place to face in a clockwise direction to do the Circle Right. They will take two steps straight forward, then circle toward the center of the training area. After completing one circle, they will be back at the starting point.

(9) TURNS IN PLACE (RIGHT & ABOUT)—Sequence 2:

Review: Review Sequence 1. For the Right Turn, handlers place their right foot at a 90 degree angle, one large step to the right, then command and turn. For the About Turn, handlers take two steps forward, turn away from the dog, keeping their feet together, then they take two steps forward, stop and sit the dog.

Instructions: Instruct Sequence 2.

Demonstration: Demonstrate emphasizing the Command/Motion Sequence. For the About turn, emphasize the one *full* step forward, turn and one *full* step forward again.

Articulation: "Hold your leashes in Control Position. When I say 'Right Turn,' say your dog's name, heel, *then* step to the right, close with your left and sit your dog with your right hand on the leash snap, left hand tucks.

"When I say 'About Turn,' say your dog's name, 'heel,' take *one* step forward, turn 180 degrees away from your dog, keeping your feet together take *one* step forward and sit your dog."

Repetitions: 4 of each turn.

Watch for: The Command/Motion Sequence and straight sits. The Command/Motion Sequence is giving the command **before** moving.

246

For the About Turn, handlers take one *full* step forward, turn and take one *full* step forward.

Hints for Traffic Control: Depending on the size of the class and training area, one or two straight lines facing the same direction. Allow sufficient room for the students to spread out and for the Instructor/Assistants to observe from front and rear.

(10) SIT STAY—Sequence 1:

Object: "To teach your dog what to do when he wants to jump on you."

Instructions: Instruct Sequence 1.

Demonstration: Demonstrate facing sideways to the class emphasizing the hand signal, the demonstrator's proximity to the dog, his straight body posture and the return, pause, relax tension, praise and release at the end.

Articulation: "Bring the rings of the collar to the back of the dog's neck and fold the leash accordion style into your left hand. Hold the leash directly above the dog's head and maintain slight tension on the leash. When I say 'leave your dog,' give the signal with your right hand, palm open, brought across your body to in front of your dog as you say 'stay,' return your right hand to your side, stand erect and pivot directly in front of your dog. Pause for a silent count of 10, then pivot back to your dog, pause, release the tension on the leash, quietly praise, then release with 'Okay!' If your dog moves before you release him, check him back into position by using the leash and collar and repeat 'stay.' Prepare to leave your dogs, fold the leash into your left hand . . . leave your dogs. Say 'stay,' signal with your right hand, return your right hand to your side, stand erect and pivot directly in front. . . . Back to your dogs, pause, praise, release."

Repetitions: 3 times.

Watch for: A dog will rise up on his hind legs or paw the leash, if there is too much pressure on the collar.

   The hand signal comes across the body from right to left rather than in a hitting motion toward the dog, which he might construe as a threat. There is no physical contact with the dog's nose.

   The handler's feet and the dog's forefeet are almost touching. The handler is *directly* in front.

   The handler stands erect, not hovering over the dog.

   The count to 10 is *silent.* Counting out loud will teach the dog that the exercise ends when the handler says "ten."

   When the handler pivots back to the dog's side, he pauses before

Sequence 1 of the Sit Stay, then handler . . .

pivots in front of dog.

248

releasing the tension, praises quietly while the dog maintains position, and then releases. Until the dog is released, he holds position. The pause is to prevent the dog from associating the handler's return with his release. This association would quickly result in the dog getting up as soon as his handler returns to heel position.

Hints for Traffic Control: One straight line or a circle facing the center.

(11) SLIP RELEASE:

Object: "To teach you how to start your dog heeling off leash."

Instructions: Using the back of a chair to demonstrate, explain to the students that the chair represents a dog, and the back of the chair is the dog's collar. In class, students practice this on their dogs, who by the end of the class are usually lying down and tired.

Demonstration: Demonstrate on a chair twice, then demonstrate while they are doing it, pausing each step of the way to allow them to look at your hands and check on their own hand position.

Articulation: "Thread the loop of the leash, stitched portion facing down, through the dog's collar at the top of the neck, front to back. Place the loop over your left thumb, and grasp the leash lightly with the fingers of your left hand, left hand in Control Position. Hold the clasp of the leash in your right hand and accordion fold the excess into your right hand until both hands are in Control Position. Keeping your left hand absolutely still, when I say 'release,' drop the loop off your thumb, but keep the fingers of your left hand around the leash. Draw the leash out of the collar and through your left hand by accordion folding it neatly into your right hand."

Repetitions: Three times.

Watch for: All motion is with the right hand, leash slipping through the left. The left hand does not move and remains in Control Position.

The loop end threaded from front to back with the stitched portion facing down. If the stitched portion is up, it will catch on the dog's collar when it is drawn out.

Hints for Traffic Control: A line or semi-circle.

(12) LONG SIT—Sequence 1—AND LONG DOWN—Sequence 2 (Homework Assignment):

Object: "To teach your dog self-discipline."

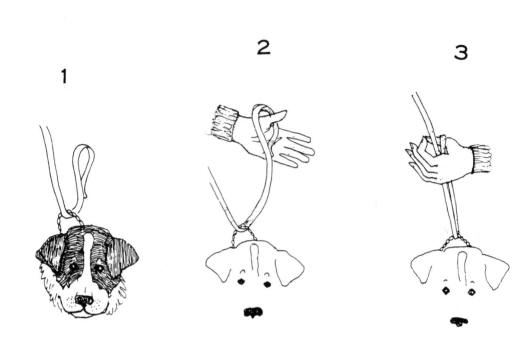

1

2

3

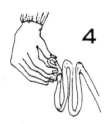

4

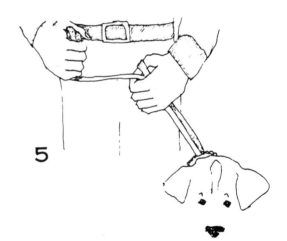

5

Diagram for the . . .

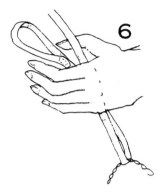

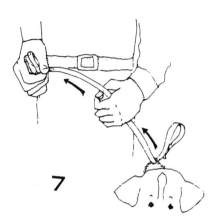

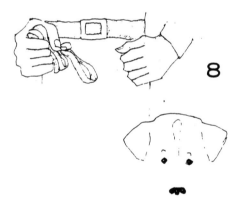

Slip Release.

Instructions: For the Long Sit—Instruct handlers to sit in a chair and do a ten-minute sit, three times a week. This is not a Sit Stay. If the dog goes down, they are to reposition him with "sit." If he starts to walk away, they are to replace him with "sit." At the end of ten minutes, they will release with "Okay." Do this on alternate days with the Long Down.

For the Long Down—Instruct the handlers to sit in a chair and do a 30-minute Down just as they did last week sitting on the floor. Those who had difficulty with this exercise are assigned five Long Downs this week.

Watch for: The handler who is "working his way up to 30 minutes." Remind him that the assignment is to **do** the Long Down for 30 minutes, even if it is 30 minutes of continuously putting the dog back into position. This handler needs the Long Down more than those who are having an easy time. Instruct him to repeat it five times this week.

(13) REMINDERS:

Inform the students to use their training whenever they want their dogs to be under control. The training equipment is not for use only when they are working in class or at home. The equipment and the training are used any time they need control of their dogs, such as heeling their dogs to their cars right now.

Answer questions.

(14) PREVIEW:

"Next week we will start to teach your dog to come when called!"

(15) HAND OUT HOMEWORK SHEETS & COLLECT NAME TAGS.

WEEK 3

(1) CHECK COLLARS, NAME TAGS, CALL ROLL.

(2) SIT & DOWN—Sequence 3:

Review: Sequence 2. Hand out treats or toys and review with the object of attraction from the dog's side.

Instructions: Instruct Sequence 3.

Demonstration: Demonstrate facing sideways to the class emphasizing the pressure downward, even if the dog voluntarily follows the object down.

252

Articulation: "Sit your dogs, say 'stay,' pivot in front, and kneel directly in front of them. When I say 'prepare to down your dogs,' fold the leash into your left hand, and place two fingers of your left hand, palm down, in the collar under your dog's chin. Hold the object of attraction in your right hand directly in front of the dog's face. When I say 'down your dogs,' say 'down,' lower the object of attraction and apply downward pressure in the collar with your left hand. When your dog is down, release the pressure, give him the object and praise. . . . Down your dogs. . . . Praise. . . .

When I say 'prepare to sit your dogs,' bring your left hand to the top of the dog's neck and place two fingers, palm up, in the collar. When I say 'sit your dogs,' say 'sit,' raise the object and apply upward pressure with the left hand to sit your dogs. Give them the object and praise. . . . Sit your dogs."

Repetitions: Repeat 3 times each.

Watch for: Handlers not applying pressure downward. Even if the dog goes down voluntarily, it is important that the handler apply downward pressure on the collar, as it prepares the dog to go down with pressure alone, which is part of next week's lesson. This exercise conditions the dog to accept this pressure without resisting.

Hints for Traffic Control: Handlers in a circle or semi-circle facing center.

(3) SIT STAY—Sequence 2:

Review: Sequence 1. Leash is folded in the left hand held above the dog's head, count to 30, pivot back.

Instructions: Sequence 2.

Demonstration: First, facing sideways or with the dog's back to the class, demonstrate Sequence 2 of the Sit Stay, emphasizing the slack leash when leaving the dog, hand positions on the leash and the direction of the leash slap.

Articulation: "Prepare to leave your dogs. Bring the rings of the collar underneath the dog's chin, let out three feet of slack and hold the leash in your left hand. When I say 'leave your dogs,' give the signal and command 'stay,' and go three feet in front of your dog, turn and face him. Hold your left hand at your belt buckle, and poise your right hand, palm open, under the leash about midway between you and your dog. At the first sign that your dog is *thinking* about moving, slap the leash with your right hand, upward and toward the dog, but not above your waist. At the same time, repeat 'stay.'"

Repetitions: 2 times.

Reinforcing the Stay command.

Watch for: Handlers do not praise after reinforcing the stay with the slap on the leash. This is training for abstention and is not followed by praise.

In case the dog manages to move before the handler reinforced with the slap on the leash, he is repositioned as quickly as possible at the exact spot where he had been left. This is done with a minimum of physical handling, using the leash and collar to reposition the dog. Physical handling at this point may be construed by the dog as praise, not the impression we want to create.

The dog holds his position until he is released. If the dog gets up when he is being praised, before the "Okay," he is repositioned, told "stay," and is made to wait until the release.

Hints for Traffic Control: One straight line or two lines facing each other. Allow enough room behind the handlers for the instructor/assistants to observe from both sides.

(4) RETURN TO DOG ON STAY:

Instructions: Instruct the return around behind.

Demonstration: The demonstrator faces the class, dog's back to the class to demonstrate the return. Emphasize leash handling, the left hand remaining in front of the dog as the demonstrator walks around behind.

Articulation: "When I say 'prepare to return,' place the loop of the leash over your right thumb, and hold the leash loosely in your left hand, leaving about three feet of slack. When I say 'return to your dogs,' keep your left hand in front of your dog as you walk by your dog's left side, then behind him, and then stop at his right side (your left) in heel position. When I say 'exercise finished,' praise your dog. When I say 'release,' release your dogs with 'Okay!'"

Repetitions: Repeat Sequence 2 of the Sit Stay twice with two returns.

Watch for: On the return, there is no pressure on the collar as the handler walks around behind. The left hand prevents the leash from pulling against the collar or dragging across the dog's face or neck.

The handler will check the dog back to his original position, if he tries to move with the handler who walks behind him. Tentative walking, or body posture that implies trying to sneak back without the dog knowing it will make the dog turn to see what is happening behind him. The handler returns by confidently walking around behind the dog.

Hints for Traffic Control: One straight line or two lines facing each other.

Returning around . . .

behind . . .

the dog.

256

Allow enough room behind the handlers for the instructor/assistants to observe from both sides, and for the handlers to walk around behind.

(5) SIT FOR EXAMINATION:

Instructions: Instruct the Sit for Examination.

Articulation: "Bring the rings of the collar to the top of the dog's neck. Fold your leash into your left hand and hold it above the dog's head as you did for Sequence 1. Give the hand signal with 'stay,' but remain at your dog's side. We will approach your dog from in front, allow him to sniff our left hand, and then touch the dog's head and back. If your dog begins to get up, check straight up with 'stay.'"

Watch for: Dogs that are shy or aggressive. For information on desensitization, see Chapter 12, Behavior Problems.

Hints for Traffic Control: One straight line or two lines facing each other.

(6) HEEL ON LEASH:

Review: Briefly review with leash over shoulder, including an about turn.

Instructions: Instruct Changes of Pace. For the slow pace, handlers will take normal-sized steps at a **slow** pace. For the fast, they will gradually move into a trot, taking short choppy steps.

Demonstration: Demonstrate without a dog.

Articulation: "When I say 'slow,' slow your pace so you are moving very slowly with normal-sized steps. When I say 'normal,' return to a normal, brisk pace. When I say 'fast,' break into a trot with short, choppy steps, then return to 'normal' on my command."

Repetitions: Two times around the training area with two changes of pace.

Watch for: Handlers changing pace abruptly.
For the slow, they will have to hold the dogs back in heel position with their left hand on the leash. For the fast, if the dog becomes overly exuberant, have the handler check the dog back to heel, remove his hand and praise. The fast pace is a trot, not a gallop.

Hints for Traffic Control: Start out in a counterclockwise direction. If the dogs are still difficult to control, do the majority of the heeling practice in a clockwise direction.

(7) TURNS IN PLACE (RIGHT & ABOUT):

Review: Sequence 2. For the Right Turn, step to the right *after* the command. For the About Turn, take one step forward, turn, take one step forward and sit the dog with the right hand on the leash snap, left hand tucks.

Repetitions: Four of each turn.

Hints for Traffic Control: One or two straight lines facing the same direction.

(8) STAND—Sequence 3:

Review: Sequence 2. The handler stands his dog, and keeping the right hand in the collar under the dog's chin, stands erect next to him.

Instructions: Leashes off, placed to the right and behind. Instruct Sequence 3.

Articulation: "Stand your dog, stand erect next to him and take your right hand out of the collar. Give the stay command and signal and remain standing at your dog's side. When I say, 'exercise finished,' praise, put your leashes back on, but keep the dog standing still. When I say 'release,' release.

Repetitions: Brief review of Sequence 2, then Sequence 3 dogs standing still for 1 minute.

Hints for Traffic Control: A circle facing the center.

(9) CIRCLES RIGHT & LEFT:

Review: From stationary, leashes held in Control Position. The circles are 4' in diameter, with handlers going slow on the left and trotting on the right. They complete one circle, stop and sit their dogs.

Repetitions: Two of each circle.

Hints for Traffic Control: As in Week 2.

(10) DOWN & DOWN STAY:

Instructions: The handler *places* his dog in the down position. With 3' of slack in the leash, the handler will give the stay command and signal, go 3' in front, turn and face his dog. If the dog starts to get up, he will step toward the dog, grasp the leash snap with his left hand and check straight *down*

258

Reinforcing the Down Stay.

with "stay." The handler returns to his dog as he did for the Sit Stay, keeping his left hand in front of the dog.

Demonstration: Demonstrate the step toward the dog for the check.

Repetitions: One one-minute Down Stay.

Watch for: Handlers who pull on the leash from 3′ away rather than stepping toward the dog to check when the dog starts to get up. Pulling on the leash causes the dog to come toward the handler.

Hints for Traffic Control: A straight line on the opposite side of the training area from where the Sit Stay was done.

(11) AUTOMATIC SIT:

Review: Sequence 2. The leash is held in Control Position. The rings of the collar are at the top of the dog's neck. The handler plants his left foot in front of the right, grasps the leash snap with his right hand and checks straight up as he tucks the dog into a sit with his left hand.

Repetitions: Repeat 5 times.

Hints for Traffic Control: A counterclockwise circle.

(12) HEEL FREE:

Review: Leash handling for the Slip Release.

Instructions: Instruct Circle Left, normal pace, with release.

Demonstration: Demonstrate emphasizing the release as you *enter* the circle.

Articulation: "With the leash in Slip Release position, when I say 'Circle Left,' say your dog's name and 'heel,' take two steps forward and begin to circle left at a normal pace. As you enter the circle, release your leash. Complete the circle, stop and sit your dog by placing your right hand on his chest, left hand tucks him into a sit with 'sit.' If your dog *begins* to leave heel position, place your right hand on his chest and tuck him into a sit."

Repetitions: Twice.

Watch for: Dogs who have not yet been conditioned to walking on a loose leash will have difficulty with this exercise. With handlers whose dogs take off as soon as the leash is released, stress the importance of teaching them to heel with **no tension** on the leash.

Watch handlers for proper leash handling. The left hand is kept still, not yanking the leash out from under the collar.

260

Alternate Technique: For small dogs and dogs with excessive hair, the slip release is executed with a leash from which the spring has been removed from the snap so all that remains is a hook similar to a fish hook.

With the rings of the collar under the dog's neck, have the handler hook the snap into the live ring of the collar so that it faces the dog. When the handler begins his circle, he maintains a light tension on the leash so the hook remains attached to the collar. To release, he lowers to leash so the hook comes out of the ring and gathers the entire leash into his right hand through his left as for the slip release.

Hints for Traffic Control: Begin with handlers spread out in a large circle facing counterclockwise.

(13) RECALL—Sequence 1:

Object: "To teach the dog to come when called."

Instructions: This is done individually. Each handler will heel his dog out of the line-up, walk 15' in front, make a Left U-turn and face the vacated spot. He will remove the leash, take it with him, leave the dog on a Sit Stay (assistant or instructor holds dog, if necessary), and returns to the line-up. He turns to face his dog, counts to five, kneels down and sits on his heels, putting the leash behind him on the floor, counts to five again, places his hands, palms up, on his thighs, smiles and calls the dog with "(Name), come!" When the dog arrives, the handler **pets** and praises the dog for one minute.

Demonstration: Demonstrate the posture and the vocal inflection. It is not necessary to demonstrate with a dog.

Repetitions: Each handler does this one time.

Watch for: Handlers executing a Left U-turn rather than an About Turn. From now on, whenever the handlers are instructed to line up in a particular place, they will do so with a Left U-turn.

Handlers count to five before kneeling and then count to five again before calling the dog. To call the dog without pausing will teach the dog to come without waiting for the command.

Hands remain on the thighs until the dog arrives. Reaching out toward the dog may cause him to stop before he gets to the handler, or bolt.

It is rare for a dog not to go directly to his handler the first time this exercise is done in class. However, if a dog runs away from his handler, the instructor or assistant walks the dog up to the handler, who is instructed to pet and praise the dog for one minute. The handler tries again, only this time with food as an added inducement.

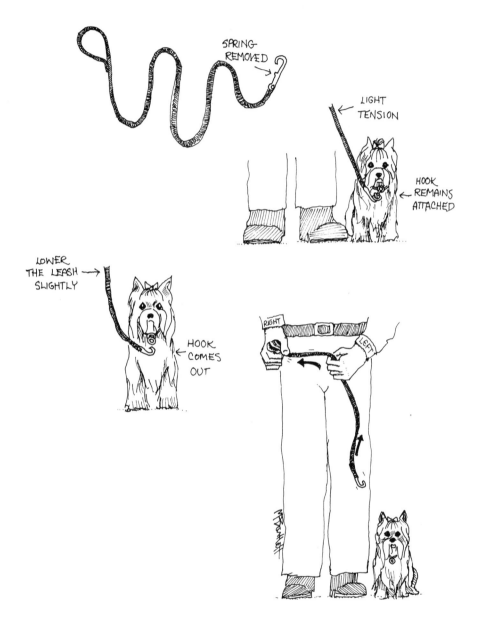

Alternate technique for the Slip Release.

262

Hints for Traffic Control: One straight line.

(14) LONG SIT & DOWN (Homework Assignment):

Instructions: This week the handler sits across the room from the dog for the 10-minute Sit and the 30-minute Down. Each is done three times, on alternate days.

(15) REMINDERS:

"This week train in three different locations that are free of distractions. For example, if you have been training only in the back yard, train in the front yard as well as a neighbor's yard or some other place. This teaches the dog to pay attention in new places.

When practicing off leash exercises—Heel Free and Recall—do so in a safe area where there is no danger of your dog running away."

(16) PREVIEW:

"Next week your dog will learn the hand signal for down."

(17) NAME TAGS & HOMEWORK SHEETS.

WEEK 4

(1) NAME TAGS & CALL ROLL

(2) HEEL ON LEASH:

Review: With leash over shoulder, including Changes of Pace and About Turn.

Instructions: Instruct Circles Right and Left in motion. While handlers are heeling, command "Circle (Right/Left)" and have them execute a circle 4′ in diameter at a trot to the right, slow to the left. Instruct handlers to grasp the leash close to the snap while making the circle(s) and then release it again. Handlers continue heeling at a normal pace after completing the circle(s).

Demonstration: Demonstrate the traffic pattern without a dog.

Repetitions: Heeling for 3 minutes, including two of each circle.

Hints for Traffic Control: The majority of the heeling can be done in a clockwise direction for a bouncy class, or counterclockwise for the class that has more control.

(3) SIT STAY—Sequence 3:

Review: Sequence 2. The leash is held in the left hand at the belt buckle, ready to reinforce with right hand under the leash. Return to the dog after one minute.

Instructions: Sequence 3—Sit Stay Test.

Demonstration: Demonstrate emphasizing the pressure is applied by twisting the wrist rather than leaning backward.

Articulation: "Transfer the leash snap to the dead ring of the collar and fold the leash into your left hand so it is coming out from under your little finger, leaving 3′ of slack. When I say 'leave your dogs,' signal and command stay, go 3′ in front, turn and face your dogs. Place your left hand holding the leash at your belt buckle, right hand prepared to reinforce. When I say 'pressure,' twist your left hand to apply gradually increasing pressure on the collar. If necessary, reinforce with your right hand slapping the leash with 'stay.' When I say 'release,' release the pressure.... Pressure ... Release ... Prepare to return ... return ... exercise finished ... release. Transfer the leash snap back to the live ring."

Repetitions: Three pressure/release tests, each lasting five to ten seconds, followed by a release.

Watch for: The pressure is gradual and not a check. It is not hard enough to pull the dog out of position, but is sufficient for the dog to pull against.

Watch the handler's body motion. Many handlers will rock backward rather than twist the wrist.

Hints for Traffic Control: One straight line or two lines facing each other, leaving enough room behind the dogs for handlers to walk around behind and for the Instructor/Assistants to observe and help the handlers.

(4) SIT FOR EXAMINATION:

Instructions: Instruct Sit for Examination. After the Sit Stay Test, the handler returns the leash to the live ring for the Sit for Examination. With rings of the collar at the back of the dog's neck, the handler will stand directly in front of the sitting dog, leash held in his left hand directly over the dog's head, ready to reinforce as the Instructor/Assistant examines the dog.

Repetitions: One Sit for Examination.

Hints for Traffic Control: The same position as for the Sit Stay Test.

264

(5) TURNS IN PLACE (RIGHT & ABOUT):

Review: Sequence 2. For the Right Turn, command then step. For the About Turn, one step, turn, one step.

Repetitions: Four of each turn.

Hints for Traffic Control: Move the class to a different area and have them line up in one or two straight lines facing the same direction.

(6) DOWN STAY:

Review: Handlers place dogs down, leave and go 3' in front for two minutes.

Remind them that the reinforcement is to step toward the dog and check straight down under the dog's chin.

Hints for Traffic Control: One straight line in a different area from the Sit Stay.

(7) TURNS:

Object: "To teach your dog to remain in heel position when you turn."

Instructions: Place a chair in each corner of the training area. Handlers are instructed to heel around the training area with leashes in Control Position, staying on the outside of the chairs and squaring their turns at the corners.

Demonstration: Demonstrate the turns at a corner without a dog.

Articulation: "For the left turn, slow down and draw back on the leash as you approach the corner, make the turn and resume a normal pace. For the right turn, keep moving at a normal pace and verbally encourage the dog to make the turn. Keep your feet together as you turn the corner."

Repetitions: One time around the training area in each direction so the students do four of each turn.

Watch for: Hands remaining in Control Position, and holding the dog back on the left turn.

Hints for Traffic Control: Begin in a counterclockwise direction for left turns, call an about turn, then one time around in a clockwise direction for right turns.

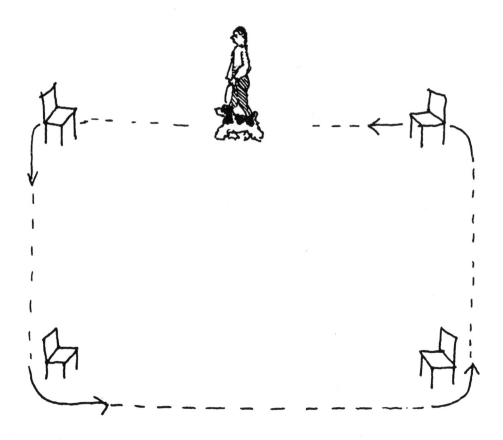

A chair is placed in each corner
of the training area. Handlers square
their turns at each corner.

Traffic control for Turns in Motion.

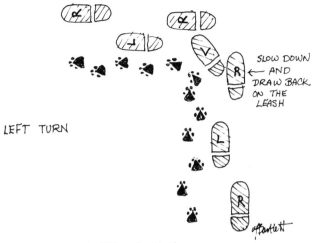

Left Turn in Motion.

Right Turn in Motion.

(8) STAND—Sequence 4:

Review: Sequence 3. Handlers remove their leashes and pocket them, stand their dogs, give stay command/signal and stand erect at the dog's side.

Instructions: From now on, when the handlers remove their leashes for the Stand, they will pocket them, out of sight of the dog. Instruct Sequence 4.

Articulation: "Take the leash off and put it in your pocket. Stand your dogs. When I say 'leave your dogs,' you will give the stay command and signal and pivot directly in front of your dog. When I say 'back to your dogs,' you will pivot back, pause and praise. When I say 'exercise finished,' put the leash back on and when I say 'release,' release. Your dog remains standing until you say 'okay.'"

Repetitions: Repeat two times. Handlers are in front of the dogs for a count of 10.

Watch for: Hovering and not standing erect.
   If the dog moves, he is replaced from in front with "stand, stay."

Hints for Traffic Control: A circle facing the center.

(9) AUTOMATIC SIT—Sequence 3:

Review: Sequence 2. Leash in Control Position, rings of the collar at the top of the dog's neck. The right hand grasps the leash snap and checks straight up as the left hand tucks.

Instructions: Instruct Sequence 3.

Demonstration: Demonstrate emphasizing the left arm remaining in line with the dog's spine and parallel with the ground. The action is upward and not backward, toward the handler or away from the handler. Demonstrate what to do if the dog does not sit straight. Repeat the demonstration so the entire class can see the arm position.

Articulation: "Hold your leash in Control Position, rings of the collar at the top of the dog's neck. When I say '... and ...' move your left hand down the leash so it is close to the leash snap. When I say '... halt ...' say 'sit,' plant your left foot in front of your right and check straight up with your left hand, keeping your forearm parallel with the ground and in line with the dog's spine. When your dog is sitting, close with your right foot. If your dog does not sit straight, say 'heel,' take one step forward and sit him as you have been doing for the last two weeks, right hand on the leash snap checking straight up, left hand placing him in a sit with 'sit.'"

Sequence 3 of the . . .

Automatic Sit.

Repetitions: Repeat 5 times.

Watch for: Incorrect checking with the left hand. The action is **straight up,** not backward or to one side. If the dog is not sitting straight, look to the handler. **If the handler's action is correct, the dog's response will be correct.**
Handlers who, when the dog does not sit straight, pull the rear end into heel position rather than taking a step forward and repositioning with Sequence 2. This incorrect action will teach the dog to sit incorrectly and wait to be pulled in, whereas taking the step forward and repositioning the dog correctly teaches the **dog** to assume the responsibility of where to sit.

Hints for Traffic Control: A counterclockwise circle.

(10) HEEL FREE:

Review: Slip Release and Circle Left from stationary.

Instructions: Instruct Circle Left plus 5 steps.

Demonstration: Demonstrate without a dog, emphasizing normal body posture and normal pace.

Articulation: "When I say 'Circle Left,' say '(Name), heel,' take two steps forward and begin to circle left. Release the leash, complete the circle and take five steps in a straight line forward, stop and sit your dog with your right hand on his chest."

Repetitions: Once with the Circle Left and halt. Twice with the Circle Left plus five steps straight forward.

Watch for: Handler's body posture. The tendency to hover over the dog as soon as the leash is off is strong. This change in body posture may cause the dog to take off. Handler's posture is confident and normal throughout the Heel Free.

Hints for Traffic Control: A counterclockwise circle.

(11) SIT & DOWN:

Review: Sequence 3. With object of attraction, handlers in front of the dog, using downward pressure in the collar for the down.

Repetitions: Twice.

Hints for Traffic Control: A straight line leaving sufficient room for the instructor/assistants to observe from both sides.

Reaching in to reinforce the Down Signal.

(12) HAND SIGNALS:

Object: "To teach your dog to respond to hand signals."

Instructions: Instruct Sit and Down Hand Signals.

Demonstration: Demonstrate the Down emphasizing the **back and down** pressure of the left hand and the position of the right arm for the signal. Demonstrate the Sit emphasizing the left hand against the right hip, the signal starting backward and the slapping motion toward the dog. Position for the demonstration is with the dog's back to the class, the demonstrator facing the class.

Articulation: "Kneel in front of your dogs and prepare to down your dogs—fold the leash into your left hand and place two fingers of your left hand in the dog's collar under his chin. When I say 'down your dog,' say 'down,' raise your right arm straight up over your shoulder and apply pressure against your dog's chest **back and down** with your left hand in the dog's collar. When he is down, release the pressure and praise.

"Stand up in front of your dog, fold the leash in your left hand and place your left hand against your right hip. When I say 'sit your dog,' say 'sit' and signal with your right hand, palm open toward the dog, brought back six inches, then forward toward the dog, slapping the leash with 'sit.' Praise him and return your hand to your side."

Repetitions: Repeat each signal 4 times, pausing for a count of ten between repetitions. Inform the handlers to count to ten between repetitions at home as well. Otherwise the dog will learn to bounce up and down, but will not learn to respond to the signals.

Watch for: For the Down, the handler keeps his back erect, not hovering over the dog. If the handler leans forward, his signal is behind the dog's head and the dog cannot see it.

The signal is the right hand remaining erect over the shoulder, not going up and coming down in a sweeping motion.

The left hand pushes **back and down.** If the handler pulls forward, his dog will get up. The backward pressure moves the dog slightly off balance so he cannot resist the downward pressure.

For the Sit, if the dog is slow in getting up, or is reluctant to get up, the handler slaps the leash harder. If the dog rolls over onto his back, the handler still checks upward with the leash.

Hints for Traffic Control: The same line as for the Sit and Down.

(13) RECALL—Sequence 2:

Instructions: Done individually. The handler brings the dog out of the line-up, makes a Left U-turn and faces the vacated spot. He removes the leash, taking it with him, and leaves the dog on a Sit Stay. The Instructor/Assistant will hold the dog, if necessary. The handler returns to the line-up, turns to face his dog, counts to five, kneels down and sits on his heels, putting the leash behind him on the floor, counts to five again, places his hands, palms up, on his thighs, smiles and calls the dog with "(Name), come!" When the dog arrives, he places his right hand against the dog's chest, reaches over with his left hand and tucks the dog into a sit with praise. **No "sit" command.** He continues to praise and pet the dog for one minute.

Demonstration: Demonstrate the posture and hand action for the sit. It is not necessary to demonstrate with a dog.

Repetitions: Each handler does this one time.

Watch for: Handlers who have practiced all week without counting to five. Have them pause before kneeling and again before calling.

New wrinkles. Handlers may have added their own embellishments, such as clapping or slapping the backs of their hands against the thighs as they call, repeating "come," encouraging with "come on, come on" or saying "come" before the dog's name. Now is the time to correct the handlers so they don't learn any bad habits.

Now is also the time to emphasize the importance of working on Sit Stays. If the dog needed to be held, the handler needs to work harder on the stays. Remind them to work on Sit Stays as a separate exercise, and not call the dog every time he is left on a stay.

Hints for Traffic Control: One straight line.

(14) LONG SIT & DOWN (Homework Assignment):

Instructions: The ten-minute Long Sit and 30-minute Long Down are done this week with the handler moving around the room, but not going out of sight of the dog. Each is done three times, on alternate days.

(15) REMINDERS:

"Three times this week, train in new locations without distractions."

(16) PREVIEW:

"Next week your dog will learn to respond to 'come' around distractions."

(17) HOMEWORK SHEETS & NAME TAGS.

WEEK 5

(1) NAME TAGS & CALL ROLL.

(2) HEEL ON LEASH:

Review: Briefly review heeling with leash over shoulder including Changes of Pace, About Turn and Circles Left and Right.

Instructions: Instruct the Heeling Hand Signal. With the dog sitting at heel position, the signal is given with the handler's left hand, palm toward

The hand signal to Heel.

the dog, swept from left to right in front of the dog's face as he says "(Name), heel" and starts to walk.

Demonstration: Demonstrate emphasizing the direction of the signal. It is from **left** to **right.**

Repetitions: Repeat the signal three times. Heeling is practiced for two to three minutes.

Watch for: Incorrect hand signal, or the signal done with the right hand.
    It is not necessary to repeat the signal each time the handlers start.

Hints for Traffic Control: At this stage of the training, heeling begins in a counterclockwise direction, dogs on the inside. A logical sequence is: Forward at a normal pace, slow, normal, circle left at a slow, return to normal, about turn, normal, fast, normal, circle right at a trot, return to normal, halt. The changes of pace are preparatory for circles.

(3) SIT STAY:

Review: Sit Stay Test. Leashes attached to the dead ring, handlers 3' in front for pressure/release.

Instructions: Instruct handlers to return the leash snap to the live ring. Then have them leave their dogs and go 6' in front for 30 seconds.
    For the Sit for Examination, the handlers are 3' in front, prepared to reinforce as the Instructor/Assistant examines the dogs.

Repetitions: Three pressure/release tests each lasting no more than 10 seconds. Thirty-second Sit Stay with handlers 6' in front. One Sit for Examination with handlers 3' in front.

Watch for: When the handlers are 6' in front for the Sit Stay, if it is necessary to reinforce, the handler steps *toward* the dog when he slaps the leash.

Hints for Traffic Control: One straight line or two lines facing each other.

(4) TURNS IN PLACE (RIGHT, LEFT & ABOUT):

Review: Sequence 2 of Right and About Turns. For the Right Turn, command then step. For the About Turn, one step, turn, one step.

Instructions: Instruct Left Turn in Place—Sequence 1.

Demonstration: Demonstrate emphasizing the left foot position before giving the command and the large step beyond with the right foot. Demonstrator faces the class so they can see the left foot position.

Articulation: "Hold your leash in Control Position. When I say 'prepare for the left turn,' place your left foot directly in front of your dog's front feet, facing 90 degrees to the left. When I say 'left turn,' say '(Name), heel,' take a large step with your right foot past your left and close with the left foot, guiding your dog into heel position with 'sit.'"

Repetitions: Two Right Turns, two About Turns and four Left Turns.

Watch for: Placing the left foot in front of the dog's feet **after** giving the command to heel. This is a 90 degree turn, not 180 degrees. Watch to see that handlers take a **large** step with the right foot beyond the left, and that the dogs sit straight at heel.

Hints for Traffic Control: Move them to a different area and have them line up in one or two straight lines facing the same direction. Leave sufficient room for observation and help.

(5) TURNS:

Object: To teach the handlers to make turns in response to the instructor's commands.

Instructions: Place three chairs in a line six feet apart. Line up three handlers six feet apart, the first one parallel with the first chair, two feet away from the chair to his left. The dogs are sitting at heel position and leashes are in Control Position. On your command, the handlers will heel their dogs forward and, using the chairs as guideposts, execute the turns as you call them—forward, left turn, about turn, right turn and halt.

① "Fido, heel"

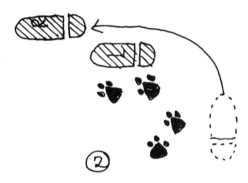

②

③

"Sit"

Diagram for the Left Turn in Place.

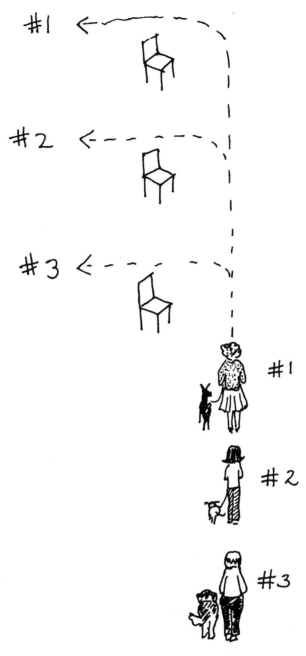

Traffic control for Turns in Motion.

277

Demonstration: Demonstrate the starting position and turns on command without a dog.

Articulation: "When I say 'forward,' say '(Name), heel' and start to walk straight forward. Follow my commands. . . . 'Forward . . . left turn . . . about turn . . . right turn . . . and halt.'"

Repetitions: One sequence for each handler.

Watch for: Handlers' pace.

Some handlers do not have any sense of direction, and cannot execute a square turn. They will need to be guided through the turns in order to learn them.

Hints for Traffic Control: The class is lined up along one side of the training area and the handlers are brought out to take their positions by the chairs. The first three students in line come out and do the turns, then return to the end of the line and the next three come out to take their turn.

(6) STAND—Sequence 5:

Review: Sequence 4. Leashes pocketed, have handlers stand dogs, pivot directly in front and pivot back.

Instructions: Instruct Sequence 5. The handler leaves his dog, goes 3′ in front, turns and faces his dog for ten seconds, then pivots back to heel position, pauses, praises and releases.

Instruct Owner Examination

Object: "To accustom your dog to being examined."

Instructions: The handler stands his dog, leaves him and pivots directly in front, then pivots back and begins his examination. He thoroughly checks his dog all over, looking at the teeth, ears, and feeling the legs. At the completion of his examination, the handler stands erect next to his dog, pauses, praises, puts the leash back on and releases.

Articulation: "Stand your dogs. Leave your dogs and pivot directly in front. Pivot back and begin your examination. Start at the dog's head and thoroughly check him all over, from head to tail. . . . When you are finished, return to heel position, pause, praise, put your leash back on and release."

Repetitions: One review of Sequence 4. Two repetitions of Sequence 5. One repetition of Owner Examination.

Watch for: When doing Sequence 5, some dogs may walk forward toward the handler. The handler bodily moves his dog back to the original position with "stand, stay." Avoid allowing the handlers to take the dog by the collar

278

and walk him back to position. If the dog is not ready for this sequence, have the handler remain by the dog's side or directly in front, and tell him to work harder on Stand this week.

For the Owner Examination, some handlers become overly enthusiastic. The examination is gentle and non-threatening to the dog.

Hints for Traffic Control: A circle facing the center.

(7) AUTOMATIC SIT:

Review: Sequence 3. Left hand grasps the leash near the snap and checks straight up.

Instructions: Instruct the handlers to start and stop **briskly** and to concentrate on getting quick responses to the "sit" command.

Repetitions: Repeat 5 times.

Watch for: Remind the handlers if the dog fails to sit straight, say "heel," take one step forward and sit the dogs with the right hand on the leash snap checking straight up, left hand tucking.

(8) HEEL FREE:

Review: Completing the Circle Left, taking 4-5 steps and sitting the dog.

Instructions: Complete the Circle Left and then take **ten** steps. Remind the handler to keep his body posture erect, facing straight forward, and his left hand motionless.

This particular exercise tells you whether or not the training is getting through to the dogs. Repeated failures are indicative of incorrect collar position, incorrect collar (you may have to recommend the pinch collar) or incorrect use of the check (the handler may be pulling on the leash and maintaining pressure instead of checking), or the checks may not be firm enough.

Demonstration: Demonstrate the Slip Surprise, if necessary. See Alternate Technique below.

Repetitions: Practice one of the review sequence, followed by two repetitions of the Circle Left and ten steps.

Watch for: Watch the handler's body posture after the release. Dogs that bolt do so for one of two reasons: either they have not been properly conditioned to **no tension** on the leash or a change in the handler's body posture causes the dog to leave.

Alternate Technique: If necessary, instruct the Slip Surprise for those dogs who are bolting as soon as the leash is released. Have the handler begin the Slip Release again, but this time leave the snap attached to the training collar. He grasps the leash approximately in the middle with his right hand so there is **no tension** on the leash snap and executes the release as before. When the dog bolts, the handler allows him to go out to the end of the leash then firmly and emphatically checks him.

Instruct the handler to repeat this procedure three times, checking firmly each time, even if the dog no longer attempts to bolt. If, after this, the dog is still not performing the exercise, examine their Heeling on Leash and whether or not the dog is responding to the check.

The Slip Surprise is also used for Off-Leash Heeling if the handler is unable to practice in a safe area.

Hints for Traffic Control: A counterclockwise circle.

(9) HAND SIGNALS—Sequence 2:

Review: Sequence 1. For the Down, handlers kneeling in front of the sitting dogs, signal/command and pressure back and down with left hand in collar. For the Sit, handlers stand erect, leash in the left hand against the right hip, command/signal and slap the leash.

Instructions: Instruct Sequence 2.

Demonstration: Demonstrate the Down emphasizing the check downward as opposed to pulling the dog down. Also point out the Command/ Motion Sequence—the signal/command is given **before** reaching in to check, not simultaneously. Demonstrate the Sit emphasizing the step *toward* the dog on the right foot, then bringing the foot back. For both demonstrations, the demonstrator is sideways to the class so they have a clear view of his actions.

Articulation: "Sit your dogs, leave them, go three feet in front and kneel down. When I say 'down your dogs,' give the signal and command, then reach in with your left hand, grasp the leash snap and check straight down under the dog's chin. . . . Down your dogs. . . . Praise . . . Stand up and prepare to sit your dogs—hold the leash in your left hand and place it against your right hip. When I say 'sit your dogs,' give the command/signal and as you slap the leash with your right hand, step toward the dog on your right foot. When your dog is sitting bring your right foot back again. . . . Sit your dogs. . . ."

Repetitions: One of the review sequence. Then three of Sequence 2, each

280

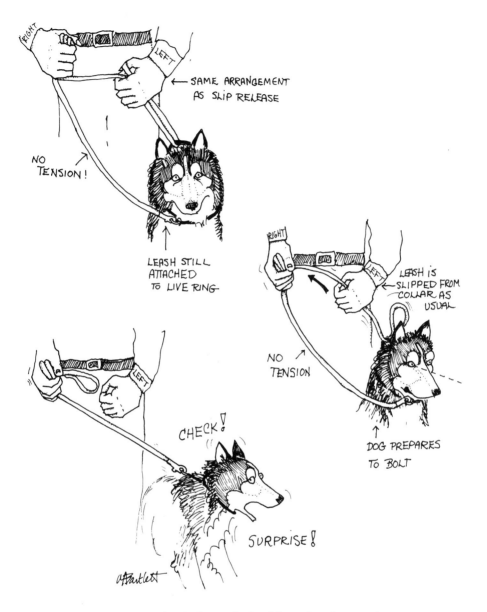

For the dog that bolts on the heel free, the Slip Surprise.

signal. Pause between repetitions, and remind handlers to pause between repetitions in their practice at home.

Watch for: For the Down—handlers that pull the leash toward them rather than reaching in to check. The action is *reaching in* to grasp the leash snap to check, not checking the leash from three feet away.

Watch for improvisations on the signal. Some handlers have invented their own signals at this point, either holding the arm very close to the body with the hand at shoulder height—a signal which would not be visible to the dog from a distance—or motioning downward using the entire body as a signal.

For the Sit—if the dog sits, then immediately lies down again, the handler repeats the slap on the leash.

For both signals, it is not necessary for the dog to be looking directly at the handler in order for him to see the signal. Many handlers will engage in all manner of arm waving, foot stomping, calling the dog's name or saying "psssst" to get the dog's attention prior to giving the signal. Dogs have excellent peripheral vision and can see very well to the side, even if they are looking away. Therefore, instruct handlers to give the signals as though the dogs were looking directly at them.

In any case, even if the dog is not paying attention and doesn't see the signal, the check teaches him that it is his responsibility to be aware of what the handler is doing.

(10)   DOWN ON COMMAND AND DOWN STAY:

Object: "To teach your dogs to respond to the voice command 'down.'"

Instructions: With the dog sitting at heel position, instruct Down on Command.
   Then review the Down Stay 6' away for two minutes.

Demonstration: Demonstrate Down on Command emphasizing the Command/Motion Sequence—the command is given **before** pressure is applied. The demonstrator faces the class.

Articulation: "When I say 'prepare to down your dogs,' fold the leash into your left hand and place two fingers of your left hand in the dog's collar at the side of his neck. When I say 'down your dogs,' say 'down' and, if necessary, apply pressure with your left hand **straight down.** When your dog is down, release pressure and praise.

Repetitions: Repeat 3 times, then do a Down Stay for 2 minutes with handlers 6' in front.

Down . . .

on command.

Watch for: A hand signal or pointing to the floor. The purpose of this exercise is to teach the dog to respond to the verbal command *only*. Some handlers cannot keep their hands still when they give a command. Instruct these handlers to place the right hand in a pocket or grasp the seam of their pants when giving the command.

If the dog strongly resists this sequence, have the handler return to the object of attraction for another week, then try this exercise again. Do not allow this to become a contest of strength.

(11) FRONT—Sequence 1:

Object: "To teach your dog what to do when he comes to you."

Instructions: Instruct Sequence 1. Each handler is given an object of attraction which can be a ball, a toy or a treat.

Demonstration: Demonstrate emphasizing that the motion with the object is toward the body and upward in an 'L,' and that *both* hands hold the object. The demonstrator positions himself either sideways to the class or with the dog's back to the class so the students can see his position.

Articulation: "Remove your leash and pocket it. Stand your dogs, leave them and step directly in front, toe-to-toe. When I say 'sit your dogs,' hold the object of attraction in both hands directly in front of your dog's face just below his chin, say 'come' and motion toward you and up to your chest in an 'L.' When your dog is sitting, praise and reward with the object of attraction. If he does not sit, kneel down, place your right hand on his chest, reach over with your left hand and tuck him into a sit. Remove your hands and praise."

Repetitions: Repeat 3-5 times. Have the handlers pivot back to re-stand their dogs between repetitions.

Watch for: Handlers motioning straight up or back rather than toward them and up in an 'L.'

Handlers keep their backs erect, bending their knees, if necessary, to place their hands under the dog's chin. Hovering over the dog is a threatening posture that will cause the dog to back into a sit.

Hints for Traffic Control: A circle facing center.

(12) RECALL ON LEASH:

Object: "To teach the handlers how to reinforce the 'come' command."

284

The Sit . . .

in Front.

Instructions: The Instructor or Assistant crouches in the center of the training area, holding a bag of dog treats.

Demonstration: Demonstrate the action without using a dog.

Articulation: "Walk your dog up to the distractor saying 'Let's go' rather than 'heel.' Allow your dog to sniff the bag of treats. While he is investigating, back up to the end of the leash and call your dog '(Name), come!' If your dog fails to respond, guide him toward you on leash and crouch to welcome him with praise and petting when he arrives."

Repetitions: Have each handler do this twice.

Watch for: Use of the "heel" command to walk the dog up to the distraction. Since the dog is going to be allowed to leave heel position and go to the bag of treats, the handler walks him forward with an alternate command such as "let's go."

The distractor does not feed the dog. The goodies are there only as an enticement to get the dog's attention away from the handler.

Hints for Traffic Control: The class is lined up along one side of the training area, with the distractor about 10′ in front of the line, or centered in the area. Starting at one end of the line, the handlers bring their dogs out to the distractor and then back up. When they have done their repetitions, they go to the end of the line and the next person comes out. The line keeps moving forward until everyone has had a turn.

(13) REMINDERS:

Instruct handlers to take three trips to shopping centers or parks so the dog learns to respond around distractions.

To keep the dog under control when company comes, use the Long Down.

Safety—As a safety precaution, instruct handlers to teach their dogs to let them go through doorways first. They practice by opening doors and verbally reprimanding the dog with "ah, ah" if he tries to go through first. If he does not respond, they shut the door as he rushes it.

(14) NOTE:

The first "learning plateau" may begin toward the end of this week. If the dog seems to have forgotten everything he has learned so far, instruct handlers not to despair. They should be patient and continue with training.

Recall on leash—dog investigates . . .

is called . . .

and guided toward handler . . .

where he is warmly welcomed.

"Next week you're going to learn the Recall Hand Signal."

(16) NAME TAGS & HOMEWORK SHEETS.

WEEK 6

(1) HEEL ON LEASH:

Review: Briefly review heeling with leash over shoulder including Changes of Pace, About Turn and Circles Left and Right. Review the Heeling Hand Signal.

Repetitions: Heeling is practiced for two or three minutes.

Hints for Traffic Control: Begin with a counterclockwise circle, normal pace, then slow, normal, Circle Left, normal, About Turn, normal, fast, normal, Circle Right, normal, halt.

(2) SIT STAY:

Review: Sit Stay Test. Leashes attached to the dead ring, handlers 3' in front for pressure/release.
   Then review a Sit Stay with handlers 6' in front for 2 minutes.

Repetitions: Three pressure/release tests each lasting no more than 10 seconds. Two minute Sit Stay with handlers 6' in front.

Homework Assignment: Instruct handlers that their homework includes working on three different surfaces to accustom the dog to different types of flooring. They will incorporate Sit Stays into their daily routines, such as while they are preparing the dog's dinner, setting the table, and so forth.

Hints for Traffic Control: One straight line or two lines facing each other.

(3) TURNS IN PLACE:

Review: Sequence 2 of the Right and About Turns. For the Right Turn, command then step. For the About Turn, command then one step, turn, one step.
   Review Sequence 1 of the Left Turn. The handler's left foot is placed in front of the dog's forefeet. With "(Name), heel," the handler takes a large step with his right foot and closes with his left.

Repetitions: Two of each turn.

Hints for Traffic Control: Move the handlers to a different area and have them line up in one or two straight lines facing the same direction.

(4) TURNS:

Instructions: Instruct the handlers to count off in 2's. They will begin heeling in a counterclockwise circle with the leashes in Control Position. After both groups have made their turns and heeled across the circle, call an about turn and repeat going clockwise.

Demonstration: Demonstrate the turn and walk across the circle without a dog.

Articulation: "While you are heeling, when I say '1's, left turn,' all the 1's will turn toward the center of the circle, heel their dogs across the circle and rejoin the 2's who have continued heeling around the outside of the circle. When I say '2's, left turn,' all the 2's will turn toward the center of the circle, heel their dogs across the circle and rejoin the 1's who have continued heeling around the outside of the circle. Then I'll call an About Turn to do the same thing going in the other direction."

Repetitions: One left turn and one right turn for both sections of the class.

Hints for Traffic Control: Begin with a counterclockwise circle and after both the 1's and 2's have done their left turns, call an About Turn so they are moving in a clockwise circle for the right turns.

(5) STAND—Sequence 6:

Review: Sequence 5. Leashes pocketed, have handlers stand dogs, go 3' in front, pause for 30 seconds, then pivot back.

Instructions: Instruct Sequence 6. The handler leaves his dog, goes 6' in front, turns and faces his dog for ten seconds, then pivots back to heel position, pauses, praises and releases.
Instruct Return
Instruct Stand for Examination
With the dogs standing, the handlers leave and stand directly in front while the Instructor/Assistant goes over the dogs as on the Sit for Examination. After the examination, the handlers return, pause, praise, replace their leashes and release.

Demonstration: Demonstrate the Return with two fingers of the left hand on the dog's withers.

Articulation: "When I say 'return to your dogs' you will return as for the Sit or Down Stay. Place two fingers of your left hand lightly on the dog's

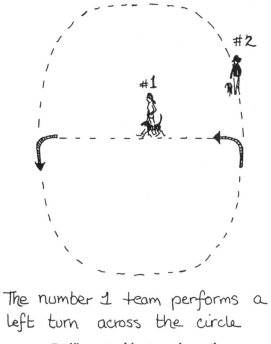

The number 1 team performs a
left turn across the circle

Traffic control for turns in motion.

Return around behind on the Stand.

withers as you walk around behind him. Stop in heel position. . . . Exercise finished, praise, replace your leashes . . . Release."

Repetitions: One Stand Stay 3′ in front and two 6′ in front with the Return. Then one Stand for Examination.

Homework Assignment: Refer the handlers to the Stand Stay progressions on the homework sheet.

Hints for Traffic Control: A circle facing the center.

(6) AUTOMATIC SIT:

Review: Sequence 3. Left hand grasps the leash near the snap and checks straight up. Have handlers start and stop briskly.

Instructions: Instruct the handlers to eliminate the "sit" command.

Repetitions: Repeat 5 times.

Watch for: Those who continue to say "sit."

Hints for Traffic Control: A counterclockwise circle.

(7) HEEL FREE:

Instructions: With leashes in Slip Release position, handlers heeling briskly in a large circle, they give a Pay Attention Check to reinforce heeling, then release. They continue moving at a brisk pace, and when you call a halt, stop and sit their dogs with right hand on the chest. If the dog begins to leave heel position, they stop and sit him.

Articulation: "Position your leash in Slip Release position. When I say 'release' give a Pay Attention Check to get your dog's attention on you and to create slack in the leash, then release. Continue moving briskly. When I say 'halt,' stop and sit your dog with your right hand on his chest. If your dog begins to leave heel position, stop and sit him."

Repetitions: Twice.

Watch for: Changes in posture or slowing down which may cause the dog to leave heel position.

Hints for Traffic Control: A counterclockwise circle.

(8) HAND SIGNALS—Sequence 3:

Review: Sequence 2. For the Down, handlers are on their knees, 3′ in front; for the Sit, they are standing 3′ in front.

292

Instructions: Instruct Sequence 3. For the Down, the handlers stand erect 3' in front of their dogs. Giving the signal and command "down," the handler steps toward his dog on his right foot and grasps the leash snap with his left hand to check straight down under the dog's chin. When the dog is down, he brings his right foot back and praises.

For the Sit, he steps toward the dog with his right foot as he did in Sequence 2, slapping the leash with his right hand with "sit," and bringing his right foot back.

Repetitions: Do each signal 3 times, pausing between repetitions.

Watch for: Handlers pulling the leash toward them for the Down rather than checking downward under the dog's chin.

Hints for Traffic Control: One straight line leaving sufficient room for the Instructor/Assistants to observe from both sides.

(9) DOWN ON COMMAND & DOWN STAY:

Review: With fingers in the collar prepared to reinforce, handlers give command "down."

Instructions: Down Stay 6' in front for 3 minutes.

Repetitions: Down dogs twice, then leave on Down Stay for 3 minutes, 6' in front.

Hints for Traffic Control: A straight line on the opposite side of the training area to where the Sit Stay was done.

(10) RECALL HAND SIGNAL & SIT IN FRONT:

Object: "To teach your dog to come on signal."

Instructions: Instruct the Recall Hand Signal.

Demonstration: Demonstrate facing toward the class, the dog's back to the class, so they can see the hand signal and leash check, if necessary.

Articulation: "Stand 6' in front of your dog with the leash held in your left hand at your left side. When I say 'call your dogs,' you will give the signal with your right hand brought up to shoulder height and to your chest as you say 'name of dog, come!' If the dog does not respond, check toward you with your left hand. When he arrives, praise and guide him into a sit in front with your hands under his chin."

Repetitions: Have the handlers repeat the exercise 3 times by saying "stay" after the dog is sitting and backing up 6' away to do it again. **There is no hand signal for Stay from in front of the dog.** The verbal command is sufficient.

Watch for: Invisible hand signals—those that are done too close to the body for the dog to see.

Hints for Traffic Control: One straight line, moving across the training area with each repetition. If necessary, have the handlers turn the dogs around to do the necessary number of repetitions. Handlers turn by executing a Left U-turn.

(11) RECALL—Sequence 3:

Instructions: The Instructor or Assistant crouches in the center of the training area, holding a bag of treats. Handlers individually bring their dogs up as last week.

Demonstration: Demonstrate the action without using a dog.

Articulation: "Walk your dog up to the distractor with 'let's go' and allow him to sniff the bag. Back up to the end of the leash and call your dog '(Name), come!' If your dog fails to respond, emphatically check the leash toward you, crouch and welcome the dog with praise and petting when he arrives. The purpose of the check is to train the dog to respond to the command, not to reel him in. Check **after** saying 'come.'"

Repetitions: Have each handler do this twice. In the case of a handler who is not checking properly or timing the command and check incorrectly, it may be repeated once or twice more.

Watch for: Incorrect timing of the check. It is given **after** the command "come," not simultaneously.

Handlers hauling their dogs to them rather than checking and letting the dog move voluntarily.

(12) REMINDERS:

This is the week the dogs may reach a learning plateau. Instruct the handlers to be patient and continue working on the training exercises.

They are to take three more trips to new areas with distractions.

Safety—Instruct the handlers to practice making the dog wait while they go up and down stairs, rather than allowing the dog to bolt past them.

Pay particular attention this week to firming up stays.

294

(13) GRADUATION REQUIREMENTS:

To graduate from Level 1, the dog must heel on a loose leash, hold a stay in the sit, stand and down position, and come when called. If any of these areas present problems, the handlers should review the progressions in the homework sheets.

(14) PREVIEW:

"Next week you get to evaluate us."

(15) HOMEWORK SHEETS & NAME TAGS.

WEEKS 7 & 8

*(1) HEEL ON LEASH:

Review: Briefly review heeling with leash over shoulder including Changes of Pace, About Turn and Circles Left and Right. Review the Heeling Hand Signal.

Instructions: Instruct handlers to use the Heeling Hand Signal with no voice command.

Repetitions: Heeling is practiced for two or three minutes.

Hints for Traffic Control: Begin with a counterclockwise circle, normal pace, then slow, normal, Circle Left, normal, About Turn, normal, fast, normal, Circle Right, normal, halt.

*(2) SIT STAY:

Review: Sit Stay Test. Leashes attached to the dead ring, handlers 3' in front for pressure/release.

Instructions: Have the handler do a 6' Sit Stay for two minutes, then return, drop the leash at the dog's side, leave again, stand 6' away for ten seconds, return, etc.

Repetitions: Three pressure/release tests each lasting no more than 10 seconds. Two minute Sit Stay with handlers 6' in front, followed by ten seconds with leashes dropped.

---

*8th week lesson plan, followed by graduation.

295

*(3) TURNS IN PLACE:

Review: Sequence 2 of the Right and About Turns. For the Right Turn, command then step. For the About Turn, command then one step, turn, one step.

Review Sequence 1 of the Left Turn. The handler's left foot is placed in front of the dog's feet, then a large step with the right foot.

Instructions: Left Turn Sequence 2. Instruct the handler to place his left foot directly in front of his dog's feet, then take a small step with the right foot beyond the left and guide the dog into heel position.

Articulation: "When I say 'prepare for a left turn,' place your left foot directly in front of your dog's feet. When I say 'left turn,' take a small step with your right foot beyond your left, close with your left and guide the dog into heel position."

Repetitions: Two of each of the Right and About Turns, Sequence 2. Two reviews of the Left Turn Sequence 1. Two repetitions of the Left Turn Sequence 2.

Hints for Traffic Control: Move handlers to a different area and have them line up in one or two straight lines facing the same direction.

*(4) TURNS:

Review: Counting off in 2's and executing turns across the circle.

Instructions: Call a right or left turn across the circle for the entire class.

Articulation: "One's right turn . . . Two's right turn . . . Everyone right turn."

Repetitions: One left turn for each half of the class, followed by the entire class turning left. Then one About Turn and do the same with the right turn.

Hints for Traffic Control: Begin with a counterclockwise circle.

*(5) STAND—Sequence 7:

Review: Sequence 6. Handlers are 6' in front and return around behind.

Instructions: Instruct Sequence 7—Stand for Examination with the handlers 3' in front while the Instructor/Assistant goes over the dogs. Handlers return around behind, pause, praise, replace leashes and release on your command.

Repetitions: One repetition of Sequence 6 and one of Sequence 7.

Hints for Traffic Control: A circle facing center.

*(6) AUTOMATIC SIT:

Review: Without voice command. Left hand grasps the leash and checks straight up. Remind handlers to start and stop briskly.

Repetitions: Repeat 5 times.

Hints for Traffic Control: A counterclockwise circle.

(7) HEEL FREE:

Review: With leashes in Slip Release position, heeling in a large circle, giving a Pay Attention Check before releasing.

Repetitions: Twice.

Hints for Traffic Control: A counterclockwise circle.

*(8) HAND SIGNALS:

Review: With command and signal, handlers erect 3' in front, stepping toward the dog to check for the Down and slap the leash for the Sit.

Instructions: Instruct signal *only* from 3'. Have the handlers give the signal with no voice command. For the Sit, the handler will continue to slap the leash as he gives the signal. For the Down, if the dog does not respond, the handler steps in to check.

Repetitions: One of review sequence and two with signal only.

Watch for: Double signals or double commands. Some handlers will give the hand signal without slapping the leash, and when the dog doesn't respond, will signal again, this time slapping the leash. This teaches the dog the double signal just as saying "sit, sit" teaches him a double command. Have the handler slap the leash the *first time* he gives the signal.

Some handlers will give a double command as well for the Down. If the dog does not respond to the first signal, they will say "down" as they step in to check. There is no second command or signal. If the dog does not respond to the signal the first time it is given, he is checked *without* a second command.

Hints for Traffic Control: One straight line leaving sufficient room for the Instructor/Assistants to observe from both sides.

*(9) DOWN ON COMMAND & DOWN STAY:

Review: Down on Command. The handler's left hand is in the collar prepared to reinforce before giving the command.
Review Down Stay with the handlers 6' in front for 2 minutes.

Instructions: Have handlers return to their dogs, drop their leashes and go 6' in front for 1 minute.

Repetitions: Two Down on Command; one 6' Down Stay on leash for 2 minutes; one 6' Down Stay for 1 minute with leashes dropped.

Hints for Traffic Control: A straight line on the opposite side of the training area to where the Sit Stay was done.

*(10) RECALL HAND SIGNAL:

Review: Hand signal with leash check, if necessary. The handler guides the dog into a sit in front with his hands under the dog's chin.

Repetitions: Three times.

Hints for Traffic Control: One straight line moving across the training area with each repetition.

(11) RECALL—Sequence 4:

Instructions: Done individually.

Demonstration: Demonstrate the positions of the dog and handler.

Articulation: "Heel your dog out of the line-up and sit him perpendicular to the group. Remove your leash, pocket it, leave your dog on a Sit Stay, go 15' away, turn and face your dog. Count to five, crouch, count to five, smile and call '(Name), come!' As your dog arrives, stand up and guide him into a sit in front with your hands under his chin. Remove your hands, praise, count to five, say 'stay' and pivot back to heel position. Pause, praise, put your leash back on and release. Heel your dog to the end of the line."

Repetitions: Each handler does this once. If a dog takes off, it is repeated using the long line (see Watch for).

Watch for: Handlers reaching out toward the dog before he arrives or leaning forward as they stand up. Both these postures have the effect of stopping the dog in his tracks or causing him to veer away from the handler. This is not, however, the same as a bolting dog.

298

Recall perpendicular to group.

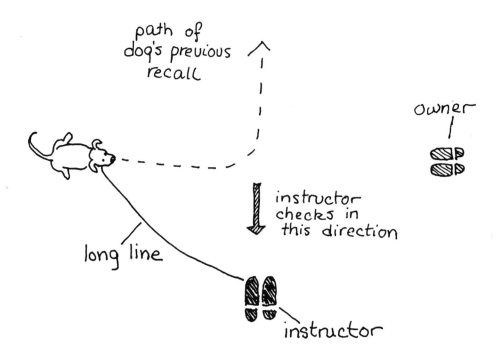

Reinforcing the Come command for the dog that bolts.

The Instructor uses the long line for the dog who still bolts. After the dog takes off, the Instructor/Assistant brings him to the handler who praises him, replaces his leash on the dog and takes him back to the starting point. Before the leash is removed, the long line is attached to the dog, coming out from under the dog's chin in front of him. The handler again leaves the dog. The Instructor stands opposite the point where the dog first bolted. The handler is instructed to call his dog. At the exact spot where the dog previously bolted, the Instructor will emphatically check him, and the handler calls him again. When the dog arrives, he is enthusiastically praised, the leash is put back on and the exercise is repeated.

After three repetitions, with the Instructor checking the dog each time, the long line is removed and the dog is called again. For all but the chronic

If the dog runs to the owner
and then bolts past...

the instructor stands behind the dog
and checks as the dog heads past....

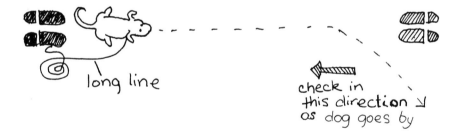

long line

check in
this direction ↘
as dog goes by

Reinforcing the Come command for the dog that shoots past the handler.

runaway, this will be sufficient to teach the dog that it is much more advantageous to come when called than to run the other way. For the chronic runaway, further analysis of the situation and behavior modification may be required. Refer to Chapter 11, Analyzing Problems, and Chapter 12, Behavior Problems.

Hints for Traffic Control: The class is lined up along one side of the training area. Starting at one end of the line, each handler brings his dog out and sits him. After the Recall, he heels his dog to the end of the line.

(12) EVALUATIONS:

If time allows, and if the Instructor desires to do so, have the class fill out evaluation forms at this time.

This is a good time to privately discuss repeating the course for those who, as a resut of their class work the last few weeks, are not going to graduate. Do so quietly.

(13) REMINDERS:

Talk about further training. Level 2 teaches the handlers greater control in situations where the dog is distracted. More emphasis is placed on off leash work and further development of the dog's responses to commands.

Inform the class about AKC competition. Describe the Novice routine and what it entails. Stress that with only one exception, their dogs are performing all the requisite exercises.

Demonstrate the Novice routine with a trained dog, including the Finish as an example of what the handlers will learn in Level 2.

Talk about graduation next week. Friends and family are invited to share the celebration. Refreshments will be provided (or invite them to contribute refreshments if you so desire). The order of business will be a short class during which they will show off what they have learned for the past 8 weeks, as a group. This will be followed by the awarding of diplomas and a party.

(14) HOMEWORK SHEETS & NAME TAGS.

SAMPLE INSTRUCTOR OUTLINE

WEEK 4

(1) NAME TAGS & CALL ROLL.

(2) HEEL ON LEASH: **Review** Leash Over Shoulder with Changes of Pace & About Turn. **Instruct** circles in motion.

(3) SIT STAY—Seq. 3: **Review** Seq. 2 (L hand holds leash at belt buckle, R hand reinforces). **Review** return. **Instruct** test. Leash on dead ring, rings under muzzle. 3′ away, pressure/release. Return leash to live ring.

(4) SIT FOR EXAMINATION: **Instruct** rings at back of neck, handlers directly in front, leash in L hand directly over dog's head ready to reinforce as instructor/assistant goes over dogs.

(5) TURNS IN PLACE: **Review** Seq. 2 (RT—command then step; AT— 1 step, turn, 1 step).

(6) DOWN STAY: **Review**—place dogs down. Go 3′ in front for 2 minutes.

(7) TURNS: **Object**—"To teach dog to remain at heel when you turn." **Place** chairs at 4 corners. **Instruct** Control Position. LT—slow down & draw dog back, come out normal. RT—maintain normal pace & encourage dog to remain at heel.

(8) STAND—Seq. 4: **Review** Seq. 3 (Leashes off, remain at dog's side). **Instruct** Seq. 4—Pivot in front, count 10 & pivot back again. Pause, praise, replace leashes & release.

(9) AUTOMATIC SIT—Seq. 3: **Review** Seq. 2 (Plant L foot, R hand on leash snap, L hand tucks). **Instruct** Seq. 3—Rings at top of neck, grasp leash snap with L hand & check straight up keeping L arm parallel with ground and in line with dog's spine. If not straight, take 1 step forward & sit as with Seq. 2.

(10) HEEL FREE: **Review** circle left & halt. **Instruct** from stationary circle left, release, complete circle and continue in a straight line for 5 paces. Sit Seq. 1.

(11) SIT & DOWN: Review Seq. 3 (from in front with OA).

(12) HAND SIGNALS: Object—"To teach dog to respond to hand signals." **Instruct**—For down—on knee in front of dog, leash folded in L hand, palm down, 2 fingers in collar. With "down" raise R arm & apply pressure back & down. Watch body posture. For sit—stand in front of dog, leash in L hand against R hip. Signal, slap toward dog, return hand to side. Pause 10 seconds between repetitions.

(13) RECALL—Seq. 2: Instruct—Take out of line, leave, count 5, kneel, count 5, smile, call, while praising tuck into sit facing handler, with R hand on chest, L hand tucks (no "sit" command). Praise, replace leash.

(14) LONG SIT & DOWN (Homework): 10 min. Sit & 30 min. Down, handler moving around room (not out of sight), 3X each, alternate days.

(15) REMINDERS: Alternate Recalls & Sit Stays. Again, 3X train in new locations without distractions.

(16) PREVIEW: "Next week your dog will learn to respond to 'come' around distractions."

(17) NAME TAGS & HOMEWORK SHEETS.

HOMEWORK SHEETS

WEEK 1

SIT: Kneel next to dog. Place right hand on dog's chest, left hand on withers. With "sit," stroke down dog's back, over tail and tuck forward behind knees (stifles), until dog sits. Praise with "GOOD" while holding dog in position. Do not pet at this time.

DOWN: Sit dog at your left side. Place your left arm across dog's back, and left hand behind his left foreleg. Place your right hand behind his right foreleg. With hands open, thumbs out, say "down" and **lift** and **lower** dog down. Praise with "GOOD." Do not pet at this time.

STAND: Sit dog and remove leash. Place 2 fingers of right hand in collar under dog's chin. Pull forward and parallel with the ground with right hand, as you say "stand." Block rear legs with the back of your left hand. Praise with "GOOD . . . stand." Practice for 1 minute, keeping the dog standing still.

HEELING: Sit your dog at heel and throw the leash over your right shoulder. With "(Name), heel" in a pleasant voice, start walking at a brisk pace in a straight line. If your dog begins to leave heel position, bring him back with your left hand on the leash and immediately let go of the leash. Praise. When the dog is in heel position, do not touch the leash. After 10 paces, stop and sit dog (as above). Practice until you can heel for 10 paces without having to bring the dog back.

ABOUT TURN: While heeling, call dog's name, turn away from the dog (to the right), face in the opposite direction and continue walking at a brisk pace. Keep moving and keep the dog at heel position throughout your turn.

AUTOMATIC SIT: Stop on your left foot slightly in front of your right, bend your knees and sit your dog.

RIGHT TURN IN PLACE: Sit dog in heel position. With leash in Control Position, both hands in front of your legs, place your right foot at a 90 degree angle, one large step to the right. With "(Name), heel" bring left foot together with right and sit dog as above. Praise but do not pet. Repeat 5 times per session.

ABOUT TURN IN PLACE: Sit dog in heel position. With leash in Control Position, both hands in front of your legs, say "(Name), heel" and take two steps straight forward, turn in place 180 degrees away from your dog, and take two steps straight forward again. Sit dog as above. Praise but do not pet. Repeat 5 times per session.

LONG DOWN: Sit on the floor beside your dog and place him down. Every time he gets up, replace him down with "down." If he **begins** to get up, apply pressure to the withers with "down." Keep your hands off the dog when he is down and do not pet him during this exercise. Remain patient and calm throughout. At the end of the 30 minutes, release him with "OK!" Repeat 3 times this week.

GENERAL INSTRUCTIONS: It is recommended that you get some information about your particular breed of dog. This may be obtained from your breeder or from books. Find out what special characteristics apply to your breed, and how you can make use of these in training. If your dog is a mixed breed, determine what breeds he is a mixture of and find out this same information about those breeds.

Use your dog's training collar only for training sessions and when you need control. When you are not training, it is safer to keep a buckle collar on your dog. Two short periods of training are better for your dog than one long one. Call your instructor or assistants if you have any questions.

HOW TO PUT ON THE TRAINING COLLAR: The collar consists of a **loose ring,** a **stationary ring** and a **clasp.**

1. Facing your dog, hold both rings of the collar in your right hand and the clasp in your left.

2. Place the collar under the dog's neck, and bring the ends up to the top of the dog's neck.

3. Attach the clasp to the **loose** ring. Place the smooth side of the clasp next to the dog's skin so that the hook part of the clasp will not hurt your dog.

4. The leash is attached to the **stationary** ring of the collar.

DO NOT LEAVE THE TRAINING COLLAR ON YOUR DOG WHEN HE IS NOT BEING TRAINED.

HOW TO HOLD THE LEASH—CONTROL POSITION:

1. Put your right thumb through the loop of the leash.

2. Fold the excess leash back and forth, accordion style, into your right hand. Be sure the part of the leash attached to the dog's collar comes out from under your little finger. Tighten your right hand into a fist around the leash.

3. Place your right hand against the front of your right leg, palm toward your leg.

4. With your left hand, grasp the leash in front of your left leg, palm facing down.

5. Keep both hands below your waist at all times, and keep your elbows straight and close to your sides.

6. Keep the leash short; when the dog is in heel position there is no tension on the leash.

From now on this will be referred to as **CONTROL POSITION.**

HEEL POSITION: You and your dog are in **heel position** when the dog is at your left side, facing the same direction you are facing. Whether the dog is sitting, standing, lying down or moving next to you, he is in proper heel position when the area from his head to his shoulder is in line with your left hip.

SLIP RELEASE:

1. Thread the loop of the leash under the collar, toward the tail, with the stitched portion facing down so it doesn't get caught under the collar.

2. Slip the loop over your left thumb and grasp the leash lightly with the fingers of your left hand.

3. Hold the clasp in your right hand and accordion fold the excess leash into your right hand.

4. With hands in Control Position, keep your left hand **ABSO-LUTELY MOTIONLESS** as you drop the leash off the thumb and slip it

through the fingers of your left hand. Fold the entire leash neatly into your right hand.

5. Practice this several times a day without your dog, using the back of a chair.

YOUR INSTRUCTOR IS: **ASSISTANTS:**

WEEK 2

REVIEW: If and when you have difficulty with any sequence of an exercise, review the previous sequences.

SIT ON COMMAND: Object of attraction held in your right hand. Motion above and slightly behind the dog's head with "sit." Tuck into sit if necessary. Praise. Repeat 5 times.

DOWN ON COMMAND: Sit dog, place left hand on withers, hold object in right hand. Lower hand quickly as you say "down." Place down if necessary. Praise and give object to dog. Repeat 5 times with Sit on Command. To take object from dog, say "give," remove object and praise.

STAND: Remove leash, stand dog and remain in position 2 minutes. Keep right hand in collar, but try not to touch him with left hand except as necessary to reposition with "stand." Work up to standing up, keeping your right hand in the collar under his chin.

RETRIEVE BALL: Leash on dead ring of collar, you and dog 5 feet away from wall, get him interested in ball, roll toward wall with "take it." Praise when he picks ball up, coax him back to you, say "give," remove ball & praise. Repeat 3X.

HEEL ON LEASH: Call "(Name), heel" **before** starting to walk. Walk in a straight line. Practice until you can walk 15 paces and make 2 about turns without having to touch the leash with your left hand.

CIRCLES RIGHT & LEFT: Leash in Control Position. Say "(Name), heel" and circle 4' in diameter to the **left** at a *slow* pace. Stop and sit your dog. Then circle to the **right** at a *trot*, stop and sit your dog. Keep hands in front of your legs throughout. Repeat 3 circles to the right and 3 to the left.

TURNS IN PLACE: Seq. 2. **Right Turns** say "(Name), heel" then step 1/4 turn to the right. **About Turn** say "(Name), heel" then take 1 step forward, turn, take 1 step forward and sit dog. Praise. Repeat 5X each.

AUTOMATIC SIT IN MOTION: Rings between ears. Stop on your left foot, slightly in front of your right. Grasp leash snap in right hand and check straight up with "sit." Tuck into a sit with left hand. Praise. Say "(Name), heel" each time you start to walk. Repeat 5 times.

SIT STAY: Leash folded in your left hand, rings between the ears, left hand held above dog's head. Give hand signal and say "stay." Pivot in front for 10 seconds. Pivot back, release pressure, pause, praise and release with "OK!" Check straight up and repeat "stay" if your dog **thinks** about moving. Work up to a 30 second Sit Stay. After 3 days of success at 30 seconds, release the tension above dog's head, but remain standing directly in front.

SLIP RELEASE: Practice the leash handling for this exercise. Instructions are on last week's homework sheet.

LONG SIT: (10 minutes) Sit in a chair next to your dog. Keep him sitting there 10 minutes. Release at end. Repeat 3 times this week.

LONG DOWN: This week sit in a chair and place your dog down. Repeat 3 times for 30 minutes each. Do not pet during this exercise. Alternate days with the Long Sit.

REMINDER: PRACTICE AT HOME IS WHAT BRINGS SUCCESS. CLASS IS TO TEACH *YOU* WHAT TO TEACH YOUR DOG AT HOME.

WEEK 3

GENERAL INSTRUCTIONS: Three times this week train in different locations, free from distractions. Review previous sheets if confused.

HEEL ON LEASH: Practice until you can heel 20 paces, do an about turn and go another 20 paces without having to touch the leash.

CHANGES OF PACE: Gradually change pace from normal to slow, walk slowly for 10 steps and return to normal pace. Gradually change pace from normal to a trot, trot for 10 steps, then return to normal pace. Goal: Moving at the different paces without touching the leash.

CIRCLES: Practice 3 of each circle each training session.

SIT STAY: Seq. 2. Rings under muzzle. Stand 3' in front of dog, leash in left hand against belt buckle, right hand poised under leash. Slap leash with right hand at first sign of dog's **thinking** about moving. Goal: A 1-minute Sit Stay without slapping the leash.

RETURN AROUND BEHIND ON STAY: Loop over right thumb, keep left hand in front of dog as you return around behind to heel position, pause, praise and release.

SIT FOR EXAMINATION: Have a friend or relative run a hand down your dog's back while he is on a Sit Stay at your side.

TURNS IN PLACE: Seq. 2. **Right Turn:** Say "(Name), heel" then step 1/4 turn to the right. **About Turn:** Say "(Name), heel" then take 1 step forward, turn, take 1 step forward and sit dog. Praise. Repeat 5X each.

STAND STAY: Leash off, stand dog with "stand," stand erect, say "stay" and remain at heel. Begin with 30 seconds and work up to a 3-minute Stand Stay at your dog's side.

SIT & DOWN: Seq. 3. Kneel in front of dog, leash folded in left hand, 2 fingers in collar. Object in right hand, say "down," motion and **apply pressure** to help dog down. Praise. To sit dog, motion upward over head with object, say "sit" and help dog into sit. Praise. Repeat 3X.

DOWN STAY: Begin with a 1-minute Down Stay and work up to 3 minutes.

AUTOMATIC SIT: Practice 5 Automatic Sits in motion each session.

HEEL FREE: Position leash for Slip Release. Give command "(Name), heel" and begin to circle left. Release leash. Complete circle and sit dog with "sit," hand on chest. Repeat 3 times per session.

RECALL: Leave dog, go 15', turn, count to 5, kneel, sit on your heels, count to 5, place palms up on legs, smile and call "(Name), come." Praise and pet for 1 minute. Make this exercise **very pleasant and fun for you and your dog.**

LONG SIT: Seq. 2. Sit across the room from your dog for 10 minutes. 3X.

LONG DOWN: Seq. 3. Sit across the room from your dog for 30 minutes. 3X. Alternate days with Long Sit.

WEEK 4

GENERAL INSTRUCTIONS: Again, 3 times this week train in different locations, free from distractions. Begin practice with a review of the steps your dog knows before introducing new steps. **Be patient with all work—old and new.**

HEEL ON LEASH: Begin each session with a 2-minute heeling drill including **Changes of Pace** (fast & slow) and **Circles Right & Left** (3 of each).

RIGHT & LEFT TURNS IN MOTION: Practice going around trees or other objects making right and left turns. Hold dog back for the left turn, and encourage him to keep up with you on the right. Practice 3 of each per session.

SIT STAY WITH TEST & SIT STAY: Leash on dead ring, from 3' in front, apply pressure until dog physically resists. Be prepared to reinforce with right hand under leash. Test 3 times for 5 to 10 seconds each. From 3' in front of your dog, increase to a 2-minute Sit Stay.

TURNS IN PLACE: Do 4 Right and 4 About Turns in place. Sit dog by checking straight up with left hand above his head. Keep your left arm parallel with the ground and in line with dog's spine. Say "sit" and praise.

SIT FOR EXAMINATION: Seq. 2. Leave dog on Sit Stay. Have a friend or relative go over your dog while you are 3' in front.

SIT & DOWN: Sequences 2 & 3. Review with object of attraction twice by dog's side, then twice in front of dog.

DOWN HAND SIGNAL: Kneel in front of dog, leash folded in left hand, 2 fingers of left hand in collar. Give hand signal and command "down" as you push back and down. Praise. Repeat 4X.

SIT HAND SIGNAL: Stand in front of dog, leash in left hand placed against right hip. Slap leash with right hand toward dog as you give signal and "sit." Praise. Repeat 4X with Down Signal.

DOWN STAY: From 3' in front of dog, work up to 3 minutes.

AUTOMATIC SIT: Seq. 2. Rings of collar between dog's ears. When you halt, check straight up with left hand holding leash snap. Keep left arm parallel with the ground and in line with dog's spine. Repeat 5X.

HEEL FREE: Review as last week. Then position leash for slip release, enter circle left, release, complete circle and continue walking in a straight line for 5 steps. Stop and sit dog. Repeat 3X.

STAND STAY: Seq. 2. Stand dog and leave on Stay. Step directly in front and remain there 30 seconds. Pivot back, pause, praise and release.

RECALL: Seq. 2. Leave dog, pause for count of 5, kneel for count of 5, hands on tighs, smile & call dog. When he arrives, continue praising while you tuck him into sit. Praise 1 minute. Repeat 3X.

LONG SIT & DOWN: This week move around the room during the 10 min. Sit and the 30 min. Down. Do each 3 times. Do not go out of sight.

GENERAL INSTRUCTIONS: This week take several excursions to a park or shopping center parking lot. Your dog should now pay attention to you around distractions.

HEEL ON LEASH: 2-minute heeling drill with Changes of Pace and Circles (2 of each).

HEEL HAND SIGNAL: Left hand, palm open from left to right as you say "heel."

SIT STAY & SIT STAY TEST: Test 2X each session from 3′ in front prior to doing Sit Stay. Then go 6′ in front for Sit Stay. This week work up to 2 min.

TURNS IN PLACE: Practice 3 Right, 3 About and 3 Left Turns in place per session. For the Left Turn, place left foot in front of dog's feet, say "(Name), heel" and take a large step with your right foot beyond your left.

STAND STAY: Stand dog and leave on Stay. Go 3′ in front, turn & face him. After 10 seconds, step back, pause, praise and release. Work up to 1 minute.

STAND FOR EXAMINATION: Leave your dog on Stand Stay, pivot back after 10 seconds, then examine your dog as though you were looking for something. Then pause, praise and release.

DOWN HAND SIGNAL: Seq. 2. Review right in front of dog. Then move 3′ away, and kneel. Give signal and command, reach in with left hand, grasp leash snap & check straight downward. Praise. Repeat 4X with Sit Hand Signal.

SIT HAND SIGNAL: Seq. 2. Stand erect 3′ in front of dog, leash in left hand against right hip. As you give command and signal, slap leash with your right hand and take 1 step toward dog with right foot. Then return right foot to original place. Repeat 4X with Down.

DOWN ON COMMAND & DOWN STAY: Fold leash in left hand and place 2 fingers of left hand in dog's collar. Command "down" **then** help with pressure as necessary. Praise. Leave on Stay and go 6′ away. Begin with 1 minute and work up to 3 minutes. Return around behind, pause, praise & release.

AUTOMATIC SIT: Review with rings of collar between ears, checking straight up with left hand as you halt and say "sit." Repeat 5X.

HEEL FREE: Position for slip release. Enter the circle left, release leash, complete circle and walk in a straight line for 10 steps before you stop and sit your dog.

SIT IN FRONT: Stand your dog and step directly in front. Say "come" and motion toward you and up with the object of attraction. If he does not sit, kneel, place your right hand on his chest and tuck him into a sit with your left hand. Praise and reward. Pivot back, re-stand him and repeat 5X.

RECALL: Allow dog to become interested in something. As he walks away from you, call "(Name), come!" and guide him toward you with the leash. Crouch and enthusiastically praise and pet when he gets to you. Practice in different areas with different distractions.

SAFETY: Teach your dog to wait for you to go through doorways first. Use verbal reprimand or the door to prevent your dog's rushing through. Practice going through various doorways.

WEEK 6

GENERAL INSTRUCTIONS: This is **Patience Week.** Be patient if your dog seems to have forgotten everything. Take him to 3 shopping centers or parks.

HEEL ON LEASH: 2-minute drill including Changes of Pace, Circles and the Heeling Hand Signal. Use voice command with & without the signal.

SIT STAY TEST & SIT STAY: Review test once before doing Sit Stay. Then go 6' in front of dog and increase time of stay. Work up to a 3-minute Sit Stay. Work on 3 different surfaces and in different areas.

TURNS IN PLACE: Review 3 Right, 3 About and 3 Left Turns in place per session.

STAND STAY: Review the Stand Stay progressions on reverse side.

STAND FOR EXAMINATION: Stand your dog, step directly in front of him and have a helper go over him. Return, pause, praise and release.

RIGHT, LEFT & ABOUT TURNS: Do 3 of each turn in motion per session, keeping your body facing straight ahead. Have a helper call commands to you.

DOWN HAND SIGNAL: Stand erect 3' in front of your dog. Give command/signal and step toward dog with right foot. Grasp the leash snap with left hand and check straight downward. Step back with right foot. Praise. Repeat 4X with Sit Signal, pausing for a count of 10.

SIT HAND SIGNAL: 3′ in front of dog, give signal/command as you slap leash and step toward dog with right foot. Return right foot. Repeat 4X.

DOWN ON COMMAND: Have your left hand in position **before** giving command. Left hand helps your dog if he fails to respond to your voice command. Repeat 3X.

DOWN STAY: From 6′ in front, work up to 1 minute on different surfaces.

AUTOMATIC SIT: Practice 5 per session. If dog *begins* to sit crooked, say "heel," take one step and make him sit straight.

HEEL FREE: Practice in a straight line or large circle. Check prior to releasing dog. Keep pace constant. Heel 20 paces off leash, stop & sit dog.

RECALL HAND SIGNAL & SIT IN FRONT: Hold leash in left hand at your side. Give signal with right hand as you call dog. Guide with leash if necessary. Guide into straight sit by motioning toward you and upward with both hands.

RECALL: Allow dog to become interested in something. As he walks away from you, call "(Name), come!" If he does not respond, emphatically check leash toward you. Crouch and enthusiastically praise and pet when he gets to you. Practice in different areas with different distractions.

REMINDERS: Use the Long Sit & Long Down at home when you have guests.

SAFETY: Practice having dog wait going up and down stairs.

STAND STAY REVIEW: Each day practice the previous day's procedures, in order, one time. Then practice the new procedure five times. If you encounter any difficulty on any day, do not proceed to the next day's exercise until you have successfully accomplished what you are working on. Remove the leash before beginning this exercise.

Praise with your voice, keep your hands off your dog as much as possible. Keep your dog in a Stand as you praise. Release with much enthusiasm.

DAY 1: Stand your dog. Remain at his side. Keep him standing perfectly still for 2 minutes, pause, praise and release.

DAY 2: Review Day 1, then stand your dog, command "stay," pivot in front, count to ten and pivot back. Pause, praise, release.

DAY 3: Review Days 1 & 2, then stand your dog, command "stay," pivot in front, count to 20, pivot back to your dog, pause, praise, release.

DAY 4:   Review Days 1, 2, & 3, then stand your dog, command "stay," go 3 feet in front of your dog, turn and face him. Count to 30, then step back to his side, pause, praise, release.

DAY 5:   Review previous days, then stand your dog and command "stay." Go 6 feet in front of your dog, turn and face him. Count to 30 and **return around behind** your dog, pause, praise, release.

DAY 6:   Review previous days, then stand your dog and command "stay." Go 6 feet in front of your dog and face him. Count to 60 and return around to heel position, pause, praise, release.

WEEK 7

HEEL ON LEASH: 2-minute drill including Changes of Pace, Circles and the Heel Hand Signal. Use voice command with and without the signal, then use the hand signal with no voice command.

SIT STAY TEST & SIT STAY: For the test, from 3' in front apply pressure for 15 seconds with your dog visibly resisting. Then practice a 1-minute Sit Stay from 6' in front. Return to your dog, pause, drop leash by his side, repeat "stay" and go 6' in front for 10 seconds. Work up to a 1-minute Sit Stay with leash dropped.

TURNS IN PLACE: Review 3 of each turn per session. For the Left Turn, take a smaller step with your right foot.

STAND FOR EXAMINATION: Stand your dog, go 3' in front and have a helper go over him. Return, pause, praise and release.

STAND STAY: Practice a 1-minute Stand Stay 6' in front. Return around behind.

DOWN HAND SIGNAL: From 3' in front, review signal/command. Then try signal only. If he fails to respond, **step in** and check as last week. Repeat 4 times pausing for count of 10 before giving Sit Hand Signal.

SIT HAND SIGNAL: Review from 3' in front. Then try without voice command, slapping the leash.

DOWN & DOWN STAY: Down your dog by voice command only, then leave him and go 6' in front for 1 minute. Return around behind, drop your leash, say "stay" and go 6' in front again. Remain in front for 2 minutes before returning.

AUTOMATIC SIT: Practice 3 Automatic Sits with the check and "sit" command, then do 2 with no voice command, just checking upward.

HEEL FREE: Incorporate 1 About Turn off leash. Call dog's name before turning.

RECALL HAND SIGNAL & SIT IN FRONT: Review with command and signal. If dog fails to respond, check toward you with left hand. Motion into a straight sit in front. Repeat 4X.

RECALL: Seq. 4. Leave dog, pause for count of 5, crouch for count of 5, hands on thighs, call dog. Stand erect so you are standing when he arrives. Guide him into a sit in front with both hands under his chin. Praise. Pause for count of 5, say "stay" and pivot back to heel.

GENERAL INFORMATION: Now is the time to think about further training for your dog. We offer Advanced Classes for greater control of your dog under more difficult conditions and for those who think they might be interested in obedience competition. You are always welcome to observe any of our classes. Next week is graduation. You are invited to bring family and friends to celebrate with you.

Appendix II

INSTRUCTING MODEL—LEVEL 2

INTRODUCTION

Level 2 is for individuals who have graduated from Level 1 and who are interested in more control and perhaps AKC titles. Having graduated from Level 1 presumes that the dog will walk on a loose leash, stay when told and come when called.

To graduate from Level 2, the dog must be able to heel with the "Umbilical Cord" including one About Turn, a Fast and a Slow without having to reinforce; do a Sit, Stand and Down Stay off leash; and do a Recall with 2nd Degree Distraction.

In Level 2, unless otherwise specified, all exercises start with the leash in Control Position (with the hands held correctly and the dog at heel position, there is no more than 1/2″ of slack).

Explain that "reinforce" can be inducive (food or praise for the desired response), or compulsive (check).

WEEKLY SESSIONS

WEEK 1

(1) HEEL ON LEASH:

Object: "To teach you to concentrate on your dog while heeling."

Instructions: Passive use of leash—the dog checks himself when he leaves heel position (will work only with snap-around or pinch collar). Review with Changes of Pace, About Turns and Circles. Minimum of two minutes and not more than five.

Articulation: "While heeling, pay attention to your dog. Concentrate! Look at him by turning your head, but not your shoulder. Keep your hands in Control Position at all times. Don't worry about the dog, if he strays from heel position, he will check himself."

Watch For: Handlers maintaining Control Position with passive use of leash and keeping their shoulders straight.

(2) SIT STAY:

Object: "To teach your dogs the Sit Stay off leash."

Instructions: Review Sit Stay Test from 3' in front with leashes on the dead ring. Review Sit Stay on leash with handlers 6' in front of dogs for 1 minute. Handlers return to their dogs. Instruct handlers to remove leashes, place them behind the dogs and go 6' in front for 10 seconds. Handlers return, pause, praise, put leashes back on and release on the instructor's command. Dogs must maintain position while being praised and the leash is being put on. If dog breaks, reinforce stay by checking dog back into position with "stay."

Articulation: ". . . when I say 'exercise finished,' praise your dog and put the leash back on. Your dog must remain in position while being praised. When I say 'release,' release your dogs." This is the articulation for every stay exercise from now on.

Watch for: When a dog is off leash and breaks a stay, have the handler put him back from the *front* so the dog can distinguish between starting the exercise and an undesired response. The handler places his hands, palms up, in the collar at either side of the dog's neck, *facing the dog,* and emphatically re-places the dog in position with "stay."

(3) TURNS IN PLACE:

Instructions: Review Sequence 2 of the Right, Left and About Turns in Place (for the Right and About Turns, one step; for the Left Turn, place left foot in front of dog's feet, and take a small step with the right, closing with the left).

(4) DOWN & DOWN STAY:

Object: "To teach your dog the Down Stay off leash."

Instructions: Review Down on voice command (two fingers of the left hand in the collar, reinforcing, if necessary). Review Down Stay on leash

317

with handlers 6' in front for two minutes. Handlers return to dogs. Instruct handlers to remove the leashes, place them behind their dogs and go 6' in front for 30 seconds. If dog breaks, reinforce by checking straight down with "stay." Return to dogs, pause, praise, replace leashes and release on the instructor's command. Dogs must maintain position while being praised and the leash is being put back on.

(5) TURNS:

Instructions: Review. Have handlers count off in 2's. On instructor's command, 1's heel across circle while 2's continue heeling, then vice versa. Then instructor commands "everybody (right/left) turn."

(6) STAND:

Instructions: Review Stand in circle, handlers 6' in front with instructor/ assistant examining dogs. (The Stand is done off leash and the leash is pocketed by the handler.)

(7) AUTOMATIC SIT:

Instructions: Review three times with handlers checking dogs. Then do one Automatic Sit with leash over shoulder and no check to evaluate progress. Emphasize stopping briskly and checking emphatically.

Watch For: Observe handlers' body posture and the direction of the check (straight up) with left hand.

(8) ATTENTION:

Object: "To teach your dog to pay attention."

Instructions: Handlers and dogs in a circle, dogs on the inside at heel. Handlers look at their dogs, call the dog's name, then release and run forward five steps. Then have handlers call their dogs, and the instructor silently counts to two before giving release command. Repeat to the count of five before releasing.

Demonstration

Articulation: "On my command, 'name of dog,' say your dog's name, then release and run forward five steps, stop and sit your dog at heel. Let's do it again, only this time wait until I tell you to release your dogs. Sit your dog, 'Name of dog,' . . ."

318

(9) FRONT—Sequence 3a:

Object: "To teach your dog to sit straight in front of you when you call him."

Instructions: Instruct Sequence 3a.

Demonstration

Articulation: "With the leash in Control Position, when I say, 'call your dogs,' command '(Name), come,' take two steps forward, extend your arms in front to guide the dog around, take two steps back and sit your dog by motioning upward with both hands together to visually guide the dog into a sit directly in front. Hands are used to condition the dog to a **reference point** (face, center of chest, belt buckle). If the dog does not sit straight, reposition him by putting the right hand through the collar, palm up under the dog's chin, leave the left leg where it is, bring the right leg straight back, and place him into position with pressure on the collar, tuck him into a sit with the left hand, close with the left foot, let go, stand up and praise the dog."

Demonstration

Watch for: **Two** steps forward and not just one. Command/motion sequence—handler gives command then moves.

(10) HAND SIGNALS:

Instructions: For Sit & Down, review from 3' in front, handlers standing erect, on leash, with command and signal. Then review signal without voice command. For Recall have handlers go 6' in front and call dogs with signal and command (left hand checks, if necessary). Handlers guide dogs into a straight sit in front with hands under chin.

(11) RECALL:

Instructions: Review Recall on Leash with distraction (instructor/assistant with food) and with particular emphasis on prompt response. Handler crouches, pets and praises dog when he arrives.

Watch for: Timing of command/check sequence—give the dog a chance to respond and only check if he does not.

(12) REMINDERS:

Remind handlers to continue doing Long Downs and Long Sits on alternate days, two of each per week. These can be incorporated into daily

319

The Sit in Front . . .

on leash.

The Sit in Front . . .

off leash.

routines, for instance while watching TV or during meals. Also remind handlers to continue on Safety exercise through doorways and on stairs. Instruct handlers to introduce all new material in an area free from distractions and review familiar material in areas with distractions. Admonish handlers to be consistent and to give a command only when they are in a position to reinforce it, if necessary. Explain that "reinforce" can be positive (food or praise for the desired response), or negative (check to get the desired response).

WEEK 2

(1) HEEL ON LEASH:

Object: "To teach you how to reinforce your dog for looking at you."

Instructions: Instruct handlers to smile and praise everytime their dog looks at them while heeling. Incorporate Changes of Pace, Circles and About Turns. In preparation for the Figure 8, spend time on Circles. Remind handlers to concentrate on their dogs. Minimum of five minutes but not more than 10.

Articulation: ". . . when your dog looks at you, smile and praise."

Watch for: Timing of praise so that handlers do not praise at the moment the dog looks away.

(2) SIT STAY:

Instructions: Review Sit Stay Test with emphasis on more pressure by the handler and increased resistance by the dog. Instruct a Sit Stay off leash with handlers 10′ in front for 30 seconds. Then have handlers stand two steps closer (6′ in front of dogs) for one additional minute. Return, pause, praise, put leashes back on and release.

(3) TURNS IN PLACE:

Instructions: Review Sequence 2 of the Right, Left and About Turns. Instruct Sequence 3 of each turn. For the Right and About Turns, handlers turn in place. For the Left Turn, handlers command "(Name), heel," place their right foot directly in front of their left foot in a "T", close with the left and guide the dog back into heel position with backward pressure of the left hand on the leash snap.

Demonstration

Watch For: On the Left Turn, many handlers will try to guide the dog back by either bringing their left hand up, or twisting their left wrist, or bringing the dog forward. In order to go to heel, however, the dog must first back up, so the action of the left hand is pressure straight back.

(4) DOWN & DOWN STAY:

Object: "To teach your dog to respond to the Down command reliably."

Instructions: Review Down with fingers in collar. Instruct handlers to let out enough leash so the dog can go down. With the hands in Control Position, handlers give the Down command. Instruct handlers, if the dog fails to respond, to slide the left hand down the leash to the snap and to check the dog down, keeping the left arm straight. Instruct off leash Down Stay at 10' for 2 minutes. Return, etc.

Demonstration

Watch For: On the Down on Command, watch for visual cues by the handler such as bending over, sliding the hand down the leash, but stopping if the dog starts to go down first, giving a hand signal or pointing to the ground. Re-emphasize that the dog has to respond to the command *alone*. Watch for the command / motion sequence. The command is given, the dog has a chance to respond, then, if he fails to respond, he is checked.

(5) TURNS:

Instructions: Have the handlers count off in 2's and review heeling across a circle one group at a time. When completed, have everybody cross circle together.

(6) STAND:

Object: "To steady your dog for this exercise."

Instructions: Have handlers stand dogs and go 6' in front. Instruct handlers to take a step to the right, step back in front of their dogs, then take a step to the left and back in front of their dogs. Instruct handlers "if your dog moves, reposition him, repeat 'stay' and leave." Return, etc.

(7) AUTOMATIC SIT:

Instructions: Review three times with check (stopping briskly), then once with leash over shoulder and no check.

(8) ATTENTION:

Instructions: Instruct handlers to wait for your command to release. Instruct "Name of dog," silently count to 5 and release. Repeat two times.

Articulation: "When I say 'name of dog,' say your dog's name and wait for my command to release."

(9) HAND SIGNALS:

Instructions: Review Sit & Down from 3' in front, with voice and signal; check, if necessary. Review with signal only. For the Recall, from 6' in front, with voice and signal; left hand checks, if necessary. Guide into a straight sit in front with hands under chin.

(10) FRONT—Sequence 3b:

Instructions: Review Sequence 3a (2 steps forward, 2 steps back). Instruct Sequence 3b. Control Position, with "(Name), come," the handler takes *one* step forward, extends his arms, takes one step back and sits his dog as in Sequence 3a. If the dog is not straight, reposition as in Sequence 3a.

Demonstration

(11) RECALL:

Instructions: Review individually on leash with food as a distraction.

WEEK 3

(1) HEEL ON LEASH:

Instructions: Review heeling noting the progress in the dog's attention. Include Changes of Pace, About Turns and Circles. Minimum of two minutes but not more than five.

(2) SIT STAY:

Instructions: Review Sit Stay Test. Instruct Sit Stay off leash with handlers 15' in front for 30 seconds. Then have handlers return to their dogs, pause briefly, then go 10' in front for 2 minutes. Return, etc.

Sit in Front from heel . . .

with one step forward . . .

and back.

325

(3) TURNS IN PLACE:

Object: "The Left U-turn is the first step to teaching your dog to go to heel from in front."

Instructions: Review Sequence 3 of the Right, Left and About Turns (Right and About, turn in place; Left, place right foot in front of left, close with left). Instruct Left U-turn in place—two Left Turns in Place.

Demonstration: Demonstrate the Finish with a trained dog, then the Left U-turn.

Articulation: ". . . when I say 'Left U-turn', place your right foot directly in front of your left, close with your left, place your right foot directly in front of your left again, and close with your left. Apply backward pressure on the leash with your left hand. . . Left U-turn . . . Right, left, right, left."

Watch For: On the Left U-turn, many handlers will try to guide the dog in a circle rather than backward. To have the dog move with the handler, the left hand remains in Control Position throughout the turn, guiding the dog back with backward pressure on the leash.

(4) DOWN & DOWN STAY:

Instructions: Review response to Down command (slack in leash, give command, if dog fails to respond, check, keeping left arm straight.) Instruct Down Stay 15′ in front for 2 minutes. Return, etc.

(5) TURNS:

Object: "To teach your dog to stay at heel position when you turn."

Instructions: Place a chair in each corner of the training area and have handlers make a Motivational Left Turn around the chairs. Instruct handlers to slow down before the turn, draw back on the leash, make the turn keeping their feet together and **trot** for five steps.

Demonstration

Watch For: Body posture, facing forward and not looking back; and left hand remaining in Control Position, not drifting back. Also, some handlers will start to accelerate before having completed the turn.

(6) STAND:

Instructions: Have handlers stand their dogs facing the center of the circle

326

and go 6' in front. Then have each handler examine first the dog to his right and then the dog to his left. Have handlers go in front of their own dogs, pause, return, etc.

(7) FIGURE 8:

Object: "To teach your dog to remain in heel position when you move around objects."

Instructions: Place pairs of chairs 12' apart. Have handlers individually position themselves and their dogs centered between the chairs, two feet back. Instruct handlers to take two steps straight forward, then trot around the post to the right, continue trotting until they have crossed the center of the Figure 8, then move very slowly around the left post.

Demonstration

Watch For: Body posture facing forward and not looking back; and left hand remaining in Control Position and not drifting back. Also, many handlers will execute some geometric shape other than a Figure 8. The Figure 8 is a Circle Right joined with a Circle Left both 4' in diameter. Smaller circles or sharp turns will cause the dog to fishtail.

(8) AUTOMATIC SIT:

Instructions: Review three times with check (stopping briskly), then once with leash over shoulder and no check.

(9) ATTENTION:

Instructions: Review handlers waiting for your command to release. Instruct "Name of dog," silently count to 5 and release. Repeat two times.

(10) HAND SIGNALS:

Instructions: Review Sit & Down from 3' in front with voice and signal, check, if necessary. Review with signal only. Then have handlers go 6' in front for the Sit & Down with voice and signal. For the dog who does not respond, handler steps toward the dog to reinforce—check *straight* down for the down and check *straight* up for the sit. For the Recall, review from 6' with voice and signal and left hand check, if necessary. Guide into a straight sit in front with hands under chin.

Watch For: Many dogs will not respond to the signal/command, but will wait until the handler steps in to check before going down. When this happens, the handler's inclination is to praise the response without checking. If the dog has not responded to the signal/command, but has responded to the handler's forward movement, the dog is checked even if he is already down. In this way the dog will learn that rather than being praised for his slow response, he is checked for it. He can avoid the check by responding to the signal/command.

(11) FRONT—Sequence 3c:

Instructions: Review Sequence 3b (1 step forward, 1 step back). Instruct Sequence 3c. Conrol position, with "(Name), come," the handler extends his arms to guide the dog around to the front without moving his feet. If the dog is not straight, reposition as in Sequence 3a.

(12) RECALL:

Instructions: Review individually off leash, handlers standing erect, hands at their sides.

WEEK 4

(1) HEEL ON LEASH:

Object: "To establish smoothness and rhythm."

Instructions: Instruct handlers that heeling is teamwork between handler and dog. Stress working together and establishing rhythm (music helps). No more than 5 minutes.

Watch For: Pacing dogs, or those that move from a trot to a walk and back again and are not in rhythm. A smooth team is one in which the dog is trotting.

(2) SIT STAY:

Instructions: Review Sit Stay Test. Instruct a Sit Stay off leash with handlers 20′ away for two minutes. Instruct handlers to return, put leashes back on and go 3′ in front for distraction. First Degree Distraction— handlers jump up and down, jump to the right, jump back to the center, jump to the left, jump to center, jump toward the dog and jump back. Then return, etc.

Watch for: Handlers reinforcing *from in front* with check and "stay."

(3) TURNS IN PLACE:

Instructions: Review Sequence 3 of the Right, Left and About Turns in Place. Review the Left U-turn (two Left Turns).

328

(4) DOWN & DOWN STAY:

Instructions: Review the Down on command (slack in leash with hands in Control Position, check if dog fails to respond to command). Instruct Down Stay off leash with handlers 20′ in front for 3 minutes. Return, put leashes back on and go 3′ in front for distraction. Have handlers jump as on the Sit Stay, then return, etc.

(5) TURNS:

Instructions: With chairs at the 4 corners, review the Motivational Left Turn (slow down, make turn, come out at a trot). Instruct the Motivational Right Turn, the right turn keeping feet together, then trot for 5 steps.

Watch For: Body posture (looking back) and left hand leaving Control Position (drifting). Also, some handlers will pivot in the turn, or will accelerate before completing the turn, thereby causing the dog to fishtail.

(6) STAND:

Instructions: Review in a circle, handlers examining the dogs to their right and left. Return, etc.

(7) FIGURE 8:

Instructions: Handlers with dogs as posts, 12′ apart. Review Motivational sequence (fast on the outside, slow on the inside). Concentrate on handlers' body posture and pace. When handlers change pace watch for smooth transition so the dog can keep up.

(8) AUTOMATIC SIT:

Object: "The step-to-the-right-halt teaches your dog to find heel position."

Instructions: Review three times with handlers checking, then once with leash over shoulder and no check. Instruct step-to-the-right-halt. On the command "halt" have handlers take one step to the right, close with the left and halt. Remind handlers if dog begins to sit crooked to take a step forward and sit with check.

Demonstration

Watch For: Hands remaining in Control Position without drifting left.

(9) HEEL FREE:

Object: "To create the feeling of Off Leash Heeling with the security of the leash."

Instructions: Instruct handlers to place the leash around their waists by passing the leash behind the back, holding the loop in the left hand, threading the snap through the loop with the right hand and reattaching the snap to the collar (from now on called "Umbilical Cord"). Instruct the reinforcement: If the dog leaves heel position, reinforce by *slowly* placing two fingers of the left hand in the collar, bringing the dog back to heel position, letting go and praising. For the small dog or the longhaired dog, the handler grasps the leash snap.

Demonstration

Watch For: Slow, deliberate movements, without snatching, lunging for the dog or using the leash to bring the dog back to heel. Also, watch for timing of praise—let go, then praise.

(10) HAND SIGNALS:

Instructions: Review Sit, Down and Recall from 6' in front with command and signal. Then review signal without voice command.

(11) FRONT—Sequence 4a:

Instructions: Review Sequence 3c (0 steps forward and back). Instruct Sequence 4a. Handler removes leash, pockets it and leaves dog on Sit Stay. From 3' in front, handler takes a step to the right/left, calls, and as the dog arrives, takes two steps backward visually guiding him into a straight front with object of attraction motioning upward to reference point. If dog does not sit straight in front, handler repositions dog.

Demonstration

Watch For: Handlers moving as they call and *before* dog arrives.

(12) RECALL:

Object: "To teach your dog to ignore distractions when you call him."

Instructions: First Degree Distraction—Distractor crouches midway between the dog and handler, two feet from the dog's line of travel, facing the dog. Instruct handlers that if the dog goes to the distractor, to *walk* to the dog, grasp the collar under his chin with both hands, palms up, and, *without saying anything,* trot backwards to the spot from which the handler called, sit the dog in front, let go and praise. For those dogs that go to the distractor, repeat until they ignore him and do the exercise correctly. Instruct handlers, after the instructor says "call your dog," to pause to the count of 5 before calling.

Heeling with "Umbilical Cord."

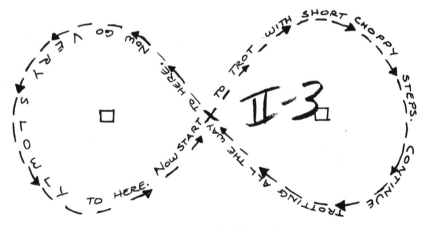

GO VERY SLOWLY

NOW GO TO HERE.

TO HERE.

NOW START.

TO THE WAY AL TROT — WITH SHORT CHOPPY STEPS. CONTINUE TROTTING ALL THE WAY TO

II-3.

Diagram for the Figure 8.

Recall with First Degree Distraction.

Dog goes to distractor . . .

handler *walks* to dog . . .

and shows him . . .

what to do.

333

Watch For: Handlers rushing toward their dogs. Have handlers take their time, moving slowly, but deliberately. Then make sure they trot back without saying anything.

WEEK 5

(1) HEEL ON LEASH:

Instructions: Review heeling with emphasis on concentrating on the dogs and rhythm. No more than five minutes.

(2) SIT STAY:

Instructions: Review Sit Stay Test. Review distractions—dogs on leash, handlers 3' in front, jumping up and down, to right, center, left, center, forward and back. Instruct Second Degree Distractions—handlers begin clapping softly, gradually increasing intensity. Instruct handlers to return to their dogs, remove the leashes, go 25' in front for 2 minutes. Return, etc.

(3) TURNS IN PLACE & FINISH:

Object: "To teach your dog to go to heel from in front."

Instructions: Review Sequence 3 of the Right, Left and About Turns in Place. Review the Left U-turn. Instruct the Finish. Handlers are instructed to step directly in front of their dogs. The leash is folded in the right hand, with the left hand near the leash snap. On the instructor's command "finish your dogs," handlers say "(Name), heel," and guide their dogs to the left into heel position. The leash guidance is the same as on the Left U-turn.

Demonstration

Watch For: Correct guidance with the leash. Some handlers will attempt to steer the dog rather than use pressure on the leash to have the dog move to heel on his own.

(4) TURNS:

Instructions: Review the Motivational Left and Right Turns (completing the turn, then trotting for 5 steps). Instruct the Motivational About Turn. Have handlers keep their feet together, complete the turn, then trot for 5 steps.

Watch For: Straight body posture with no looking back, left hand remaining in Control Position (no drifting back), or handlers accelerating before the dog has completed the turn.

(5) STAND:

Instructions: Have handlers line up in a straight line, stand their dogs and go 6' in front. Instructor/Assistant examines dogs. Instruct the Motivational Release.

Hints for Traffic Control: A straight line, because in a circle, handlers would crash into each other when releasing.

Articulation: "When I say 'exercise finished,' praise your dogs, put the leashes back on and hold it in Control Position. When I say 'release,' release your dogs and run *straight forward* for 5 steps."

(6) FIGURE 8:

Instructions: Instruct handlers and dogs as posts, 10' apart. Review Motivational Sequence.

(7) DOWN & DOWN STAY:

Instructions: Review voice command for the Down. Instruct Down Stay 3' in front, on leash, with distractions (jumping, then clapping as on the Sit Stay). Return, remove leashes, and do a 30' Down Stay for two minutes.

(8) AUTOMATIC SIT:

Instructions: Review Automatic Sit three times with check, then once with leash over shoulder. Review step-to-the-right-halt.

(9) HEEL FREE:

Instructions: Review heeling with "Umbilical Cord" (two fingers in collar to bring dog back to heel), stress *emphatically* bringing the dog back, hands off, praise. Instruct About Turn—have handlers call the dog's name before making the turn, reinforcing, if necessary.

(10) HAND SIGNALS:

Instructions: Review Sit, Down and Recall Hand Signals from 6' in front with no voice command. Reinforce, if necessary.

(11) FRONT—Sequence 4b:

Instructions: Review Sequence 4a (from 3' in front with 2 steps back). Instruct Sequence 4b. From 3' in front to the right/left, handler calls dog and takes one step backward as dog arrives. If dog does not sit straight in front, handler repositions dog.

(12) RECALL:

Instructions: Review First Degree Distraction with 4-corner Recalls.

Hints for Traffic Control: One handler/dog team in each corner of training area, facing counterclockwise, remainder of class in the center with dogs left on Down Stay and their handlers acting as distractors. Those doing the Recalls go to the corner they are facing and call their dogs. Those whose dogs ignored the distraction are finished and trade places with a student in the middle. Those who had to reinforce, start from where they stopped and do it again. They do not go back to the leg where the dog became distracted.

Watch For: If after four corners, the dog is still not responding correctly, review **THE THREE PHASES OF TRAINING,** *The Practicing Phase* in Chapter 7.

WEEK 6

(1) HEEL ON LEASH:

Instructions: Review heeling with emphasis on concentrating on the dogs and rhythm. Include *long* fast and slow to overcome the tendency of most handlers to change pace always for the same number of steps. No more than five minutes.

(2) SIT STAY:

Instructions: Review Sit Stay Test. Review Second Degree Distractions (clapping), and add handlers cheering, first quietly, then increasing in intensity. Review off leash Sit Stay at 25′ for 2 minutes. Return, etc.

(3) TURNS IN PLACE & FINISH:

Instructions: Review Sequence 3 of the Right, Left and About Turns in Place. Review three Left U-turns, then do a Finish.

(4) TURNS:

Instructions: Review the Motivational Left, Right and About Turns (completing the turn, then trotting for 5 steps).

(5) STAND:

Instructions: Have handlers line up in a straight line, stand their dogs and go 6′ in front. Instruct handlers to step in front of the dog to their right, examine him, and stand in front of their own dogs. Repeat with the dog to their left. Return to their dogs, praise, put leashes back on, assume Control Position and do a Motivational Release.

(6) FIGURE 8:

Instructions: With the posts 10' apart, review the Motivational sequence (fast on the outside, slow on the inside).

(7) DOWN & DOWN STAY:

Instructions: Review voice command for the Down. Instruct Down Stay 3' in front with distractions (clapping and cheering as on the Sit Stay). Return, remove leashes, and do a 30' Down Stay for two minutes. Return, etc.

(8) AUTOMATIC SIT:

Instructions: Review Automatic Sit three times with check, then once with leash over shoulder. Review step-to-the-right-halt.

(9) HEEL FREE:

Instructions: Review heeling with "Umbilical Cord." Instruct reinforcement. When a dog leaves heel position, the handler now *slowly* but firmly grasps him by the scruff of the neck, emphatically brings him back to heel position, lets go and praises. Instruct changes of pace.

Watch For: Handlers grasping the dog at the top of the head and not the scruff; snatching; letting go before the dog is in heel position; and praising before they let go, or not praising at all.

(10) FRONT—Sequence 4c:

Instructions: Review Sequence 4b (from 3' in front with 1 step back). Instruct Sequence 4c. From 3' in front to right/left with handler standing still as dog arrives. If dog does not sit straight in front, handler repositions dog.

Watch For: Command/motion sequence.

(11) HAND SIGNALS:

Instructions: Review Sit and Down Hand Signals from 6' in front signal only. Instruct signal and command from 3' in front, off leash. If necessary, handlers take a step toward the dog and reinforce. Review Recall Hand Signal from 6′ in front on leash. Instruct Recall Hand Signal from 6′ in front, off leash, with command and signal.

(12) RECALL:

Instructions: Instruct 4-corner Recalls with 2nd Degree Distractions. Distractors crouch midway between the dog and handler, two feet from the dog's line of travel, facing the dog. As the dog comes, the distractor tries to entice the dog to come to him by clapping his hands and calling, "here puppy, puppy, puppy" (the dog's name is **not** used). If necessary, handlers reinforce as before.

Watch For: Some dogs will veer to avoid the distractor, in which case the exercise is repeated with a distractor on both sides of the dog's line of travel. The dog is taught to come in a straight line.

REMINDERS: Remind students that in order to graduate from Level 2, the dog has to be able to heel with the "Umbilical Cord" including an About Turn, a Fast and a Slow, without reinforcement; do a Sit, Stand and Down Stay off leash; and do a Recall with 2nd Degree Distraction.

WEEKS 7 & 8

*(1) HEEL ON LEASH:

Instructions: A two-minute *brisk* heeling drill with changes of pace and circles. Have handlers concentrate on their dogs and establishing rhythm.

*(2) SIT STAY:

Instructions: Review Sit Stay Test. Instruct distraction—with the dogs on leash, handlers 3′ in front, the instructor/assistant stands in front of each dog, points to the ground and says "down." Remind handlers to reinforce from in front with "stay." Return, etc.

*(3) TURNS IN PLACE & FINISH:

Instructions: Review Sequence 3 of the Right, Left and About Turns in Place. Review 3 Left U-turns, then do a Finish. Repeat the Finish *only* for those who did not do it correctly.

---

*8th week exercises.

*(4) TURNS:

Instructions: Review Motivational Right, Left and About Turns.

*(5) STAND:

Instructions: Review having handlers examine the dogs to their right/left from 6' in front. Return, etc.

(6) FIGURE 8:

Instructions: Instruct handlers and dogs as posts, 8' apart. Review Motivational Sequence.

*(7) DOWN & DOWN STAY:

Instructions: Review voice command for the Down. Instruct Down Stay 3' in front on leash with distraction—instructor/assistant giving command and signal to sit from directly in front of dog.

*(8) AUTOMATIC SIT:

Instructions: Review Automatic Sit three times with check, then once with leash over shoulder. Review step-to-the-right-halt.

*(9) HEEL FREE:

Instructions: Review heeling with "Umbilical Cord" including changes of pace and an About Turn.

*(10) FRONT—Sequence 5:

Instructions: Review Sequence 4c (from 3' in front with 0 steps back). Instruct Sequence 5. Off leash, handler stands directly in front of dog. Holding object of attraction, with "come," handler turns 90 degrees to the right/left and takes one step backward. If dog does not sit straight, handler repositions dog.

*(11) DOG COMING ON NAME:

Object: "To teach your dog to come on the command and not his name."

Instructions: On leash, handlers 6' in front. Handlers say "(Name), stay" and if dog breaks, reinforce stay. When dog holds stay with "(Name), stay," repeat with "(Name)" and, if necessary, reinforce stay. Then do a Recall on Leash with "(Name), come."

(12) RECALL:

Instructions: Review 4-corner Recalls with 2nd Degree Distractions.

(13) DEMONSTRATION:

Demonstrate Novice Routine with a trained dog and talk about Level 3 for those who will graduate. Next week is graduation. Invite friends and family. Privately inform those who will not graduate and invite them to repeat Level 2.

SAMPLE INSTRUCTOR OUTLINE

WEEK 2

(1) HEEL ON LEASH: **Instruct** reinforcing desired response—smile & praise when dog looks. **Review** not less than 5 minutes, not more than 10, with changes of pace, circles & AT (Control Position). Spend time on circles in preparation for the Figure 8. Emphasize concentrating on dog.

(2) SIT STAY: **Review** test with more pressure (3', dead ring). **Instruct** 10' for 30 seconds, off leash; then 2 steps closer to dog for 1 additional minute. Return, etc.

(3) TURNS IN PLACE: **Review** Seq. 2 RT, AT & LT (RT—command, then step; AT—1 step, turn, 1 step; LT—place L foot, small step with R). **Instruct** Seq. 3 of RT & AT in Place (turn in place, no steps). **Instruct** Seq. 3 of LT—place R foot in front of L ('T'), close with L & guide dog **back** & into heel position. Emphasize doing it in place.

(4) DOWN & DOWN STAY: **Review** down with fingers in collar. **Instruct** response with no fingers in collar—leash in Control Position, say "down" & if no response slide L hand quickly down to leash snap & check dog down (keep arm straight). Watch command/motion sequence (give dog a chance to respond). **Instruct** Down Stay at 10' for 2 minutes, off leash. Return, etc.

(5) TURNS: **Review** 1's & 2's across circle, then all together (Control Position).

(6) STAND: **Instruct** handlers stepping to R, back to center, to L, in preparation of handlers examining dog on R, then L. Return, etc. For those with difficulty advise review of Level 1 Homework Sheet, Week 6.

(7) AUTOMATIC SIT: **Review** with check & stopping briskly. Watch body posture and direction of check.

340

(8) ATTENTION: Control Position. "Name," count to 5, release; repeat 2 times.

(9) HAND SIGNALS: **Review** Sit & Down from 3′ in front with voice & signal; check, if necessary. **Review** with signal only. 6′ Recall with voice & signal; check, if necessary.

(10) FRONT: **Review** Sequence 3a. **Instruct** Sequence 3b—Control Position, with "(Name), come" handlers take 1 step forward, guide dog around, take one step backward and motion upward for straight sit. If not straight, handler repositions. Remind about command/motion sequence.

(11) RECALL: **Review** individually on leash with food as distraction.

HOMEWORK SHEETS

WEEK 1

HEEL ON LEASH: Begin your training sessions with a 2-minute heeling drill in a straight line or a large counterclockwise circle. Incorporate slow and fast pace, varying the number of steps, and circles right and left. Hold the leash in Control Position (1/2″ of slack). **Concentrate** on your dog (look at him).

SIT STAY: First test from 3′ in front; look for visible resistance. Then put the leash behind your dog and go 6′ in front for 30 seconds. Return, pause, praise, put leash back on and release. Work up to a 2-minute Sit Stay from 6′ in front.

TURNS IN PLACE: Review 3 Right, Left and About Turns in place.

DOWN AND DOWN STAY: **Before** saying "down," put 2 fingers of your left hand through your dog's collar. Review response to down command; reinforce, if necessary. Then put the leash behind your dog and go 6′ in front for 30 seconds. Return, pause, praise, put the leash back on and release. During the week work up to a 3-minute Down Stay from 6′ in front.

TURNS: Practice 3 Left, Right and About Turns in motion.

STAND STAY: 3 times this week, stand your dog, go 6′ in front and have a friend or relative examine him. Return, etc.

AUTOMATIC SIT: Practice 5 per session—take several steps forward, then halt. If necessary, reinforce with a check straight up with your left hand. Concentrate on keeping your body facing straight ahead.

ATTENTION: Control Position. Look at your dog and say his name, then release (release word, run 5 steps forward and **PRAISE**). Start all over. "Name," silently count to 2, release. Start again. "Name," count to 5, release.

FRONT: Dog sitting at heel, leash in Control Position, say "(Name), come," take two steps forward, extend your arms to guide dog in front of you, take two steps backward and sit dog by motioning upward. If dog is not straight, reposition by stepping back on right leg, placing right hand palm up in the collar, and placing him straight with left hand. Practice 3 times per session.

HAND SIGNALS: **Review** Down & Sit from 3' in front with voice & signal, then do 3 repetitions without voice command. **PRAISE** even if you have to step in and check. Review Recall signal on leash from 6' in front; place him into a sit in front as he gets to you.

RECALL: Practice 2 per session, standing erect, placing him into a sit in front as he gets to you. Count to 5, say "stay," return, pause, praise and release.

REMINDERS: Practice 2 Long Downs & 2 Long Sits, on alternate days. Train in different locations!

WEEK 2

HEEL ON LEASH: 2-minute heeling drill with changes of pace and circles right and left. Leash in Control Position. Concentrate on your dog and **praise** him when he looks at you.

SIT STAY: First test from 3' in front. Then put the leash behind your dog and do a 30-second sit stay from 10' in front. Return, pause, praise, put leash back on and release. During the week work up to a 1-minute Sit Stay from 10' in front. Return, etc.

TURNS IN PLACE: Do 3 of the Right and About Turns in Place (no steps). Then do the Left Turn in Place: place your right foot in front of your left ("T"), say "name, heel" and close with the left, guiding your dog **back** and into heel position. Practice 5 times per session.

DOWN & DOWN STAY: Control Position with your dog sitting at heel. Say "down" and if he fails to respond, slide your left hand down the leash to the snap and check dog down. Keep your left arm straight. **Praise.** Pause, sit dog, and repeat 3 more times. Work up to a 3-minute Down Stay 10' in front. Return, etc.

TURNS: Practice 3 right, about and left turns in motion per session.

STAND STAY: This week have 3 people who are strangers to your dog go over your dog with you 3' in front. Return, etc.

AUTOMATIC SIT: Practice 5 per session. Check, if necessary.

ATTENTION: Control Position. "Name," count to 5, release. "Name," count to 10, release; repeat 2 times per session.

FRONT: With dog sitting at heel, say "(Name), come," take one step forward, extend your arms to guide dog in front of you, take one step backward and sit dog by motioning upward to reference point. If dog is not straight, reposition by stepping back on your right leg, placing your right hand, palm up, in the collar under his chin, and placing him straight with your left hand. Practice 3 times per session.

HAND SIGNALS: Review the Down, Sit and Recall hand signals.

RECALL: Practice 2 Recalls on Leash per session and always praise your dog enthusiastically when he gets to you!

REMINDERS: Use your training at home. If your dog jumps on people at the door, use the Sit Stay while you greet your guests. If he bothers you during dinner, use the Long Down. Incorporate your training into your everyday life. Remember to **PRAISE.** Practice no less than 5 times per week and seek out unfamiliar locations so that your dog learns to respond everywhere.

WEEK 3

HEEL ON LEASH: 2-minute warm-up with changes of pace and circles. Concentrate and **praise** when dog looks at you.

SIT STAY: First test, then go 15' in front for 30 seconds. Return, etc. During the week work up to a 2-minute Sit Stay 15' in front. If you experience difficulties, reduce the distance you are away from your dog.

TURNS IN PLACE: Review the Left, Right and About Turn in Place 3 times per session. Practice the Left U-Turn in Place (2 Left Turns in Place) 3 times per session.

TURNS: Practice the "Motivational" Left Turn—keep your feet together, make the turn, **trot** for several steps and then return to normal pace. Practice 5 per session. Review all turns 3 times per session.

STAND STAY: This week have 2 more people who are strangers to your dog examine him with you 3' in front. Return, etc.

FIGURE 8: Each session, practice 3 times around each post, placed 12' apart, going slowly around the left post and trotting around the right post. Leash is held in Control Position with your hands **in front** of your body at all times.

DOWN AND DOWN STAY: 3 times per session review response to Down command, reinforcing, if necessary. 3 times this week practice a 3-minute Down Stay from 15' in front. Return, etc.

AUTOMATIC SIT: Review 4 times per session with check, if necessary.

ATTENTION: Control Position. "Name," count to 10, release. Repeat 3 times.

FRONT: With dog sitting at heel, say "(Name), come," extend your arms to guide dog around to face you. Sit dog by motioning upward. If dog is not straight, reposition by stepping back on right leg, using left hand to straighten. Practice 3 times per session.

HAND SIGNALS: Practice Down and Sit hand signal from 6' in front, stepping in to check, if necessary. Review the Recall hand signal from 6' in front.

RECALL: Practice Recall on Leash 2 times per session.

WEEK 4

REMINDER: Three times this week practice in an area unfamiliar to your dog where there are distractions, such as a supermarket parking lot.

HEEL ON LEASH: 2-minute warm-up with changes of pace and circles. Concentrate and work on **rhythm.**

SIT STAY: First test, then practice a 3-minute Sit Stay, on leash, around distractions, 3 times this week (create your own by clapping). Return, etc.

TURNS IN PLACE: 3 times this week practice 3 of each. Then do 3 Left U-Turns in Place, guiding your dog back and forward into heel position with your left hand.

TURNS: Practice 4 Motivational Left and Right Turns each session. Keep your hands in front of your body at all times. Do 3 About Turns at normal pace.

STAND STAY: Have two people who are strangers to your dog examine him with you 6' in front. Return, etc.

FIGURE 8: Review with posts 12' apart, Control Position, trotting around the right post and going slowly around the left post.

DOWN AND DOWN STAY: Say "down," **then** reinforce, if necessary. For the Down Stay, 3 times this week practice a 3-minute Down Stay from 6' in front, on leash, around distractions. Return, etc.

AUTOMATIC SIT: Vary the number of steps between starting and stopping. Practice 4 times before doing off-leash heeling.

HEEL FREE: "Umbilical cord." If dog deviates, slowly put 2 fingers of your left hand through collar, bring your dog back to heel position, let go and **PRAISE.**

FRONT: Leave your dog and go 3' in front (off leash). Take one step to the right/left and call your dog. When he arrives, take two steps backward and motion upward with object. If he is not straight, reposition. Practice 3 times per session.

HAND SIGNALS: Review from 6' in front, on leash; if no response, reinforce.

RECALL: Practice 2 times per session, off leash.

WEEK 5

REMINDER: This week take 3 more trips to unfamiliar locations with distractions to work your dog. The time spent is well worth it, because your dog is learning to respond to you no matter what is going on around him.

HEEL ON LEASH: 2-minute heeling drill. Include changes of pace and circles, and work on establishing **rhythm.**

SIT STAY: First test, then practice a 1-minute Sit Stay one day, a 2-minute Sit Stay the second day and a 3-minute Sit Stay the third day, off leash, 6' in front. Return, etc.

TURNS IN PLACE & FINISH: Practice 3 of each turn each session. Do 3 Left U-Turns in Place. Then step directly in front of sitting dog and finish. Use same leash guidance as for Left U-Turn.

TURNS: Practice "Motivational" turns, concentrating on keeping your hands in front of your body. Practice 4 turns each per session before going on to the next exercise.

STAND: 2 times this week have two strangers go over your dog with you standing 6' in front. Return, etc.

FIGURE 8: Posts 10' apart, Control Position. Practice 3 times around each post, trotting around the right post and going slowly around the left post.

DOWN & DOWN STAY: 3 times this week practice around distractions. First down your dog, then take the leash off and place it behind him and go 6′ in front for 3, 4, and 5 minutes on successive days. Return, etc.

AUTOMATIC SIT: Practice 4 per session, reinforcing, if necessary, before doing off leash heeling. Vary the number of steps between halts.

HEEL FREE: "Umbilical Cord." Incorporate an About Turn. Say dog's name before making turn.

FRONT: From 3′ in front, take one step to the right/left and call your dog. When he arrives, take one step backward and motion upward to reference point with object of attraction. Reposition, if necessary. Practice 3 times per session.

HAND SIGNALS: Review from 6′ in front, on leash, then do signals off leash.

RECALL: Practice 2 times per session. Concentrate on standing erect as you call your dog, keeping your hands at your side. When the dog gets to you, use your hands to visually guide him into a straight sit in front. If he does not sit straight, **reposition** him.

WEEK 6

REMINDER: Twice this week work in an area with distractions.

HEEL ON LEASH: 2-minute heeling drill, Control Position. Include changes of pace varying the number of steps you take at each speed.

SIT STAY: Twice this week practice in an area with distractions, 10′ in front for 2 minutes. Return, etc. Test before you take the leash off and leave your dog.

TURNS IN PLACE & FINISH: Practice 3 of the Left, Right and About Turns in Place per session. Do 3 Left U-Turns in Place. Then step directly in front of sitting dog and Finish. Use same guidance as for Left U-Turn.

TURNS: Review the Right, Left and About Turns in motion 4 times each per session.

STAND: 2 times this week have a stranger examine your dog with you 6′ in front. Return, etc.

FIGURE 8: Posts 10′ apart, Control Position. Practice 3 times around each post, trotting around on the right post and going slowly around the left post.

DOWN & DOWN STAY: Reinforce the "down" command, if necessary. Practice 4 Downs, then do a Down Stay 2 times this week 10' in front for 5 minutes. Return, etc.

AUTOMATIC SIT: Do 4 Automatic Sits before practicing Heel free.

HEEL FREE: Practice with changes of pace ("umbilical cord"). Reinforce, if necessary. Practice until your dog stays with you during changes of pace. Praise when you see him trying on his own to stay with you so that he knows this is what you want. This is a good week to spend some time on this exercise.

FRONT: From 3' in front, take one step to the right/left and call your dog. When he arrives, stand still and motion upward to reference point with object of attraction. Reposition, if necessary. Practice 3 times per session.

HAND SIGNALS: Review from 6' in front on leash, then do signals from 10' in front off leash.

RECALL: Practice 2 times per session with emphasis on straight sits in front (use hands to guide). If he does not sit straight, **reposition** him.

WEEK 7

REMINDER: Next week is graduation. Please bring your friends and relatives to celebrate with us. You should be proud of what you have accomplished in the last 15 weeks.

HEEL ON LEASH: 2-minute heeling drill, Control Position, with changes of pace. **Concentrate** and work particularly hard on **rhythm.** Everytime your dog looks at you, smile at him and tell him what a good dog he is.

SIT STAY: First review test, then 2 times this week practice a 3-minute Sit Stay 15' in front. Return, etc.

TURNS IN PLACE & FINISH: Review 3 of each turn. Do 3 Left U-Turns in Place and then a Finish. If dog's response is not correct, practice several Finishes with same guidance as for Left U-Turn.

TURNS: Review the Right, Left and About Turns in motion 4 times each per session. Concentrate on keeping your feet together and coming out of the turn at a fast.

STAND: Twice this week have someone examine your dog with you 6' in front. Return, etc.

FIGURE 8:   Posts 8′ apart, Control Position. Practice 3 times around each post, trotting around the right post and going slowly around the left post.

DOWN & DOWN STAY: Review response to down command. This week practice 2 5-minute Down Stays from 15′ in front. Return, etc.

AUTOMATIC SIT: Practice 4 Automatic Sits before doing Heel Free.

HEEL FREE: Review with changes of pace ("umbilical cord"). Reinforce, if necessary. If your dog is not readily staying with you during changes of pace, work extra hard on this exercise. Make it fun for him, getting him all excited about staying with you. **Praise** when you see that he is trying.

FRONT: From directly in front of your dog, object held in front of him, turn 90 degrees to the right/left with "come." Take one step backward and motion upward with object. Practice 3 each per session.

HAND SIGNALS: Review from 6′ in front off leash. Then practice signals from 10′ in front off leash. Concentrate on having dog respond to first signal.

RECALL: Practice 2 times per session with emphasis on straight fronts (use hands to visually guide dog). If he does not sit straight in front, **reposition** him.

Appendix III

INSTRUCTING MODEL—LEVEL 3

INTRODUCTION

Level 3 is for individuals who have graduated from Level 2 and who are interested in obtaining AKC titles. To graduate from Level 3 a qualifying Novice routine is required.

Unless otherwise specified, all exercises start with the leash in Control Position.

WEEKLY SESSIONS

WEEK 1

(1) HEEL ON LEASH:

Object: "To perfect your dog's heeling."

Instructions: Review 2-minute heeling drill including changes of pace and circles. Stress body posture and concentrating on dog.

(2) SIT STAY:

Object: "To make your dog reliable on the stays."

Instructions: Review Test. Then do a 1-minute Sit Stay, off leash, handlers across room. "Return, etc."

(3) TURNS IN PLACE & FINISH:

Instructions: Three Left U-Turns, followed by a Finish. Instruct Finish to the Right with command "place." Do 3 About Turns in Place with "place," then a Finish to the Right (leash is held in right hand, handler steps back on right leg, guides the dog around behind him and transfers the leash into the left hand behind his back).

(4) DOWN & DOWN STAY:

Instructions: Individually review response to down command. Then do a Down Stay, off leash, with handlers across the room for 3 minutes. Return, etc.

(5) TURNS:

Object: "To teach you teamwork with your dog when making turns."

Instructions: Instruct footwork for the Left Turn, first from stationary (dogs are on a Stay behind handlers), then at slow pace with dogs.

Articulation: "When I say 'left turn' stop on your right foot and bring up the left, one half the length ahead of the right, pointed in the direction of the turn, then bring the right foot into the turn."

(6) HEEL POSITION:

Object: "To sharpen your dog's understanding of heel position and teach him to adjust himself."

Instruction: Instruct handler to leave dogs on a Sit Stay and go to the end of the leash, first to the right, then behind and then in front of the dog. Handlers give command "(name), heel," and as dog arrives at handler's side, handler praises, takes two steps straight forward, guiding the dog into heel position.

Watch For: Loop of leash over right thumb, arms in Control Position.

(7) FIGURE 8:

Instructions: Review Motivational with posts 8' apart.

(8) STAND:

Instructions: Review off leash, 6' in front. Handlers examine dog to their right/left. Return, etc.

(9) READY & AUTOMATIC SIT:

Object: "To teach you to train your dog to pay attention on command and until he is released. The dog is conditioned to the word 'ready,' which signifies the start of having to pay attention; the release lets the dog know

Teaching heel position, first with handlers to the right

and then behind the dogs before giving heel command.

that he no longer has to pay attention. By gradually increasing the length of time between 'ready' and the release, the dog learns to pay attention for increasingly longer periods."

Instructions: Instruct "ready," followed by three Automatic Sits. On your command, handlers heel for five paces and release; repeat three times. Then handlers heel, halt and release; repeat three times.

Articulation: "When I say 'are you ready,' you say 'ready.' When I say 'forward,' you say '(name), heel' and step out. When I say 'release,' you release your dog."

(10) HEEL FREE:

Instructions: Review with "umbilical cord."

(11) FRONT:

Instructions: Review 90 degree turn to the right/left with object of attraction and one step backward. Instruct 45 degree turn to the right/left. Handler stands directly in front of sitting dog, hands holding object of attraction, with "come," turns 45 degrees to the right/left and takes one step backward to guide dog into a straight sit. Handler repositions dog, if necessary.

(12) RECALL:

Instructions: Review individually with 2nd degree distraction.

(13) REMINDERS:

End sessions at home with Recall(s), followed by a short play session.

WEEK 2

(1) HEEL ON LEASH & ATTENTION:

Object: "Another exercise to teach your dog to pay attention to you. The expectation of the release will condition the dog to want to pay attention to you."

Instructions: Brief warm-up with changes of pace and circles. Stress rhythm.
Instruct release while heeling—release after five steps; repeat three times.

(2) SIT STAY:

Instructions: Review Test. Then, off leash, 6' in front with handlers clapping, then clapping and cheering. Where necessary, handler puts dog back from the front without saying anything. Return, etc.

(3) TURNS IN PLACE & FINISH:

Instructions: Review Turns in Place, Finish & Finish to the Right. Before the Finish to the Left, review three Left U-Turns. Review three About Turns with command "place;" then do a Finish to the Right, eliminating the step back.

(4) DOWN & DOWN STAY:

Object: "To teach your dog to concentrate on maintaining position."

Instructions: Review response to down command individually. Instruct lying on side and tucking paw. Then do a Down Stay, on leash, handlers 6' in front with instructor/assistant trying to get dogs to sit with command and signal. Where necessary, handlers step toward dog and reinforce with left hand. Repeat until dogs hold the Stay. Return, etc.

Articulation: "Gently roll your dog onto his left hip and tuck his right forepaw. If he moves his paw, re-tuck with "stay."

(5) TURNS:

Instructions: Review Left Turn with dogs from slow, then at normal pace.

(6) HEEL POSITION:

Instructions: Review Sequence 1 (from side, behind and in front, handlers take two steps forward). Instruct Sequence 2—handlers take one step forward when dog arrives.

(7) FIGURE 8:

Instructions: Instruct normal pace, posts 8' apart.

(8) STAND:

Instructions: Review with handler directly in front and instructor/assistant telling dog to "sit." Where necessary, handler repositions dog; repeat until dog holds Stay. Return, etc.

(9) READY & AUTOMATIC SIT:

Instructions: Review "ready" with release. Instruct "ready" starting at a fast, then release; repeat three times. Then do "ready," fast, halt and release; repeat three times.

Watch For: Straight and quick sits.

(10) HEEL FREE:

Instructions: Instruct Heel Free with changes of pace and reinforcement where necessary (two fingers of left hand through collar, etc.).

(11) FRONT:

Instructions: Have handler step directly in front of his dog to what he visualizes a perfect sit in front to be. The handler's goal is to have his dog come in and sit in this position without any guidance. From now on, the handler will no longer visually guide his dog, or reposition him if he does not sit straight. The dog is being given responsibility to figure out where the perfect front is. Instruct handler to leave his dog (off leash) and go 3' in front. With his arms straight at his sides, handler calls dog, remaining motionless when dog arrives. If sit in front is perfect, dog is rewarded and praised, handler steps back to heel position and releases. If sit is not perfect, handler says "stay," backs up and calls again, using the first response as a starting point, rewarding any sit that moves the dog closer to the perfect front. With each improved response, less perfect sits are no longer rewarded. This process is called **shaping.**

(12) RECALL:

Instructions: Instruct 3rd degree distraction—distractors offer food to the dog saying "here is a cookie for you" or similar enticements. Instruct distractors to hold the food at arm's length, but not to jab at the dogs as they go by. The purpose of the exercise is to teach the dog to concentrate on what he is doing and to ignore distractions, not to frighten or overpower him. (4-corner recall; dogs that were distracted, do it again).

WEEK 3

(1) HEEL ON LEASH & ATTENTION:

Instructions: Brief warm-up with changes of pace and circles.
Review release while heeling (release after 5 steps, then release after 10 steps).

354

Recall with . . .

Third Degree . . .

Distraction.

(2) SIT STAY:

Instructions: Review Test. Then, off leash, handlers 6' in front, instructor/ assistant trying with food to entice dogs to lie down. Where necessary, handler puts dog back without saying anything, then repeat. Return, etc.

(3) TURNS IN PLACE & FINISH:

Instructions: Concentrate on Finish by doing a Finish without first having done Left U-Turns in Place. Dogs that did it correctly do not repeat; those that did not, try again. Then review Turns in Place and Finish to the Right.

(4) DOWN & DOWN STAY:

Instructions: Review response to down command individually. Then do a Down Stay (on side, paw tucked), on leash, handlers 6' in front, with instructor/assistant **gently** trying to lift dog by the collar into sit with "sit." Where necessary, handler puts dog back without saying anything, then repeat distraction. Return, etc.

(5) TURNS:

Instructions: Instruct footwork for the Right Turn—stop on the right foot, place the left foot, one half the length of the foot, ahead of the right, pointed in the direction of the turn and step into the turn on the right foot. Instruct first from stationary without dogs, then at slow pace with dogs.

(6) HEEL POSITION:

Instructions: Review Sequence 2 (one step forward). Instruct Sequence 3—handler stand still, calls with "(name), heel" and guides dog past himself and then forward into heel position.

Watch For: Guiding past and forward (the dog has to learn *how* to get to heel position); handler physically trying to maneuver the dog.

(7) FIGURE 8:

Object: "To teach you how to do a correct Figure 8."

Instructions: Instruct footwork for the Figure 8—single track around the posts with object for inside turn and elbow of post for outside turn.

(8) STAND:

Instructions: Review with handler directly in front and instructor/assistant

356

Instructor trying with food to entice dogs to lie down.

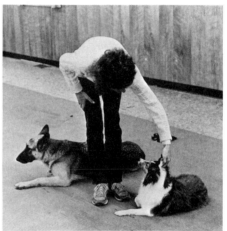

Instructor gently trying
to lift the dog by the collar
into a sit with "sit."

Teaching the Figure 8 with object for inside turn and
elbow of post for outside turn.

telling dog to sit while **gently** pushing down on rear. Where necessary, handler repositions dog, then repeat. Return, etc.

(9) READY & AUTOMATIC SIT:

Instructions: Instruct "ready" with 1st degree distraction. Instructor/ assistant at a 45 degree angle to dog, 10' away says "are you ready?" Handler says "ready!" Distractor approaches to within 2' of dog. If dog maintains attention on handler, distractor says "release" and handler releases. If dog is distracted, handler firmly checks and after dog looks up, releases. Repeat until dogs ignore distractor. Follow with fast start, stop and release, with particular emphasis on straight and quick sits.

(10) HEEL FREE:

Instructions: Review with changes of pace and reinforcement.

(11) FRONT:

Instructions: Continue shaping. Review from 3' in front and if response is perfect, increase distance to 6'. If dog seems confused, or responses deteriorate, have handler move closer. When response is perfect, handler either stops practicing this exercise or changes it by increasing distance.

(12) RECALL:

Instructions: Review 4-corner recalls with 3rd degree distraction. Dogs that became distracted repeat until they ignore the distractor.

WEEK 4

(1) HEEL ON LEASH & ATTENTION:

Instructions: Brief warm-up with changes of pace and circles.
   Review release while heeling (release after 10 steps, then release after 20 steps).

(2) SIT STAY:

Instructions: Review Test. Handlers go 6' **behind** dogs with **backs** to dogs for two minutes. Instructor/assistant tries to get dogs to lie down with command and signal. Where necessary, handler puts dog back without saying anything, then repeat. Return, etc.

358

"Ready" with First Degree . . .

Distraction.

(3) TURNS IN PLACE & FINISH:

Instructions: Finish first, then practice Turns in Place and Finish to the Right.

(4) DOWN & DOWN STAY:

Instructions: Review response to down command individually. Then do a Down Stay (on side, paw tucked) with handlers 6' behind dogs with backs to dogs for four minutes. Instructor/assistant tries to get dogs to sit with command and signal. Where necessary, handler puts dog back without saying anything, then repeat. Return, etc.

(5) TURNS:

Instructions: Review Right Turn with dogs from slow, then at normal pace.

(6) HEEL POSITION:

Instructions: Review with handlers standing still, guiding dog past and into heel position. Instruct stepping to right, forward and back together with dog—"(name), heel," then handler moves, guiding dog into heel position.

Articulation: "When I say 'step to the right/behind/forward, say '(name), heel,' take a step to the right/behind/forward and guide your dog into heel position. Keep your left hand in Control Position, close to the leash snap."

Watch For: Guiding **back** and forward into heel position.

(7) FIGURE 8:

Instructions: Review footwork with object and elbow out. Instruct check for dogs that lag on the outside turn—handler checks straight forward after he has come out of the inside turn and when the dog is straight.

Watch For: Timing of check—some handlers will try to check while they are in the turn, or worse yet, coming out of the outside turn, right before the dog has to slow down for the inside turn.

(8) STAND:

Instructions: Review with handlers 6' in front and instructor/assistant telling dog to "sit." Where necessary, handler repositions dog, then repeat. Return, etc.

(9) READY & AUTOMATIC SIT:

Instructions: Instruct "ready" with 2nd degree distraction. Instructor/ assistant at a 45 degree angle to dog, 2' away. Distractor asks "Are you ready?" Handler says "Ready!" Distractor claps hands and tries to distract dog with "here, puppy, puppy!" If dog maintains attention, distractor says "release" and handler releases. If dog is distracted, handler firmly checks and after dog looks up, releases. Repeat until dogs ignore distractor. Follow with three fast starts, stops and releases, with particular emphasis on straight and quick sits.

(10) HEEL FREE:

Instructions: Review with changes of pace and circles. Introduce an About Turn.

Watch For: Handlers' posture on About Turn.

(11) FRONT:

Instructions: Continue shaping. Review from 6' and increase distance incrementally to 15'. Handler moves closer if dog is confused or responses deteriorate. End with a perfect response by rewarding, praising, stepping back to heel and releasing.

(12) RECALL:

Instructions: Instruct individual recalls through "tunnel" (handler/dog teams in two lines, six feet apart, facing each other). The level of difficulty for this exercise is controlled by the width of the tunnel. For some dogs, six feet the first time is too close, in which case the tunnel is made wider. If the dog does not come, handler shows him what he wants him to do.

WEEK 5

(1) HEEL ON LEASH & ATTENTION:

Instructions: Brief warm-up with changes of pace and circles. Instruct heeling with 2nd degree distraction—divide class in half, one half are distractors (clapping hands & calling "here, puppy, puppy") while the other half heels. Then reverse. Handler checks dog that becomes distracted, followed by praise. Handler praises dog for ignoring distractors.

Watch For: Distractors becoming too enthusiastic and getting too loud. Handlers not reinforcing the desired response, that is, not praising the dog when he ignores the distractor.

"Ready" with Second Degree Distraction.

Down Stay on side with tucked paw.

(2) SIT STAY:

Instructions: Handlers go 6' behind dogs with backs to dogs. Instructor/ assistant tries with food to entice dogs to lie down. Where necessary, handler puts dog back without saying anything, then repeat. Return, etc.

(3) TURNS IN PLACE & FINISH:

Instructions: Finish first, then Turns in Place and Finish to the Right.

(4) DOWN & DOWN STAY:

Instructions: Review response to down command. Then do a Down Stay (on side, paw tucked) with handlers 6' behind dogs with backs to dogs for four minutes, with instructor/assistant **gently** trying to lift dogs by collar into sit with "sit." Where necessary, handler puts dog back without saying anything, then repeat. Return, etc.

(5) TURNS:

Instructions: Instruct footwork for About Turn—stop on the right foot, place the left foot one half the length of the foot ahead of the right, pointed in the direction of the turn, turn around the right, turn around the left and step out on the right. Do first from stationary, then at slow pace.

(6) HEEL POSITION:

Instructions: Review stepping to right, forward and back together with dog.

(7) FIGURE 8:

Object: "To teach your dog not to lag or crowd."

Instructions: Instruct going the other way—handler makes an about turn parallel with the outside post and reinforces with a check, if necessary; then handler makes a left U-Turn parallel with the inside post. After that, handler completes a normal Figure 8.

Articulation: "When I say 'forward,' take two steps forward, then go to your right. After you have gone around the outside post and are parallel with the inside post, make a Left U-Turn. After you have gone around the inside post and are parallel, make a Left U-Turn. On each reverse you turn *toward* the post. Then do a normal Figure 8 around each post."

Watch For: Timing of check coming out of the about turn. Some handlers will try to check too soon, before the dog is fully faced in the new direction.

363

(8) STAND:

Instructions: Review from 6' in front with handlers **thoroughly** examining dog on right/left. Return, etc.

(9) READY & AUTOMATIC SIT:

Instructions: Instruct 3rd degree distraction. Distractor at a 45 degree angle to dog, 2' away. Distractor asks "Are you ready?" Handler says "Ready!" Distractor then tries to distract dog with food. If dog maintains attention, distractor says "release" and handler releases. If dog is distracted, handler firmly checks and after dog looks up, releases. Repeat, until dogs ignore distraction. Follow with three fast starts, stops and releases, with emphasis on straight & quick sits.

(10) HEEL FREE:

Instructions: Review with changes of pace and about turn.

(11) FRONT:

Instructions: Review, continuing to increase distance.

(12) RECALL:

Instructions: Review 4-corner recall with emphasis on straight front. If dog does not sit straight in front, handler repositions dog.

WEEK 6

(1) HEEL ON LEASH & ATTENTION:

Instructions: Brief warm-up with changes of pace and circles. Instruct heeling with 3rd degree distraction—divide class in half, one half are distractors, offering food to the dogs as they go by and verbally enticing the dogs, while the other half heels. Then reverse. Handlers determine how close they want to get to the distractors. Handlers check when the dog becomes distracted and then praise, and praise when the dog ignores the distractor. Instructor randomly releases.

Watch For: Distractors jabbing at dogs and getting too loud.

(2) SIT STAY:

Instructions: Handlers go 10' in front for 2 minutes. Instructor/assistant tries to entice dogs to come, lie down and release by saying "okay." Where necessary, handler puts dog back without saying anything, then repeat. Return, etc.

(3) TURNS IN PLACE & FINISH:

Instructions: Finish first, then Turns in Place and Finish to the Right.

(4) DOWN & DOWN STAY:

Instructions: Review response to down command. Then do a 4-minute Down Stay (on side, paw tucked), handlers 10′ in front. Instructor/assistant tries to entice dogs to come, sit and release. Where necessary, handler puts dog back without saying anything, then repeat. Return, etc.

(5) TURNS:

Instructions: Review About Turn from slow, then at normal pace.

(6) HEEL POSITION:

Instructions: Review stepping to the right, forward and back together with dog ("name, heel," then handler moves), guiding dog into heel position.

(7) FIGURE 8:

Instructions: Instruct "umbilical cord" with reinforcement—if dog lags on the outside turn, the handler does nothing until he approaches the outside post the second time. The handler then firmly takes dog by the scruff of the neck, and without saying *anything* takes him all the way around the outside post, lets go and praises the dog.

Watch For: Handlers not taking the dog all the way around the outside post; handlers not praising the desired response, that is, when the dog is doing it correctly by himself.

(8) STAND:

Instructions: Instruct from 6′ in front with instructor/assistant trying to entice dogs to sit, come and release. Where necessary, handler repositions dog, then repeat. Return, etc.

(9) READY & AUTOMATIC SIT:

Instructions: Review with 3rd degree distraction. Follow with three fast starts, stops and releases, with particular emphasis on straight and quick sits.

(10) HEEL FREE:

Instructions: Review with changes of pace and introduce right turn and left turn.

(11) FRONT:

Instructions: Instruct off center fronts with shaping. From 3' in front, off leash, handler takes a step to the right/left and calls dog. Following shaping instructions.

(12) RECALL:

Instructions: Review 4-corner recall with emphasis on straight sit in front.

WEEKS 7 & 8

(1) HEEL ON LEASH & ATTENTION:

Instructions: Brief warm-up with changes of pace, circles and random releases.

(2) SIT STAY:

Instructions: Handlers go 20' in front for 3 minutes. Random distractions. Return, etc.

(3) TURNS IN PLACE & FINISH:

Instructions: Review.

(4) DOWN & DOWN STAY:

Instructions: Handlers go 20' in front for 5 minutes. Random distractions. Return, etc.

(5) TURNS:

Instructions: Review all turns at normal pace.

(6) HEEL POSITION:

Instructions: Review.

366

(7) FIGURE 8:

Instructions: Instruct off leash with reinforcement, if necessary (handler takes dog by the scruff).

(8) STAND:

Instructions: Review with instructor/assistant examining dogs.

(9) READY & AUTOMATIC SIT:

Instructions: Review response to "ready" by varying the length of time between "ready" and "forward," and fast starts and stops.

(10) HEEL FREE:

Instructions: Review with changes of pace and turns.

(11) FRONT:

Instructions: Practice random fronts using shaping.

(12) RECALL:

Instructions: Instruct with Finish.

SAMPLE INSTRUCTOR OUTLINE

WEEK 3

(1) HEEL ON LEASH & ATTENTION: Brief warm-up with changes of pace & circles. **Review** Release while heeling (release after 5 steps, then release after 10 steps).

(2) SIT STAY: Review Test. Then, off leash, handlers 6' in front, instructor/assistant trying to entice dogs with food to lie down. Return, etc.

(3) TURNS IN PLACE & FINISH: Concentrate on Finish by doing a Finish without first having done Left U-Turns in Place. Repeat for those who did not do it correctly. Then **review** Turns in Place & Finish to the Right.

(4) DOWN & DOWN STAY: Review response to down command individually. Then do a Down Stay (on side, paw tucked), on leash, handlers 6' in front, with instructor/assistant **gently** trying to lift dog by the collar into sit with "sit." Return, etc.

(5) TURNS: **Instruct** footwork for Right Turn—stop on the R, plant the L and step into the turn with the R. Do from stationary first, then at slow pace.

(6) HEEL POSITION: **Instruct** standing **still** & guiding dog **back** & into heel position.

(7) FIGURE 8: **Instruct** footwork (single track around the posts with object for inside turn and elbow of post for outside turn).

(8) STAND: **Review** with handler directly in front and instructor/ assistant telling dog to sit while **gently** pushing down on rear.

(9) READY & AUTOMATIC SIT: **Instruct** with 1st degree distraction. Follow with several fast starts and stops with particular emphasis on straight and quick sits.

(10) HEEL FREE: **Review** with changes of pace & reinforcement.

(11) FRONT: **Review** shaping from 3′ in front. If response is perfect, have handler back up to 6′ and continue working. Watch for confusion or stress.

(12) RECALL: **Review** 4-corner recalls with 3rd degree distraction. Dog(s) that were distracted, repeat.

HOMEWORK SHEETS

WEEK 1

HEEL ON LEASH: 2-minute heeling drill with changes of pace. Smile and praise dog when he looks at you. Work hard on **rhythm.** If you don't concentrate on your dog, he won't concentrate on you.

SIT STAY: Twice this week do a 3-minute Sit Stay at 20′. Return, etc.

TURNS IN PLACE & FINISH: Review Turns in Place, 3 Left U-Turns and Finish each session. Repeat Finish only if your dog did not do it correctly. Then do 3 Right About Turns in Place, step in front and Finish to the Right with "name, place."

DOWN & DOWN STAY: Each session, review response to down command. Train your dog to lie down on command, without any visual cues. 2 times this week do a 3-minute Down Stay at 20′.

TURNS: Practice footwork for Left Turn without your dog every chance you get—stop on the right foot, plant the left foot one half the foot ahead of the right, toed slightly to the left (heel to instep), and step into the turn on the right. Then practice with your dog.

HEEL POSITION: Leave your dog on a Sit Stay and go to the end of the leash to the right (Control Position). Say "name, heel" and when dog gets to your side, praise, take 2 steps forward and sit dog at heel. Practice 3 times per session to the right, in front and behind dog.

FIGURE 8:   Practice "Motivational" with posts 8' apart.

STAND: 2 times this week do a Stand, 6' in front.

READY & AUTOMATIC SIT: Say "ready!" Then say "name, heel" and step out. Practice together with Automatic Sits, reinforcing when necessary. 3 times per session.

HEEL FREE: Review with "umbilical cord." Reinforce, if necessary.

FRONT: Stand directly in front of your dog with the object held in both hands. Turn 45 degrees to the right/left with come, and take one step backward. Use the object of attraction to guide the dog into a straight sit in front. If he is not straight, reposition him.

RECALL: End every training session with 2 Recalls. Visually guide dog into front. If he does not sit straight, **reposition** him. Pivot back, etc.

REMINDERS: Follow your training sessions with a short play session. Continue to seek out different locations in which to practice. If he continues to be distracted by other dogs in class, this is especially important for him.

WEEK 2

HEEL ON LEASH & ATTENTION: 2-minute heeling drill with changes of pace. Then practice **attention:** heel for 5 steps then release; repeat 3 times. Make it fun for your dog to pay attention to you!

SIT STAY: Practice Sit Stays off leash from 6' in front with distractions (clapping & cheering). If your dog breaks, put him back without saying anything and repeat.

TURNS IN PLACE & FINISH: Each session, review Turns in Place, 3 Left U-Turns and a Finish; repeat if your dog does not do it correctly. Then do 3 Right About Turns in Place, followed by a Finish to the Right with "name, place."

DOWN & DOWN STAY: Review response to down command. Teach your dog to lie on his side and tuck his paw (gently roll him on his side and place his paw with "stay"). Practice 5 times this week a 1-minute Down Stay 6′ in front. If dog changes position or moves paw, show him what you want.

TURNS: Continue to practice footwork for the Left Turn.

HEEL POSITION: Leave your dog on a Sit Stay and go to the end of the leash to the right (Control Position). Say "name, heel" and when dog gets to your side, praise, take 1 step forward and sit dog at heel. Practice 3 times per session to the right, in front and behind dog.

FIGURE 8: Practice with posts 8′ apart at normal pace.

STAND: Practice 2 times this week from 6′ in front.

READY & AUTOMATIC SIT: Say "ready!" Then "name, heel" and take off at a fast. Control Position (keep both hands in front of your body). Practice 3 times per session together with Automatic Sit.

HEEL FREE: Practice in a safe area and incorporate changes of pace. If necessary, reinforce (2 fingers of the left hand through collar), then praise.

FRONT: From 3′ in front, off leash, hold your hands at your sides and call your dog. When he sits in front, if the sit is perfect, reward, praise, step back to heel and release. If it is not perfect, pause, say "stay," back up and repeat. Reward sits that move the dog closer to the perfect front; however, with each improved response, discontinue rewarding less perfect sits.

RECALL: Practice 2 Recalls per session visually guiding your dog into a straight front. If necessary, **reposition.** Pivot back.

REMINDERS: You know he will do it at home, but will he do it where there are distractions? Seek out new locations to practice!

WEEK 3

HEEL ON LEASH & ATTENTION: When heeling, concentrate on your dog and work on attention (release after 5 steps, then after 10 steps and one more time!).

SIT STAY: You saw what happened in class—if your dog broke, work hard on the Sit Stay (create your own distraction by clapping and cheering).

TURNS IN PLACE & FINISH: Practice the Finish before doing Turns in Place. Use left hand guidance, if necessary. Then do 3 Right Turns in Place followed by a Finish to the Right.

DOWN & DOWN STAY: Review response to down command. Then do a Down Stay, on leash, 6′ in front, on his side with paw tucked, 3 times this week for 1 minute. Reposition him, if necessary.

TURNS: Footwork for the Right Turn—stop on the right foot, plant the left foot one half the foot ahead of the right, toed slightly to the right, and step into the turn on the right.

HEEL POSITION: Leave your dog on a Sit Stay and go to the end of the leash to the right (Control Position). Say "name, heel" and guide dog **back** and into heel position (stand still). Practice 3 times per session to the right, in front and behind.

FIGURE 8: Concentrate on singletracking around the posts. Put out objects next to your posts to keep you on track.

STAND: Practice 2 times this week from 6′ in front. Return, etc.

READY & AUTOMATIC SIT: Continue to practice "ready" together with fast starts and stops. Insist that your dog pay attention to you. Vary the time between **"ready"** and the command to heel.

HEEL FREE: Practice in a safe area. Continue with changes of pace (reinforce, if necessary, and praise when you see your dog trying).

FRONT: Gradually increase your distance from 3′ to 10′. If you get an incorrect response, or your dog seems confused, move closer. When you get a perfect response, increase your distance. Always end with a correct response by praising, rewarding, stepping back to heel and releasing.

RECALL: Practice 2 Recalls per session visually guiding your dog into a straight front. If necessary, **reposition.** Pivot back.

REMINDERS: Use this week to work extra hard on the stays—the stays are exercises that can make everything else possible!

WEEK 4

HEEL ON LEASH & ATTENTION: Brief warm-up, including changes of pace and circles. Then work on **attention**—release after 10 steps 3 times.

SIT STAY: 3 times this week practice a Sit Stay with you 6′ behind your dog with your back to the dog for 1 minute. Return, etc.

TURNS IN PLACE & FINISH: Practice a Finish first and then do Turns in Place. When you finish, watch for response to command, without any visual guidance on your part. Guide only if necessary. Do 3 Right Turns in Place and Finish to the Right.

DOWN & DOWN STAY: Review response to down command each session. 3 times this week do a Down Stay (dog on his side, paw tucked) with you 6′ behind your dog with your back to the dog for 1 minute. Return, etc.

TURNS: Continue to practice footwork for the Left and Right Turns.

HEEL POSITION: With dog at heel, leash in Control Position, say "name, heel" and take a step to the right/forward/back guiding the dog into heel position. Practice 3 of each per session.

FIGURE 8:   Continue practicing your footwork going around posts. If your dog lags on the outside turn, check as you come out of the inside turn, then praise. Repeat without check and if dog is trying, praise.

STAND: Practice 2 times this week from 6′ in front. Return, etc.

READY & AUTOMATIC SIT: Continue to practice "ready" together with fast starts and stops. Work especially hard on this exercise, if your dog had difficulty in class.

HEEL FREE: Practice in a safe area and include changes of pace and about turns. Reinforce, if necessary. Praise the dog when he is trying to stay with you. Make it fun for him!

FRONT: Gradually increase your distance to 20′. If you get an incorrect response or your dog seems confused, move closer. When you get a correct response, increase your distance. Always end with a correct response by praising, rewarding, stepping back to heel and releasing.

RECALL: Practice 2 Recalls per session visually guiding your dog into a straight front. If necessary, **reposition.** Pivot back.

REMINDERS: Begin insisting that your dog works precisely. This means that you have to be precise yourself! Concentrate on what you are doing so you don't confuse your dog!

WEEK 5

HEEL ON LEASH & ATTENTION: Brief warm-up with changes of pace and circles. If your dog was easily distracted in class, work on **attention**— release after 10 steps, then after 20 steps—and heeling in locations with distractions.

SIT STAY: Your dog's performance in class tells you what you have to do.

TURNS IN PLACE & FINISH: Review Turns in Place, Finish to the Left and Finish to the Right. For the Finishes, avoid giving your dog a visual cue—see whether he responds to the command only. Guide, if necessary.

DOWN & DOWN STAY: Review response to down command each session. 3 times this week do a Down Stay (dog on his side, paw tucked) with you 10′ in front for 2 minutes. Return, etc.

TURNS: Footwork for the About Turn—stop on the right, plant the left, turn around the right one half the length of the foot ahead of the left, turn around the left and step out on the right. Practice footwork for **ALL** turns.

HEEL POSITION: Review stepping to right, forward and back with "name, heel" 3 times per session. Guide into heel position.

FIGURE 8: When you are parallel with the outside post, make an about turn (after you have completely turned, check, if necessary); when you are parallel with the inside post, make a Left U-Turn. Practice 3 times per session.

STAND: Practice 2 times this week from 6′ in front. Return, etc.

READY & AUTOMATIC SIT: Continue to practice "ready" with fast starts and stops. Get your dog all excited about this exercise.

HEEL FREE: Practice in a safe area.

FRONT: Continue your progress with increasing your distance. Always end with a correct response by praising, rewarding, stepping back to heel and releasing.

RECALL: Practice 2 Recalls per session with particular emphasis on straight fronts (visually guide dog and reposition only if necessary). Pivot back.

REMINDERS: Your dog will not learn what you want him to know unless you teach him. Work with your dog diligently several times a week and he will reward you with correct responses.

WEEK 6

HEEL ON LEASH & ATTENTION: Brief warm-up with changes of pace and circles. Continue to work on **attention**—heel for 10 steps, then release; heel for 20 steps and release. Remember to make it fun for the dog and to reinforce the desired response—praise him when he looks at you.

SIT STAY: 3 times this week practice a 3-minute Sit Stay at 20′.

TURNS IN PLACE & FINISH: Review Turns in Place and then step in front for a Finish. If dog does not Finish on command (without visual cues), practice 3 Left U-Turns in Place and try again.

DOWN & DOWN STAY: Review response to down command each session. 3 times this week do a Down Stay (dog on his side, paw tucked) with you 10′ in front for 4 minutes. Return, etc.

TURNS: Concentrate on what you are doing, so you don't confuse your dog.

HEEL POSITION: Review stepping to right, forward and back with "name, heel" 3 times per session. Use left hand for **reference point.** If necessary, guide into heel position.

FIGURE 8: Practice with "umbilical cord," reinforcing, if necessary. Concentrate on your footwork and maintaining an even pace.

STAND: Your dog's performance in class tells you what and how often you have to practice this exercise.

READY & AUTOMATIC SIT: Continue to practice "ready" with fast starts and stops.

HEEL FREE: Incorporate turns and reinforce, as necessary.

FRONT: From 3′ in front, take a step to the right/left and call your dog. If the sit is perfect, reward and increase your distance. If not perfect, back up and repeat. Continue progress as before.

RECALL: Practice 2 Recalls per session, visually guiding dog into a straight front, repositioning only if necessary. Then Finish.

WEEK 7

HEEL ON LEASH & ATTENTION: Brief warm-up with changes of pace and circles. Work on **attention** with random releases. Heel for several steps, change pace to slow and release. Repeat and release from normal and fast pace, varying the number of steps before your release. Condition your dog to pay attention at all times.

SIT STAY: 2 times this week practice a 3-minute Sit Stay at 20′. Return, etc.

TURNS IN PLACE & FINISH: Practice Turns in Place and Finishes every session.

DOWN & DOWN STAY: Review response to down command each session. 3 times this week do a Down Stay (dog on his side, paw tucked), with you 20' in front for 4 minutes. Return, etc.

TURNS: Practice all turns, concentrating on what you are doing.

HEEL POSITION: Review stepping to right, forward and back.

FIGURE 8:   Practice off leash with reinforcement, if necessary. Maintain an even pace throughout or you will confuse your dog.

STAND: Practice 3 times this week with you 6' in front.

READY & AUTOMATIC SIT: Practice "ready" with normal starts and stops. Vary the number of steps before you halt and vary the length of time between "ready" and "name, heel." If dog is distracted after "ready," check and release. Then repeat.

HEEL FREE: Work briskly and maintain rhythm—if you hesitate or become indecisive on turns, your dog will not maintain heel position. Have confidence and keep moving.

FRONT: From 3' in front, turn 45, 90 and 180 degrees to the right/left and call your dog. If perfect, reward, etc. If not perfect, do it again. Progress as before.

RECALL: Practice 1 Recall per session with Finish. If dog makes a mistake, show him what you want and repeat. Keep your hands at your side and give dog a chance to do it correctly by himself.

Figure 8 with Left U-Turn .

375

Bibliography

BEHAVIOR

Bergman, Goran, *Why Does Your Dog Do That?* New York: Howell Book House, 1973.

A lucid survey of why a dog behaves in a certain way. Explains the behavior of dogs in relation to their biological and hereditary background. The book covers all aspects of the dog as well as the difference between intelligence and association.

Campbell, William E., *Behavior Problems in Dogs.* Santa Barbara: American Veterinary Publications, 1975.

A survey of common and not-so-common behavior problems with specific instructions on how to solve them. Analyzes causes of problem behavior and suggests ways to modify the dog's behavior in his own environment. Explores in depth the influence of environmental factors on the dog's behavior.

Lorenz, Konrad Z., *Man Meets Dog.* Baltimore: Penguin Books, 1964.

Full of common sense and wit. A good guide for dog owners, especially the chapter on introducing a new animal into the household. Lorenz is considered the world's leading animal watcher and the father of ethology.

Pfaffenberger, Clarence J., *The New Knowledge of Dog Behavior.* New York: Howell Book House, 1963.

Explains the critical periods in a puppy's life and the causes of emotional blocks in adult dog behavior. Based on the research of Drs. Scott and Fuller at the Animal Behavior Division of the Roscoe B. Jackson Memorial Laboratory at Bar Harbor, Maine.

Sautter, Frederic J. and Glover, John A., *Behavior Development and Training of the Dog*. New York: Arco Publishing Company, 1978.

A thorough study of canine behavior including an analysis of the effects of genetics, critical periods, and the environment on the adult dog's behavior. Also includes the most recent research in learning and behavior, and an approach to behavioral training techniques to cure behavior problems.

Scott, John Paul and Fuller, John L., *Genetics and the Social Behavior of the Dog*. Chicago: University of Chicago Press, 1965.

The central theme is the role of heredity in the development of behavior. A report on almost twenty years of research at the Roscoe B. Jackson Memorial Laboratory at Bar Harbor, Maine, dealing with rearing methods, basic behavior patterns and the physiological and behavioral development of puppies.

Trumler, Eberhard, *Understanding Your Dog*. London: Faber & Faber, 1973.

Describes the dog from cradle to grave, including all aspects of their physical and behavioral development, the specific features common to all individuals of the same species, and the differences characterizing individual personalities. Succinctly explains the dog's developmental stages, not only as a puppy, but as an adult as well.

BREED INFORMATION

American Kennel Club, *The Complete Dog Book* (revised ed.). New York: Howell Book House, 1985.

A comprehensive compendium of the breeds recognized by the American Kennel Club. Includes breed histories and breed standards as well as general information on selecting and caring for your dog.

Howe, John, *Choosing the Right Dog*. New York: Harper & Row, 1976.

BREEDING

Harmer, Hilary, *Dogs and How to Breed Them*. London: John Gifford, Ltd., 1974.

A thorough treatment of the subject of breeding dogs from selection of breeding stock through the sale of puppies. Includes an easy reference whelping checklist.

377

Seranne, Ann, *The Joy of Breeding Your Own Show Dog*. New York: Howell Book House, 1980.

A book for everyone who wants to breed a dog for whatever purpose. Contains all the advice you need from theory to practice. You will do yourself a favor to read this book before embarking upon such an important undertaking as breeding your dog.

COUNSELING

Evans, Job Michael, *The Evans Guide for Counseling Dog Owners*. New York: Howell Book House, 1985.

Explains the nature and responsibility of counseling, interviewing and evaluating clients, teaching specific techniques and correcting behavior problems. *Invaluable* for instructors, with excellent characterizations of different owners and how to deal with them. A *must* for anyone who teaches obedience classes, and a complement to *Teaching Dog Obedience Classes—The Manual for Instructors*.

HANDOUTS

Fisher, Gail T., "Castration—Convincing Owners." *Off-Lead Magazine,* October, 1978.

Fisher, Gail T., "Castration: To Be or Not to Be." *Off-Lead Magazine,* October, 1977.

Fisher, Gail T., "Why Dogs Fight." *Pure-Bred Dogs, The American Kennel Gazette,* June, 1983.

Point, Olive S. and Volhard, Joachim J., "All About Obedience Trials." Arner Publications, P.O. Box 307, Westmoreland, NY 13490 (1977).

Volhard, Joachim J., "Teaching You to Train Your Dog—A Student Handbook." Arner Publications, P.O. Box 307, Westmoreland, NY 13490 (1975).

HEALTH

Carlson, Delbert G. and Giffin, James M., *Dog Owner's Home Veterinary Handbook*. New York: Howell Book House, 1981.

A comprehensive, easy reference health guide including what to do in an emergency.

Pitcairn, Richard H. and Pitcairn, Susan Hubble, *Natural Health for Dogs & Cats*. Emmaus: Rodale Press, 1982.

A holistic approach to the maintenance, feeding and health of a pet.

Sodikoff, Charles, *Laboratory Profiles of Small Animal Diseases*. Santa Barbara: American Veterinary Publications, 1981.

A guide to laboratory diagnosis.

HISTORY

Saunders, Blanche, *The Story of Dog Obedience*. New York: Howell Book House, 1974.

The story of the growth of dog training in America and how dog training got started in this country.

NUTRITION

Belfield, Wendell O. and Zucker, Martin, *How to Have a Healthier Dog*. New York: Doubleday, 1981.

The benefits of vitamins and minerals for your dog's life cycle are explained. Provides medical and nutritional advice to enable you to set up your own preventive medicine and health program for your dog.

Collins, Donald R., *The Collins Guide to Canine Nutrition*. New York: Howell Book House, 1976.

Explains what to look for in a commercial dog food and the needs of your dog. How to evaluate different dog foods intelligently.

Levy, Juliette de Barcali, *The Complete Herbal Book for the Dog*. New York: Arco Publishing Company, 1973.

A handbook of natural care and rearing.

Volhard, Wendy, "Back to Basics." New York: Wendy Volhard, 1980.

A guide to a balanced home-made dog food and the diet we feed our dogs.

PUPPY EVALUATION AND SELECTION

Bartlett, Melissa, "A Novice Looks at Puppy Aptitude Testing." *Pure-Bred Dogs, The American Kennel Gazette,* 31-42, March, 1979.

A detailed explanation of the aptitude test compiled by Joachim and Wendy Volhard to assist a prospective puppy purchaser in the selection of a puppy suited to his family and his life style. The following sources contributed to the development of this simple-to-administer test:

Campbell, William E., *Behavior Problems in Dogs.* Santa Barbara: American Veterinary Publications, 1975.

Fox, Michael W., *Understanding Your Dog.* New York: Coward, McCann, Geoghegan, 1972.

Humphrey, Elliot and Warner, Lucien, *Working Dogs.* Palo Alto: National Press, 1974.

Pfaffenberger, Clarence J., *The New Knowledge of Dog Behavior.* New York: Howell Book House, 1963.

Scott, John P. and Fuller, John L., *Genetics and the Social Behavior of the Dog.* Chicago: University of Chicago Press, 1965.

Trumler, Eberhard, *Understanding Your Dog.* London: Faber & Faber, 1973.

Bartlett, Melissa, "Puppy Aptitude Testing." *Pure-Bred Dogs, The American Kennel Gazette,* 31-34 & 64, March, 1985.

A review of six years of puppy testing. Includes a Puppy Aptitude Testing Questionnaire for those who would like to share their experiences in using the Volhard method of selecting puppies.

Fisher, Gail T. and Volhard, Wendy, "Puppy Personality Profile." *Pure-Bred Dogs, The American Kennel Gazette,* 36-42, March, 1985.

A detailed explanation of the specifics of the testing procedures, scoring, and interpretation of the results of puppy aptitude testing.

TRAINING

Most, Konrad, *Training Dogs.* London: Popular Dogs Publishing Company, 1954.

Most is the pioneer and father of dog training as we know it today. His manual was written in 1910 and remains the single-most important text for the serious trainer.

Volhard, Joachim J. and Fisher, Gail T., *Training Your Dog—The Step-by-Step Manual.* New York: Howell Book House, 1983.

Well-illustrated and easy to follow training techniques for basic obedience exercises. Includes a detailed explanation of how dogs learn and a chapter on behavior problems. Named Best Care and Training Book for 1983 by the Dog Writers' Association of America.

"Ready" with Third Degree Distraction.

INDEX